MILITARY
SMALL
ARMS

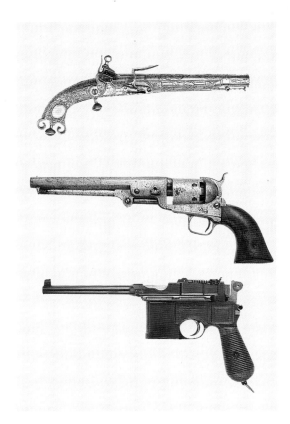

MILITARY SMALL ARMS

EDITED BY GRAHAM SMITH

FOREWORD AND INTRODUCTION BY
IAN V HOGG

a Salamander book
Published by Salamander Books Limited
LONDON

A Salamander Book

Distributed by Random House Value Publishing, Inc.
40 Engelhard Avenue
Avenel, New Jersey 07001

A CIP catalog record for this book is available from
the Library of Congress

Printed in Italy

ISBN 0-517-14292-9

All correspondence concerning the content of this volume should
be addressed to Salamander Books Ltd, 129–137 York Way,
London N7 9LG, United Kingdom

Credits

Project Editor: Graham Smith, with help from Bob Munro.
Design: Original concept by Tim Scott, with help from Mark
Holt and Paul Johnson.
Filmset by Flair Plan Phototypesetting Ltd.
Reproduction by Hong Kong Reproduction Co.

The Authors

Ian V. Hogg served in the British Army for 27 years (including
active service in Korea) before starting a second career as a writer.
He has numerous books to his credit, and has become one of the
most respected small arms experts in the world. He is the editor of
the prestigious annual publication 'Jane's Infantry Weapons'.

Graham Smith is a freelance writer and editor who has worked for
various specialist military publishers. He has written a number of
military books, including a World War II history and a guide to
modern small arms.

CONTENTS

FOREWORD

John Muller, Professor of Fortification at the Royal Military Academy, Woolwich, made a profound observation in 1756. 'The origin and rise of fortification' he said, 'is undoubtedly due to the degeneracy of mankind'. He could well have said the same thing about firearms, had that been his subject, for I can only think of one major advance in firearms technology (the percussion principle) which has been due to a demand from the sporting fraternity.

It is also chastening to think that although firearms have been in use since 1326 or thereabouts, most of the development has taken place in the last 150 years, spurred on by innumerable wars and disputes. An arquebusier of the 16th century would scarcely have been puzzled by the firearms in use at the start of the 19th century, but a soldier from the South African War would be baffled by most of the weapons in use today.

It is this progression of technology which this book sets out to explore, by looking at various classes of weapons at various times and following their development. Not from the very beginning, but certainly from the muzzle-loading flintlock, which might be considered the point at which a technical solution became a commonplace device, to the present-day period of mass-produced and almost disposable weapons. That the accent is upon military weapons is due to the tendency mentioned above, that almost all the technical advances in firearms have been driven by military demands or requirements. The two are not the same; frequently a private inventor saw what the military needed before the military did. He would then offer them a device or a complete weapon, and the usual response was to wonder where such a thing might fit into the contemporary military tactical picture. In many cases the tactical picture changed because of the introduction of a weapon, whereupon the military saw a need for something else and went back to the inventors with a demand. Perhaps the most simple example of this is not in small arms but in larger weapons; the tank and its counter-weapons. The tank came from outside the military establishment and took some swallowing by the soldiers of the day. Once it was in action, however, the next demand was from the people confronted with the new weapon, who needed an antidote. And so the anti-tank rifle, gun, mine, and eventually rocket and missile made their appearance.

A similar sequence in small arms is harder to distinguish, though currently there is an interesting see-saw going on between the high velocity rifle and the soldier. When the 5.56mm rifle appeared, its bullet delivered some remarkably savage wounds. This led to a demand for body armour, and that, in turn, has set the gun and ammunition designers searching for some combination which will defeat body armour at fighting ranges.

One should bear in mind that, like everything else, firearms fall into or out of fashion. The submachine gun was looked at with grave suspicion for the first twenty years of its life; it was used by American gangsters, and that damned it. Then the need for a compact weapon of great firepower for armour-accompanying troops and raiders led to its rise in popularity. Warfare has now, or so many would have us believe, changed into a more long-distance business conducted by missiles and smart weapons, so the close-range submachine gun has all but disappeared from the modern army and the medium-range assault rifle is the preferred arm.

Perhaps the greatest problem facing the firearms designer today is economic. We have now reached a point where the average firearm is as efficient as anyone could wish; indeed the average firearm is more efficient than the average soldier can take advantage of, so far as accuracy and reliability goes. To move forward from this standard, to develop some wholly new type of rifle or machine gun which will be capable of a significant improvement in efficiency over the present designs, is going to take some powerful thinking and ingenuity, but, more important, it is going to take a massive amount or money. The improvement likely to be gained will probably not be worth the expense of achieving it. Examples of recent developments which tend to demonstrate this are given later, and it is a situation which is currently causing a good deal of heart-searching among designers and manufacturers of military weapons.

However; as a firearms expert in Victorian days said, 'We can only see our way to the firearm of the future by studying the firearms of the past.' And this is as good a place as any to begin that study.

Ian V. Hogg
Upton-upon-Severn
England

Far left: *British soldiers with L85A1 'bullpup' rifles, which have the magazine behind the trigger.*

Left: *Even with automatic weapons, marksmanship is still an important basic skill for the modern soldier.*

Below: *The G3 rifle and HK21 machine gun fire the NATO standard 7.62mm (.3in) round.*

INTRODUCTION

The weapons of the striking element of an army - the infantry and cavalry - changed very little in the two hundred years that followed the introduction of the flintlock mechanism. There were occasional and brief forays into rifled weapons, but in general the soldier of the time was no mechanic and his masters preferred to keep his weapon as simple as possible and reduce its operation to a drill which could be mastered by anyone. As a general rule, the smoothbore musket armed the infantry, the smoothbore pistol the cavalry. The rifle, when it appeared, was usually in the hands of highly-trained skirmishers, and the short carbine for cavalry was not a common weapon.

The first, and greatest, change came with the adoption of the percussion principle, which generally took place in the 1840s. From this base, though, different armies moved in different directions. Most stayed with their existing musket, merely removing the flint mechanism and replacing it with the simpler percussion hammer and nipple. Some, however, became more adventurous; the Prussians adopted the 'needle gun', the first centre-fire bolt action breech-loader, and the French developed the Chassepot along similar lines.

In 1866 the Prussians went to war against Austria, and the breech-loading rifle easily defeated the muzzle-loading muskets of the Austrian forces. In 1870 the Prussians moved against France, but here the contest was a less one-sided affair and the Chassepot was generally considered to be the better weapon; it was artillery which won the war for Prussia, not rifle fire.

But these campaigns, plus the American Civil War, made the military minds of the time realise that the day of the muzzle-loader was over and that hasty conversions of existing muzzle-loading weapons, such as the Snider and Springfield 'trap door' mechanisms, were simply not good enough. The utility of the one-piece self-contained cartridge had also been made apparent, and much work went into cartridge development, passing through the various stages of the pinfire, rimfire and finally centre-fire patterns, with numerous excursions into 'patent ignition' systems which utilised the percussion principle in various ways, usually in an attempt to evade an existing patent. The history of ammunition development is a major study in itself and cannot be gone into here in any great detail, but it is worth bearing in mind that the last quarter of the 19th century saw many peculiar designs of ammunition appear, allied with suitable weapons. Most of the patent ammunition systems were unpractical or flawed, and only conventional designs managed to survive; and they were seized upon by ammunition manufacturers and produced by the million, so that

the man who invented a cartridge rarely saw much advantage from it.

Once the rimfire and centre-fire cartridges had reached some degree of reliability the gunmakers then set about developing practical weapons. The bolt action became the primary military system, largely because of the ease with which it could be worked by a man lying down behind cover. It was also a very strong locking system, allowing the use of powerful cartridges, and was a very simple system to operate, which meant that soldiers could easily master it. The only drawback to appear was the contortions of the soldier as he attempted to remove each cartridge from a pouch around his waist and load it into the rifle while still lying down and attempting to conceal himself from the enemy.

The answer to this was the 'quick loader', an aberration which appeared in some quantity in Europe. This took the form of a rack or clip fitted to the side of the rifle butt or stock, into which the soldier could insert several cartridges. He then lay down, took up his firing position and after opening the bolt, withdrew a cartridge from the quick loader and placed it the breech. Thus he only had to squirm around to get at his pouch every eight or ten rounds, rather than after every shot.

The quick loader was only a temporary solution; the real answer lay in providing the rifle with a magazine which could be loaded prior to action and reloaded when necessary, and from which cartridges could be fed to the breech by operating the bolt. Winchester, in the USA, had pioneered this by placing a tubular magazine under the barrel of the rifle and having a 'lifter' which lifted each round to align it with the breech. Mauser of Germany and Lebel of France adopted this idea, using a bolt action rather than the under-lever of the Winchester, but it was soon found that there were inherent drawbacks with the tubular system; firstly the danger of a cartridge exploding in the magazine, and secondly that the balance of the rifle shifted perceptibly as the magazine was emptied, so that the soldier had constantly to re-adjust his hold. Although the tubular magazine took some time to die out completely, the 1890s generally saw the adoption of box magazines on military rifles, so that by the turn of the century the bolt-action repeater was virtually the world standard.

Meanwhile, of course, other weapons had been making their own progress. The pistol was, at the beginning of the 19th century, almost entirely a cavalry weapon. Infantry officers carried swords, infantry soldiers carried muskets; only the cavalry needed pistols as a last resort should their main weapon, be it sabre or lance, be shattered or lost in the melee. But as improved rifles reached the hands of the infantry, so their officers adopted revolvers, retaining the sword as a weapon of last resort or, more usually, a symbol of authority. The design of revolvers attempted to follow the path of rifle design - from a specification and pattern by a military committee to production by government factories or contractors - but in this case it failed completely; it is remarkable that almost every revolver developed

Far left: *After hundreds of years of development. the infantryman's main weapon is still a metal tube, used to hurl small pieces of lead.*

Right: *The Beretta 92 is one of the best military pistols of the 1990s, and is the standard American service sidearm.*

Left: *An 1856 portrait of a British Colour Sergeant of Sappers and Miners. He is armed with a single-shot smooth-bore percussion musketoon.*

Below: *French Colonial troops fire from their trench during the First World War. They are equipped with the Berthier M1892 bolt-action rifle.*

under military auspices was a technical disaster, whilst every successful military revolver has been from a private manufacturer to whom the government turned in desperation.

The one common characteristic of almost all 19th Century military revolvers was their large calibre. The British adopted .445 in (11.5mm), the Germans 11.6mm (.457in), the Americans .45 in (11.4mm) and so on; among the few dissidents were the French, who adopted the same 8mm (.315in) calibre as their rifle to economise on barrel-making plant. This demand for a large calibre came from colonial wars against 'savage tribes', men who were so motivated and direct that being punctured with a small-calibre bullet made little impact upon them and rarely slowed their onward charge with sword or spear. What was needed was a bullet which would literally knock the man down, and the 1890s saw some fearsome projectiles, the ultimate probably being the British .455 'Manstopper', a soft lead cylinder with the front end scooped out into a hemisphere. What this did when it entered human tissue can well be imagined, but the St Petersburg Declaration of 1868 outlawed any projectile weighing under 400 grammes which contained explosive, so there was little alternative. However, the Hague Convention of 1899 went further and outlawed 'bullets which expand or flatten easily in the human body', which put an end to the more outrageous anti-personnel ammunition. Instead, the standard revolver bullet became a lead/antimony article with a rounded or slightly pointed nose,

which remained the case until the 1930s, when, after some very liberal interpretations of the Hague Convention, jacketed bullets became the norm.

The prospect of a weapon which would continue to deliver bullets without very much intervention from human agency, and so long as the ammunition supply lasted, had attracted designers from the 17th century onwards, but, like every other weapon, success was only feasible with a self-contained cartridge.

Gatling's hand-powered machine gun is perhaps the most famous of the many mechanical devices which appeared in the 1860-80 period; he mounted six or ten barrels in a revolving cluster, and by means of cams, opened and closed the breech blocks as they rotated. A cartridge was fed into an open breech at the top of the circle, was gradually loaded and the bolt closed as the barrel moved round, so that it fired at the bottom-most point and then unloaded during the upward movement, arriving at the top with the breech open ready for a cartridge.

It was Hiram Maxim, in 1883, who realised that the firing of a gun generates a considerable amount of power - in the form of gas, blast and recoil - which could be tapped as a means of operating a mechanism to make the gun reload and fire itself. He carefully patented almost every possible method of tapping off power, and then settled upon utilising the recoil of the weapon to drive it. He produced a working 'automatic machine gun' in 1884, but it was too cumbersome for military use and after consultation with British military officers, he

Left: *British Naval Officers practice with Webley automatics and a revolver.*

Right: *The Hotchkiss series of machine guns fed from an unusual rigid metal cartridge strip.*

Below left: *A 1916 British infantryman demonstrates his SMLE Mk III rifle.*

Below: *A New Zealand soldier aims his belt-fed FN MAG General Purpose Machine Gun.*

redesigned it into a more practical form and re-introduced it in 1885. The first recorded combat use of the Maxim gun appears to be on 21 November 1888 when a British officer who had privately acquired a gun from Maxim took it into action in the newly-formed colony of the Gambia. It was formally adopted by Britain, Germany and many other nations in the 1890s.

The success of the Maxim led other inventors to look at methods of operation, and first Browning in the USA and then Odkolek of Austria developed weapons which were driven by gas tapped off from the barrel to drive a piston mechanism. Browning later turned to recoil operation for his more famous machine guns, and the Odkolek design became the French Hotchkiss. Bergmann of Germany and Skoda of Austria developed plain blowback weapons – guns in which the breech block was kept closed simply by its own weight and inertia rather than any locking mechanism – and although somewhat over-stressed, these served until the 1920s.

The success of automatic machine guns led to the supposition that the same principles might be capable of scaling-down to fit rifles and pistols, and in the 1890s much inventiveness went into these two areas. The first successful automatic pistol, the Borchardt, was cumbersome and delicate by today's standards, but it was a revelation at the time and proved that such weapons were feasible. It was rapidly followed by designs from Bergmann and Mauser, and eventually the Borchardt was given a thorough overhaul and became the immortal Luger.

Strangely, all the running in the early automatic pistol race was made in Europe, the Americans apparently seeing little future in such delicate devices. It was not until John Browning took the matter in hand in the late 1890s that useful designs appeared from the USA, and even then he had to take them to Belgium in order to get them manufactured. Eventually, of course, the Colt company were persuaded to take an interest, and they have been industriously making Browning's 1911 pattern of pistol ever since.

Although the records are uninformative, it seems that the Danish Navy were the first organised force to adopt an automatic rifle when they purchased a small number for their marines in 1898. As a rifle it proved cumbersome and unreliable and failed to survive for long, but the basic idea was reworked into a more robust form and became the Madsen light machine gun, used to good effect in the Russo-Japanese War in 1904.

The first successful automatic rifle was the Mondragon, invented by a Mexican general of that name and made for him in Switzerland in 1912-14. The outbreak of war interrupted the contract, and the balance of the weapons which could not be shipped to Mexico were bought by Germany and used as weapons by early aviators. But although the Mondragon was workable, the appalling conditions of the Western Front soon showed that something far more robust and dirt-and-mud-proof had to be devised before the automatic rifle could ever become a standard issue.

The First World War is renowned as a machine gun war (even though artillery killed far more than did machine guns) and it focused attention on the need to devise a light and portable weapon which could be easily carried by advancing troops. In 1914 the standard machine gun was water-cooled, belt fed, tripod mounted, and heavy. The American-designed, Belgian-built Lewis machine gun showed the way towards portability, as did the Madsen and some of the French Hotchkiss designs, but they all had their drawbacks, and one of the first post-war tasks of the combatants was to look more closely at the machine gun and settle some basic tactical questions about its employment, after which they could think about its future design. This led to such weapons as the Bren light machine gun, devised in Czechoslovakia and adopted by Britain, the French Chatellerault and the Vickers-Berthier adopted by the Indian Army. It also let to an entirely new concept of machine gun employment developed by the German Army; they felt that the division of machine guns into light and medium classes, each with different weapons and characteristics, was a nuisance. A properly designed weapon, they felt, could be used on a bipod as a light weapon or on a tripod as a medium weapon. It meant belt-feed for the light gun, and it also demanded a very efficient system of quickly changing the barrel so as to prevent it overheating, but this 'General Purpose Machine Gun' philosophy served the Germans well in 1939-45 and was adopted by many countries afterwards. It was not until the 1980s that the validity of the arguments began to be questioned.

The German Army was also responsible for what is probably the greatest two upheavals in small arms seen during the entire century – the submachine gun and the assault rifle. The submachine gun came about as a result of a tactical requirement; the German Storm Troops had the task of infiltrating trench lines and required a portable, short range weapon of considerable power. Bergmann devised his 'machine pistol' and the submachine gun was born. Thompson, of the immortal 'Tommy Gun', invented the actual term 'submachine gun' , but the unfortunate connection of the Tommy Gun and Al Capone and others did little for its image in military circles, and it was disdained as a 'gangster weapon' for many years. The Second World War, and most particularly the Soviet Army's mass use of this class of weapon, soon dispelled any military doubts.

The assault rifle grew from logistic considerations; ever since the 1890s the standard infantry rifle had been influenced by the South African War or some other colonial experience, where long-range shooting was a must. But the First World War showed that in Europe, at any rate, the chances of even seeing an enemy at 500yds (460m) were thin, those of hitting him even thinner. So, argued the Germans, why waste weight on a rifle which will fire two miles when you only need to shoot 500

Below: *The M1 Carbine was a light weapon which fired a short cartridge, and was intended as a personal defence weapon for drivers, signallers and such like.*

Right: *Polish paratroops with AKM assault rifles.*

Below right: *The L1A1 is the British version of the powerful FN FAL rifle.*

yards? A less powerful cartridge would suffice, leading to a lighter and more compact rifle, and allowing more ammunition for the same weight.

The fundamental feature of the assault rifle was the reduced-power cartridge, which used a bullet of the same 7.92mm (.31in) calibre as the standard weapons but shorter and lighter and fired it a somewhat lower velocity. The muzzle energy was considerably than that delivered by the 7.92mm (.31in) Mauser bullet but still quite sufficient to do damage. In the years after the war the calibre of military rifles and assault rifles has gradually crept downwards until the current standard is 5.56mm (.223in), and even smaller calibres have been proposed and considered. There are, though, signs that this tendency may have reached its limit and that rifle calibres will creep upwards once more.

The 1939-45 war threw up a third significant factor in firearms design, the concept of throw-away weapons. Traditionally, military weapons were machined from solid billets of steel so as to be robust, to withstand arduous active service and to last a long time in peace. But the demands of war on a global scale soon showed that more economical methods of manufacture would have to be adopted, and though armies objected to 'cheap weapons' they soon realised the advantages of throwing away a cheap weapon when it failed rather than going through an expensive and time-consuming logistic exercise in returning it to a depot for repair and then shipping it back to the front. So instead of machining and forging, stamping and welding became accepted methods of manufacture. The Soviets showed the way in this field by abandoning many traditional refinements; their weapons were well-finished only where absolutely necessary.

The only drawback to this is that in peacetime the weapons do not last as well as their forebears, and thus a 25-year period has come to be recognised as the life of a service weapon. By then the annual cost of repairs and refurbishment will be uneconomic, and it is time to look for a new design and change to a new weapon. But in the 1980s it began to be apparent that revolutionary manufacturing methods – notably the introduction of computer-controlled machinery – could allow a return to the traditional machining and forging system of manufacture but without the demand for highly-paid machinists. One highly-paid programmer sets up the machine, after which it operates for 24 hours a day turning out components to a precision few of the old-time workmen could have matched. It is possible that the next generation of weapons may turn away from the sheet-metal, plastic and wire-spring wonders of the current generation and return to the more substantial construction methods of the 1890s. And the armies of the world will be grateful, for they can then stretch out their weapon life by at least ten years, reducing the frequency of the expensive changeover caused by cheap construction.

Left: *Modern weapons still need regular maintenance.*

Below left: *Sheet metal and plastic makes up the CETME L.*

Below: *A French Legionnaire struggles with his chemical warfare suit and mask as he totes a FA MAS 5.56mm (.223in) assault rifle.*

EARLY PISTOLS

The pistol – a gun capable of being easily carried and fired with one hand – came about as a result of the development of the wheel-lock. Prior to that time the only method of firing a gun was by means of a length of burning quick-match, which made it inconvenient to carry. With the adoption of the wheel-lock it became possible to cock the weapon, conceal it about the person, and then draw and fire, all of which gave impetus to a reduction in size. It also gave impetus to the concealment factor, to the extent that several cities in Europe forbade the private ownership of wheel-lock weapons.

With the general adoption of the flintlock mechanism, pistols became commonplace personal defence weapons and assumed many different shapes as gunsmiths vied with each other to produce either more elegant or more efficient designs. Moreover, while it was possible for a skilled gunsmith to make an elegantly decorated and mechanically precise weapon, it was equally possible for a blacksmith to make something less elegant and precise but equally efficient at discharging a bullet. Because of this divergence of manufacturing, and because a varied selection of people demanded pistols for various applications, different patterns emerged suited to different roles.

The first to adopt the flintlock in numbers were cavalry troops; these were generally heavy weapons of .5-.65 in (12.7-16.5mm) calibre, stocked to the muzzle and with barrels about 12in (305mm) long; the butt was usually finished with a heavy metal ornament so that in extremis the pistol could be reversed and used as a club. The civil equivalent of the cavalry pistol was the 'holster' or 'horse' pistol, so-called because the size demanded carriage in a holster, and the holster formed part of a horse harness. The style was much the same as the cavalry pistol but generally more ornate and better finished.

The small cousin of the holster pistol was known as the 'travelling pistol' from its adoption by those whose occupation required them to travel in coaches; holster pistols would have been cumbersome, but travelling pistols could be carried in an inconspicuous case and produced should a highwayman appear.

No pistol of the flintlock era strikes the imagination with so much romantic force as a duelling pistol. The prime requirements for this type were that it should 'point' naturally and instinctively as the hand came up to the 'present, and that the trigger should be light and crisp so that there could be no doubt as to the point of release. Decoration was usually minimal, the butt being chequered to provide a good grip and the metal being browned or blued so as not to reflect light and dazzle the firer.

In the middle of the 17th Century the 'turn-off' pistol appeared; this was a flintlock in which the barrel was a separate component, screwed on to the

Left: *Smooth-bore pistols were only effective at close ranges, such as in this shipboard action during the Napoleonic Wars.*

Below: *Before the flintlock, ignition was provided by a slow-burning cord or 'match' applied to a priming pan.*

breech end of the weapon. To load, the barrel was unscrewed and removed – or 'turned off' – and the chamber, which remained attached to the butt was filled with powder. The ball was dropped into the breech end of the barrel and, since it had not been rammed down the barrel it was undistorted and a more precise fit. The barrel was then screwed back in place, the pan primed, and the pistol was ready. Some designs had a loose ring on the barrel which was connected to the body by a chain so that there was no danger of accidentally dropping the barrel during the loading process.

In order to improve the firepower of the individual, double barrelled pistols were made; some could fire each barrel separately by means of individual locks, others fired both barrels at once from a single lock. This led to even greater numbers of barrels, and perhaps the most spectacular of these multi-barrel designs is the 'Ducks-foot' pistol, so-called from its splayed barrels with a lateral spread of about 30 degrees. Each barrel was loaded with a single bullet and the flint mechanism fired a common pan which discharged all barrels at once. Useful as a protection against footpads, it was also popular with ship's captains, prison guards and others who faced the prospect of attack by several opponents at once.

Another common 18th century design was the 'blunderbuss', virtually a short shotgun intended to discharge a spread of small projectiles, one or more of which would be certain to find a target. The distinctive feature of the blunderbuss was the wide bell-mouth, popularly supposed to promote the spread of shot. In fact, it did nothing whatever to the spread, and was originally a moulding to strengthen the muzzle, although it also made rapid reloading easier. The gunsmiths knew perfectly well that the bell-mouth was of little practical value, but it impressed the customers, so bell-mouths they got. And, one supposes, it must have overawed anyone at which it was pointed.

In the late 18th century the rifle began to supplant the smoothbore musket, and, of course, those who owned pistols demanded this improvement as well. The usual method of ramming the ball down the barrel was adopted, but as the rifle began to adopt improved projectile, so too did the pistol. The cavalry arm of the early 19th century became the 'pistol a tige', the 'tige' being a pillar in the central axis of the chamber. When the powder was loaded, it occupied the space around the tige; the conical bullet was then loaded by simply sliding it down on the rifling until the recessed base rested on the tip of the tige. A few brisk blows with the rammer on the nose of the bullet would cause the tige to spread the hollow base until the lead skirt bit into the rifling. When fired, the explosion pressure was firmly trapped behind the bullet, which was spun by the rifling. This meant more efficient utilisation of the propellant power, and thus better accuracy (a similar system was used by the later French Thouvenin rifle). However, by the time the 'pistol a tige' was perfected and introduced (both British and French cavalry adopted it) the day of the flintlock was over, and most were converted fairly quickly to percussion.

Below: *Many flintlock weapons were converted to the percussion system. Blanked screw holes show where the pan once was.*

Right: *This cavalry soldier from the American Civil War holds a Model 1855 single-shot percussion pistol with carbine stock.*

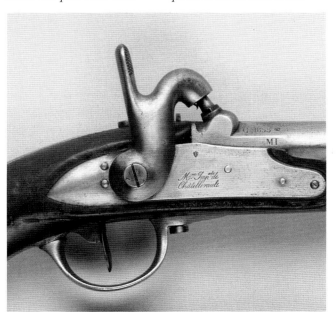

1 Snaphance Pistol
LENGTH: 15.75in (400mm)
WEIGHT: 59oz (1.67kg)
CALIBRE: .675in (17.1mm)
CAPACITY: 1
MV: c.450f/s (137m/s)

The snaphance lies midway between the wheel-lock and the flintlock in terms of firearms development. In this 16th Century example, flint is held in the jaws of the spring-loaded cocking piece, which strikes the steel plate on the hinged arm (shown swung forward in the picture).

2 Spanish Flintlock
LENGTH: 21.25in (540mm)
WEIGHT: 49oz (1.39kg)
CALIBRE: .625in (15.9mm)
CAPACITY: 1
MV: c.500f/s (152m/s)

A classic example of the flint-lock pistol, this example was made in Spain in around 1720. Superbly finished and decorated, it is one of a pair manufactured by Juan Fernandez in Madrid. The stock has elaborate decorative carvings, while the lock plate and butt cap are finely engraved. The flint is gripped in a graceful 'swan neck' cock, held in place by a small patch of leather to absorb the shocks of repeated firing. The cock is pulled back against a powerful leaf spring, to be flung forward when the trigger is pulled. The flint then strikes the steel (or frizzen), causing it to fly forwards, opening the pan beneath. The ensuing shower of sparks ignites the priming charge in the pan, causing the main charge to fire and propel the heavy ball out of the barrel. An unusually fine pistol.

3 Caucasian Flintlock
LENGTH: 13.75in (349mm)
WEIGHT: 16oz (.45kg)
CALIBRE: .4in (10.2mm)
CAPACITY: 1
MV: c.400f/s (122m/s)

Manufactured in the general area of the Caucasus mountains, these weapons often used barrels and locks imported from Spain. This is a typical example, with a slim, fragile-looking butt with an ivory ball at the tip. Pistols of this design were used all over Russia, Turkey and the Balkans.

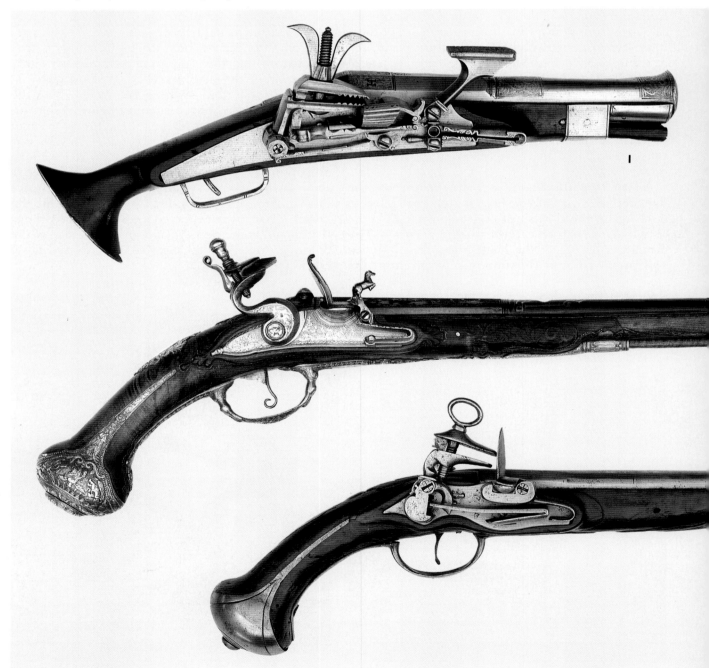

4 Scottish Steel Pistol

LENGTH: 12in (305mm)
WEIGHT: 22oz (.62kg)
CALIBRE: .556in (14.1mm)
CAPACITY: 1
MV: c.500f/s (152m/s)

During the mid-17th Century, Scottish gun-makers produced weapons such as this, with all-steel butts and stocks. This model was made in 1770, and is finely finished with extensive engravings and a traditional 'ram's horn' butt. Hidden from view is a sprung hook which allowed the wearer to slip the weapon inside his belt. Simpler versions of such weapons were carried by the Highland clan levies; and when the British Government first created regiments of Highlanders, they were also so equipped, along with their musket and broadsword. By 1776, pistols were no longer issued to the ordinary soldier, although officers continued to carry them as a badge of rank. Notice that the trigger is an unusual ball or 'button' shape, and that there is no protective trigger guard fitted.

5 Spanish Flintlock

LENGTH: 20.5in (521mm)
WEIGHT: 36oz (1.02kg)
CALIBRE: .665in (16.9mm)
CAPACITY: 1
MV: c.400f/s (122m/s)

Made in the early 18th Century, this pistol is of the Spanish 'miquelet' type, where the sear protrudes horizontally from the lockplate, holding the cock and flint back until the trigger is pulled. The large external mainspring can also be seen on this robust, no-frills cavalry weapon.

6 Screw-off Flintlock

LENGTH: 11.75in (298mm)
WEIGHT: 27oz (.76kg)
CALIBRE: .62in (15.7mm)
CAPACITY: 1
MV: c.450f/s (137m/s)

This weapon is unusual in that it is loaded by unscrewing the barrel and inserting the ball and charge from the breech end. Such a method ensures a tight-fitting ball and an accurate shot, but makes reloading slow. This specimen was made in London in about 1755 and is of 'cannon-barrelled' type.

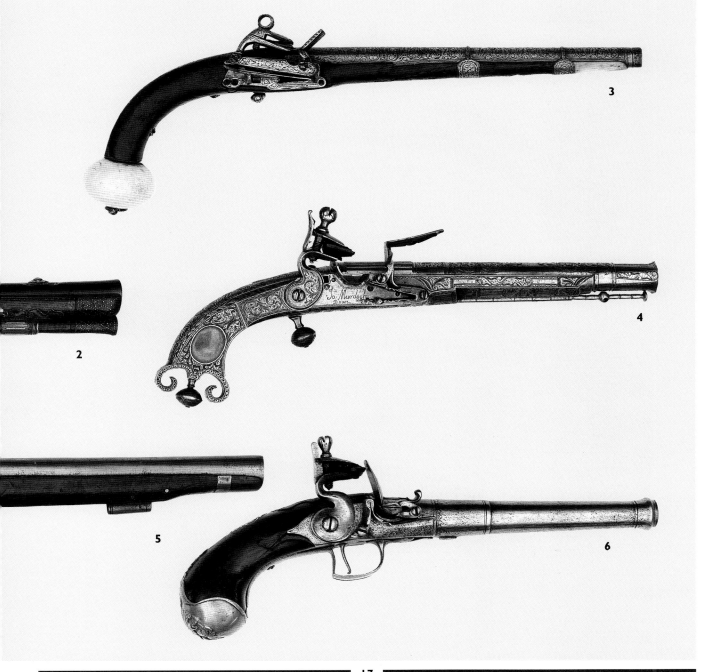

1 British Cavalry Pistol

LENGTH: 21.75in (552mm)
WEIGHT: 50oz (1.42kg
CALIBRE: .625in (15.9mm)
CAPACITY: 1
MV: c.500f/s (152m/s)

During the 16th and 17th Centuries, the pistol became predominantly a cavalry arm, useful in a close melee after the initial charge. This British service weapon was made in around 1720, and is a solid, well-manufactured piece suited to the rigours of campaign. It has long barrel (14.4in/ 368mm) which gives a reasonable muzzle velocity to the hefty .8oz (23gm) ball, enabling it to penetrate the heavy clothing or metal breast plate worn by cavalrymen of the time. The rear third of the barrel is octagonal, a configuration thought to increase the strength of the breech and allow use of a heavy charge. The pistol carries the British service monogram of King George I, although the markings on the butt indicate that it has been worked on by a Middle-Eastern gunsmith.

2 German Cavalry Pistol

LENGTH: 19.5in (495mm)
WEIGHT: 40oz (1.13kg)
CALIBRE: .55in (13.97mm)
CAPACITY: 1
MV: c.500f/s (152m/s)

Another cavalry pistol from around 1720, this model was designed to allow precision shooting against enemy skirmishers. The barrel is rifled to spin the tight-fitting bullet and increase the range. The socket at the rear of the butt was to enable attachment of an an extended butt.

3 French Army Flintlock

LENGTH: 13.25in (337mm)
WEIGHT: 46oz (1.3kg)
CALIBRE: .7in (17.8mm)
CAPACITY: 1
MV: c.500f/s (152m/s)

A solid, rugged weapon with a brass frame and walnut butt, this service pistol was manufactured at St Etienne in 1777. The cock is a straight ring-necked type, more robust than the traditional curved pattern. Pistols to this design were also manufactured in large numbers in the United States.

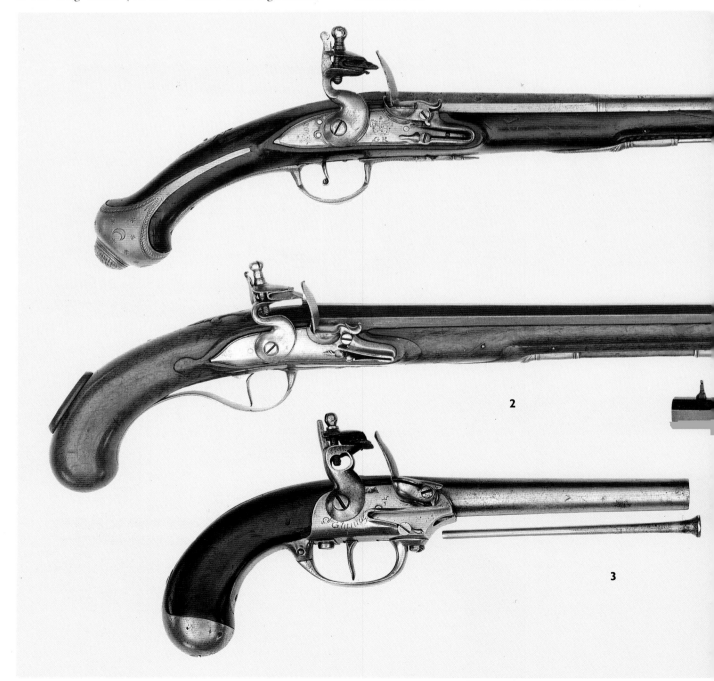

4 Napoleon I's Pistols

LENGTH: 12in (305mm)
WEIGHT: 36oz (1.02kg)
CALIBRE: .6in (15.24mm)
CAPACITY: 1
MV: c.500f/s (152mm)

This weapon is one of a pair with an unusual history. The property of the Emperor Napoleon I, they were given to a Dr Arnott after he had attended Napoleon when he was imprisoned on St Helena. They were later presented to Colonel South of the 20th Regiment, before eventually finding their way to the School of Musketry at Hythe and then the School of Infantry at Warminster. It is in no way a mere presentation model, being instead a solid, dependable service weapon. The octagonal barrel is rifled, allowing for accurate shooting at longer ranges. Rifled muzzle-loaders with their tight-fitting balls were difficult to load, however, and had to withstand much greater breech pressures than smooth-bore designs, hence the thick octagonal barrel and sturdy construction.

5 Mortimer Repeater

LENGTH: 19in (483mm)
WEIGHT: 62oz (1.76kg)
CALIBRE: .5in (12.7mm)
CAPACITY: 7
MV: c.450f/s (137m/s)

Many attempts were made to produce repeating pistols, and this is a British design from around 1800. At the breech there is a rotating cylinder with two recesses cut into it to hold a ball and charge respectively. There are also two corresponding tubular magazines in the butt, filled with shot and powder. To load, the pistol is held vertically downwards and the large lever operated to rotate the cylinder, Eventually the cylinder recesses align with the magazines, allowing one charge and a ball to drop into the cylinder. When this is rotated back, the ball drops into the breech, then the cylinder is further rotated to allow the the recess holding the powder to act as a chamber. Such weapons were often hazardous to fire, as burning gasses could easily leak to ignite the stored powder.

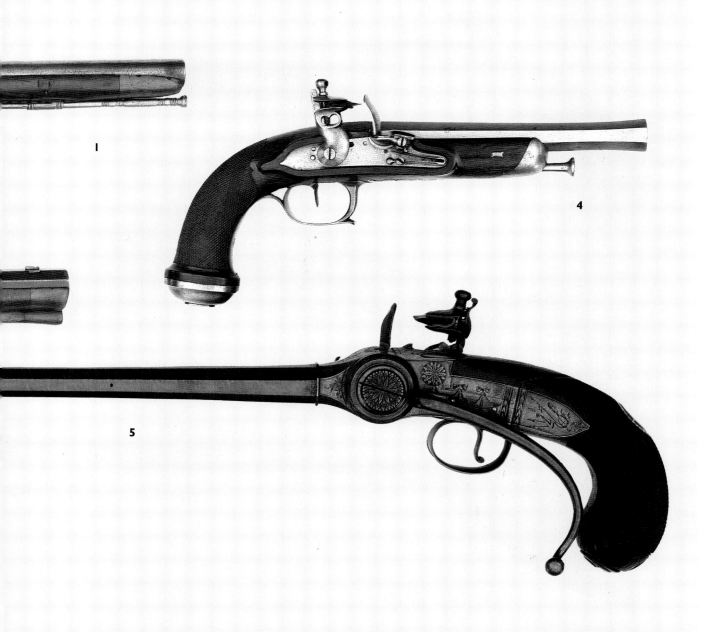

1 Naval Holster Pistol
LENGTH: 14.75in (375mm)
WEIGHT: 32oz (.91kg)
CALIBRE: .62in (15.7mm)
CAPACITY: 1
MV: c.500f/s (152m/s)

Made in 1870, this weapon represents the best of the Georgian period of British gunmaking. Finely decorated, it has a slightly bell-mouthed brass barrel, an indication that it was intended for naval use. From this time onwards, decoration was progressively reduced in gun design.

2 Sea Service Pistol
LENGTH: 16.25in (413mm)
WEIGHT: 49oz (1.39kg)
CALIBRE: .58in (14.7mm)
CAPACITY: 1
MV: c.500f/s (152m/s)

A short-barrelled weapon made in about 1790, this is a good representation of of British military pistols of the period. It is an unadorned, robust weapon with a solid walnut stock and a ring-necked cock. Even though the barrel is of steel rather than brass, the pistol is classed as a sea service model, and would have been useful in a close-range boarding action. On the far side of the stock is a spring-loaded clip allowing the pistol to be held in the belt, keeping the hands free to wield a cutlass. The "Tower' markings on the lock plate indicate that the weapon was assembled in the armoury at the Tower of London, although the components would probably have been made elsewhere by other contractors. A fine, no-nonsense fighting pistol for tough service use.

3 Turkish Blunderbuss
LENGTH: 17.5in (444mm)
WEIGHT: 46oz (1.36kg)
CALIBRE: .65in (16.5mm)
CAPACITY: 1
MV: N/a

The word blunderbuss came to describe a short carbine-like weapon with a wide barrel. Often loaded with buckshot, they were usually used at sea, although this example was made in the Middle-East from European parts, and was probably used by a Turkish or Persian horseman.

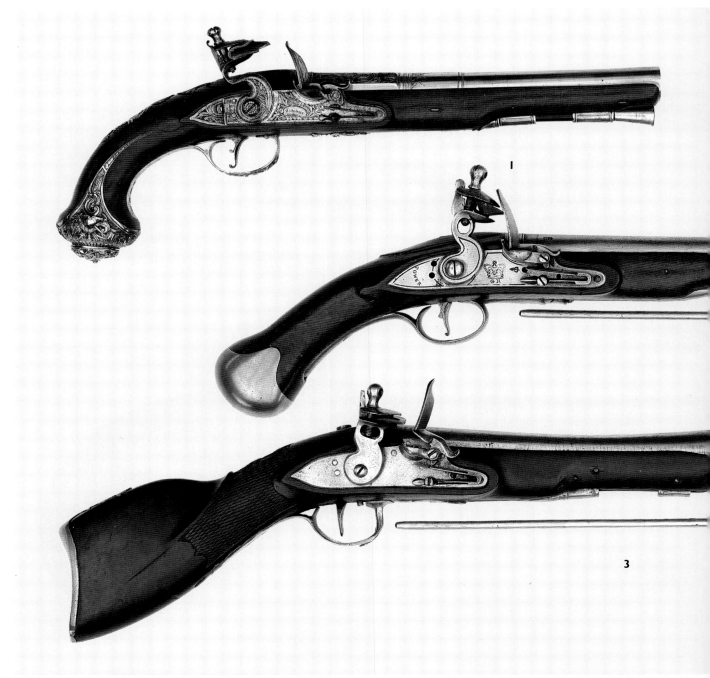

4 Irish Blunderbuss

LENGTH: 13.5in (343mm)
WEIGHT: 38oz (1.08kg)
CALIBRE: .62in (15.7mm)
CAPACITY: 1
MV: c.500f/s (152m/s)

The blunderbuss pistol was also popular in Britain for the defence of houses and coaches, although this Dublin-made item was more likely carried by a naval officer in about 1800. It is a plain service weapon, well made but with no frills. It has a curved 'swan neck' cock, while the spring holding the striking steel (or frizzen) has a roller to speed the lock action and improve accuracy. A brass-tipped ramrod lies beneath the barrel. The brass barrel resists salt-water corrosion better than steel, while the bell mouth makes it easier to reload on a moving vessel. It also has a heavy rounded butt which would make a good club in an emergency. The pistol could have been used to fire a single large-calibre ball, or more likely, to scatter a spray of buckshot at an enemy boarding party.

5 Mortimer Pistol

LENGTH: 16in (406mm)
WEIGHT: 37oz (1.05kg)
CALIBRE: .62in (15.7mm)
CAPACITY: 1
MV: c.550f/s (168m/s)

Throughout the 17th and 18th Centuries, duelling remained popular as a means of settling personal disputes for officers and gentlemen. Once the pistol became established as the weapon of choice, manufacturers produced specialised weapons such as this, made in London in around 1800. One of a pair, it is exceptionally well-made, with a smooth, fast lock and an octagonal barrel made from thin rods of steel welded together then wound around a mandrel. This method was known as the 'Damascus twist' form of construction. The flat top to the stock enables quick, instinctive sighting, while the spur below the trigger guard helps the firer to hold the weapon securely. Duelling became officially discouraged in most countries by about 1830, although it took longer to halt the practice.

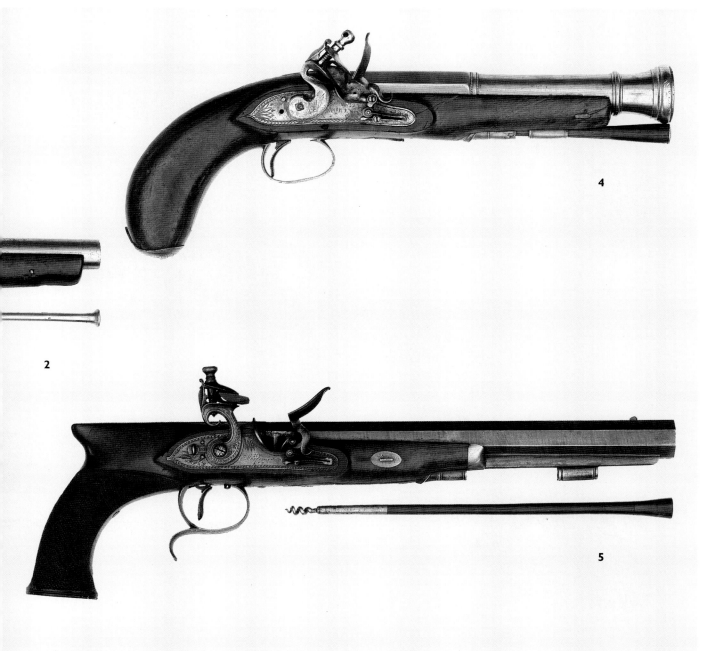

4

2

5

1 Manton Pistol
LENGTH: 14.75in (375mm)
WEIGHT: 40oz (1.13kg)
CALIBRE: .5in (12.7mm)
CAPACITY: 1
MV: c.550f/s (168m/s)

Another duelling pistol, this by Joseph Manton of London in around 1800. Superbly made, it has an octagonal barrel constructed from 'Damascus twist', with an adjustable foresight and 'U'-shaped rearsight. The stud behind the cock is a safety catch, used to lock it at half cock for loaded carriage.

2 Manton Percussion
LENGTH: 14.75in (375mm)
WEIGHT: 38oz (1.08kg)
CALIBRE: .42in (10.7mm)
CAPACITY: 1
MV: c.600f/s (183m/s)

Another Manton pistol, this time converted to the percussion system. At first glance a duelling weapon, it has a rifled barrel, a feature considered 'unsporting' by many. It may be that the owner intended to use it as a general service weapon, albeit an expensive and finely-engineered one.

3 British Percussion
LENGTH: 15in (381mm)
WEIGHT: 36oz (1.02kg)
CALIBRE: .7in (17.8mm)
CAPACITY: 1
MV: c.500f/s (152m/s)

When the percussion system became widespread, there were still vast stocks of flintlock weapons held in national armouries. The solution was to convert them to the new system, usually by removing the pan and frizzen, adding an ignition tube and nipple for the percussion cap, then replacing the cock with a simple hooded hammer. This British service pistol has been so treated, and the blanked screw holes for the pan and frizzen can be clearly seen. The conversion took place in the early 19th Century, although the pistol was first manufactured in about 1796. The new mechanism had no effect on accuracy or power, but it was easier to carry, and was much more reliable, especially in damp weather, when the primer charge in the pan of a flintlock would often fail to ignite.

4 Lang Pistol

LENGTH: 8.25in (210mm)
WEIGHT: 15oz (.42kg)
CALIBRE: .6in (15.2mm)
CAPACITY: 1
MV: c.500f/s (152m/s)

Made in about 1830 by Joseph Lang, this compact weapon is fitted with a belt hook, and was probably intended for use by a naval officer. It has an octagonal barrel, fitted underneath with a hinged or swivel rammer which swings forward to push down the barrel. This feature was often found on military weapons, as it negated the chance of the rammer being dropped when the firer was hastily reloading in action. The powder chamber of this pistol is of smaller diameter than the barrel, a feature intended to improve the ignition of the charge by the priming fulminate. The small screw beneath the nipple allows access to the chamber for cleaning. Spare percussion caps are held in a compartment at the base of the butt. The barrel is made from spiral wound 'Damascus twist'.

5 Blanch Pistol

LENGTH: 11in (279mm)
WEIGHT: 24oz (.68kg)
CALIBRE: .69in (17.5mm)
CAPACITY: 1
MV: c.550f/s (168m/s)

Of a similar design to the Lang pistol, this larger weapon was made by Blanch and Son of London in around 1830. It is a service weapon, with a barrel made from 'Damascus twist' and fitted with a swivel ramrod. The breech has a small fence to protect the user's eyes from flying fragments of percussion cap, while the hammer has a deep recess in its nose. This specimen has had the comb of the hammer broken off in an earlier accident. Spare percussion caps are held in a small recess in the butt. The weapon is well finished, with a chequered pattern engraved in the butt and little else in the way of ornamentation. It shows how the percussion concept made for a cleaner, more compact and streamlined weapon than before, one which was easier to carry in a belt, holster or pocket.

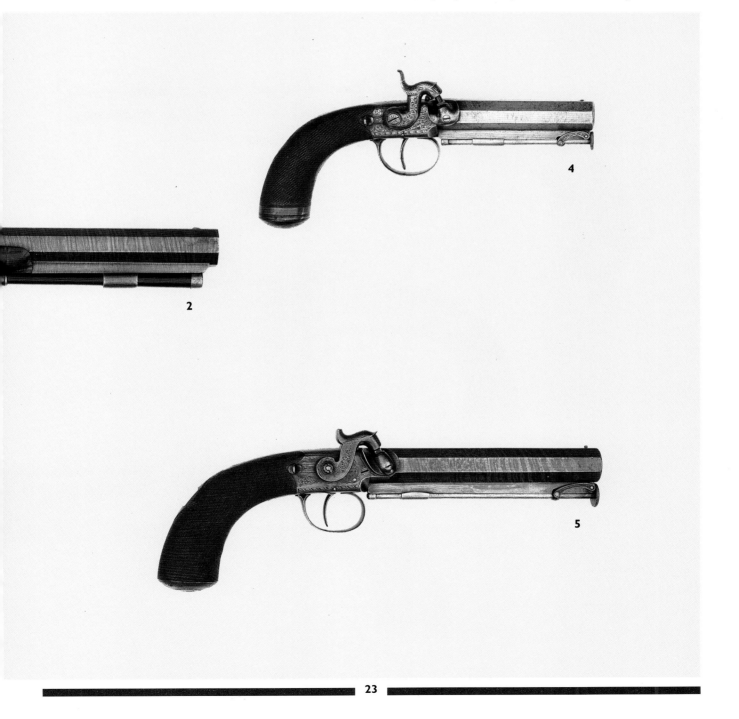

1 French Service Pistol

LENGTH: 13.75in (349mm)
WEIGHT: 45oz (1.27kg)
CALIBRE: .7in (17.8mm)
CAPACITY: 1
MV: c.550f/s (168m/s)

Stamped 1855, this is a Model 1842 service percussion pistol made at the Imperial factory at Chatellerault. It is a typical French design of the period, with the strong, solidly-built hammer and its vertical comb, combined with the slightly tapered cylindrical barrel. There are simple rear and fore-sights above the barrel, although they are of limited use at the ranges over which this pistol would be effective. The weapon is robust and simple, with a walnut butt capped in brass and with a steel lanyard ring underneath. The stock has a brass cap at the front, through which there is drilled a recess for the ramrod. Brass is also used in the wide trigger guard. It is an interesting exercise to compare this pistol with the earlier French St. Etienne flintlock weapon described on page 18.

2 Four-Barrelled Pistol

LENGTH: 8.5in (216mm)
WEIGHT: 37oz (1.05kg)
CALIBRE: .5in (12.7mm)
CAPACITY: 4
MV: c.500f/s (152m/s)

The muzzle loading pistol was a difficult and slow weapon to reload in battle, and most soldiers expected to only get one shot from a weapon before resorting to swords or hand-to-hand combat. Many attempts were made to overcome this problem, including the design of pistols with more than one barrel and chamber. This example was made by Blanch of London, and has four barrels in one solid block of metal, each with its own percussion nipple. Two independent triggers fire the upper two barrels, then the barrel assembly is unlocked by pulling back on the front of the trigger guard. The barrels are rotated until the lower two are under the hammers, where they are locked in place and the pistol cocked, ready to fire again. Once all four have fired, reloading is still painfully slow.

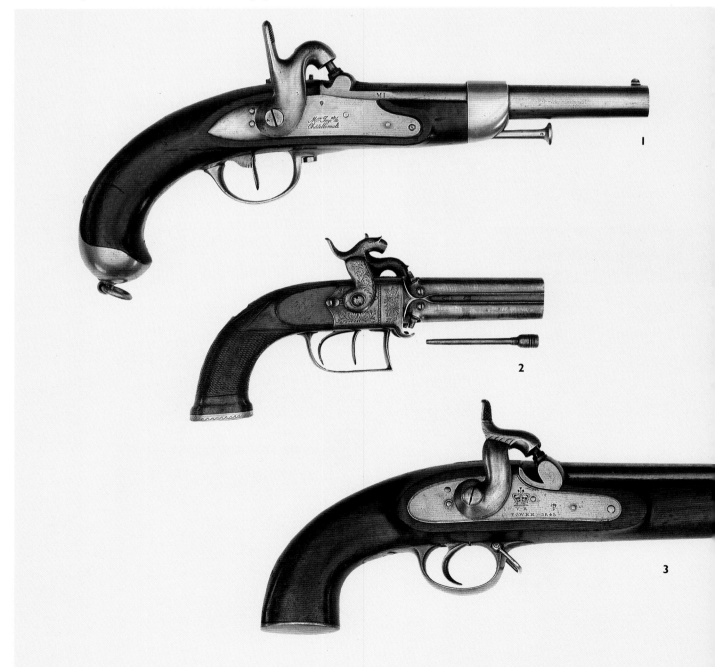

3 Tower Cavalry Pistol

LENGTH: 15.5in (394mm)
WEIGHT: 52oz (1.47kg)
CALIBRE: .75in (19mm)
CAPACITY: 1
MV: c.500f/s (152m/s)

The pistol was falling from favour as a general issue weapon for British cavalry by 1838, although some regiments retained them for quite some time. They were also kept as standard issue for sergeant-majors and trumpeters, so new designs were still required. This is the Model 1842, designed by George Lovell as a simple, tough weapon which could be easily maintained and supplied with ammunition in the field. It fires a standard musket ball and uses the lock from the 1842 pattern infantry musket. It has a permanently attached hinged ramrod under the barrel, while a sling swivel is fixed to the front of the trigger guard. The markings on the lock plate show that this specimen was assembled in the Tower of London in 1845 from contractor's components.

4 St Etienne Pistol

LENGTH: 16.5in (419mm)
WEIGHT: 32oz (.91kg)
CALIBRE: .52in (13.2mm)
CAPACITY: 1
MV: c.550f/s (168m/s)

Manufactured in around 1835, this French design was made for duelling, although it may also have been used as a general target pistol. The lock has the mainspring behind the hammer, which allows the lockplate to be set further towards the butt and the breech to be kept narrow.

5 Sea Service Pistol

LENGTH: 11in (279mm)
WEIGHT: 36oz (1.02kg)
CALIBRE: .56in (14.2mm)
CAPACITY: 1
MV: c.500f/s (152m/s)

Another Lovell pistol of 1842, this one was designed for naval use. It fires a smaller bullet than the cavalry arm, and the lock uses parts from flintlock weapons. Lovell believed in strength and simplicity in a military arm, as this tough, no-nonsense pistol demonstrates admirably.

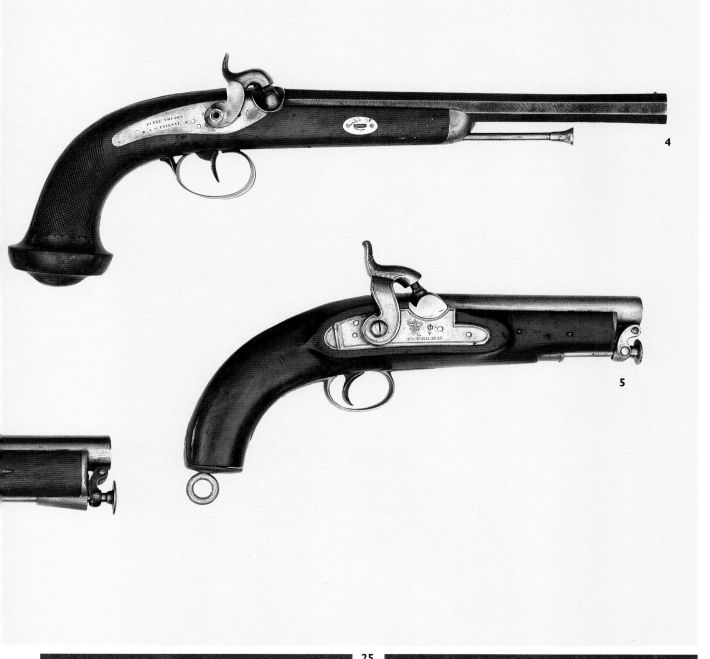

1 Gendarmerie Pistol

LENGTH: 9.5in (241mm)
WEIGHT: 23oz (.65kg)
CALIBRE: .6in (15.2mm)
CAPACITY: 1
MV: c.500f/s (152m/s)

Another French weapon from the factory at Chatellerault, this 1842 design was intended for service or militia use, and was small enough that it could be carried in a pocket if necessary. It has a short (5in/127mm) barrel and would be of use only at the closest of ranges. The percussion nipple stands well proud of the barrel while the hammer is a strongly-made item typical of service pistols of the period. Some components, including the barrel, may have been from earlier flintlock designs but it is difficult to be sure of this. Unlike the weapon on page 24, this pistol uses a back-action lock, with the mainspring behind the hammer. The mechanism is set well back into the butt, which weakens it somewhat, but this is normally not a significant problem with a pistol.

2 Double-Barrelled Pistol

LENGTH: 13in (330mm)
WEIGHT: 36oz (1.02kg)
CALIBRE: .7in (17.8mm)
CAPACITY: 1
MV: c.550f/s (168m/s)

Being much more compact than the flintlock, the percussion system allowed practical double-barrelled designs to be manufactured. This weapon would have been carried in pairs by a mounted British officer, the pistols slung in leather holsters on his saddle. It fires a musket calibre ball, and each barrel has its own lock and trigger system. The stock tapers at the rear so that the hammer mechanisms do not protrude beyond the outside edge of the barrels. Safety catches can be slid forwards to lock the hammers when they are cocked, while there are platinum plugs in the breeches which blow out if the weapon is overloaded, so avoiding serious damage. The spiral markings indicate that the barrels are made from 'Damascus twist'. This is a plain, but superbly-made weapon.

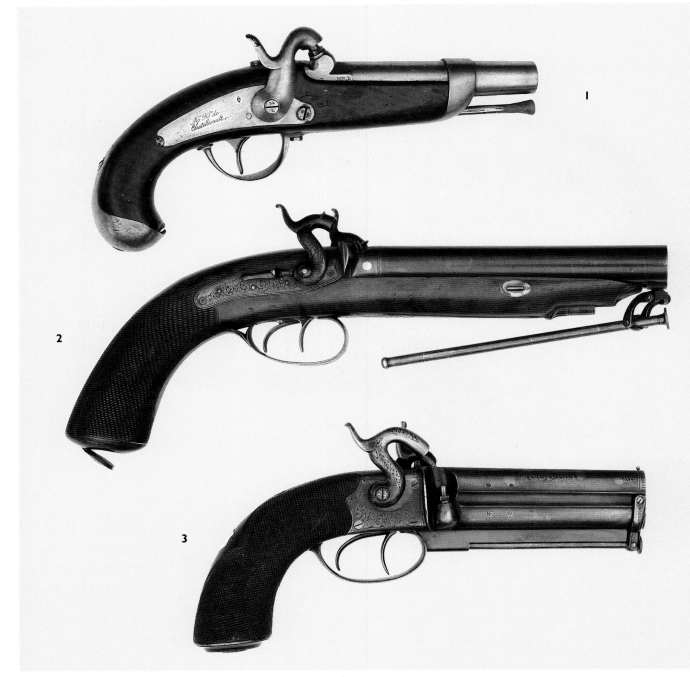

3 Over & Under Pistol

LENGTH: 9.75in (248mm)
WEIGHT: 30oz (.85kg)
CALIBRE: .5in (12.7mm)
CAPACITY: 1
MV: c.550f/s (168m/s)

Two barrels side by side still made for a wide and slightly cumbersome weapon, so many manufacturers tried to get round this by placing the barrels one above the other. Made in England by an unknown gunsmith in around 1820, this neat pistol has two barrels made out of a single block of steel. Each has its own nipple, recessed behind a shield to protect the firer from fragments of percussion cap. The left-hand hammer fires the upper barrel, while the right hand has a much longer nose to enable it to fire the lower. Both have hooded heads. Under the lower barrel is a swivel ramrod, hinged such that it can be used in either barrel. On the far side of the weapon there is a spring-loaded belt hook, indicating that this pistol was intended for a serving British army or naval officer.

4 Model 1836 Pistol

LENGTH: 14in (356mm)
WEIGHT: 44oz (1.25kg)
CALIBRE: .54in (13.7mm)
CAPACITY: 1
MV: c.500f/s (152m/s)

Based on French designs, this was the last flintlock pistol produced for the US military. From 1850 onwards most were converted to percussion operation, and a brass plug can be seen on this specimen in place of the original pan and flint. Some were also converted to use a tape primer.

5 Model 1842 Pistol

LENGTH: 14in (356mm)
WEIGHT: 44oz (1.25kg)
CALIBRE: .54in (13.7mm)
CAPACITY: 1
MV: c.500f/s (152m/s)

The Model 1842 was basically a Model 1836 built from new as a percussion pistol – the first such weapon for the US Army. It has a rounded butt and a hinged rammer under the barrel. A well-made, competent design, it saw service on both sides during the American Civil War.

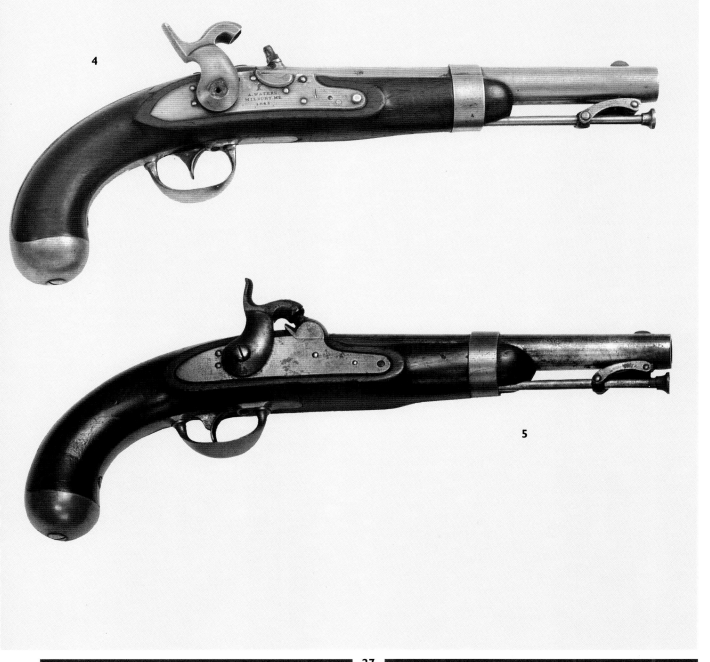

EARLY REVOLVERS

The most successful of the early revolvers was the 'pepperbox revolver', so-called from the similarity between its bunch of muzzles and a pepper-shaker. In the pepperbox, a number of barrels - usually six or seven - were rotated around a central axis. Above the topmost barrel was the usual flint and steel, and a small powder pan. The barrel cluster had to be removed to load each barrel with powder and ball, and then replaced. The cluster was turned by hand to bring one barrel beneath the flint, the pan was primed and the barrel fired, the flash from the priming passing through a small hole in the barrel. Now the owner had to unlock the barrels, rotate until the next barrel was aligned, lock them, re-cock, re-charge the pan. It was faster than re-loading a single shot pistol, but not by a lot.

What saved the pepperbox from extinction was the development of the percussion cap. The construction remained much the same, but the flint mechanism was replaced by a simple hammer. The barrels cluster was removed and loaded with shot, the nipples capped, then the cluster replaced. A shield around the rear end prevented the caps from falling off the lower barrels, and was open to expose the cap of the top barrel. The owner now revolved the cluster, cocked the hammer, fired; revolved again, cocked and fired. This was a much simpler procedure than before, and ensured a considerably faster rate of fire.

It was not long before some ingenious makers developed the self-cocking pepperbox. Instead of pulling back the hammer to cock and then releasing it by pressure on the trigger, hammer and trigger were linked so that a single long pull on the trigger would raise the hammer to full-cock and then release it to fall and strike the cap. Another lever, driven by the trigger, bore against a ratchet on the rear face of the barrel cluster and, as the trigger was pulled, revolved the cluster and brought the next barrel into line. Now the revolver could be fired as fast as the owner could pull the trigger.

Once this degree of simplicity had been reached, there seemed little point in having six barrels to bore and rifle; one barrel, with a simple rotating cylinder behind it to carry the charge and ball, with nipples behind each chamber, would be easier to make. And so the revolver was born.

Samuel Colt is often called the 'father of the revolver' with some degree of truth, but the fact is that almost all the mechanical details had been worked out before his time; his genius was to bring several ideas together, add some details, mould them into an harmonious whole, and market the idea. He was no engineer, and had his ideas translated into metal by a Baltimore mechanic called Pearson, and after several false starts Pearson finally produced a working weapon and Colt sailed for England, there to patent his revolver in 1835. He then returned to

Below: *A Confederate cavalryman poses for the photographer with a Colt 'Army' revolver in his belt.*

Right: *Colt revolvers had a hinged rammer which was used to pack the shot firmly into the cylinder.*

the USA, took out an American patent in the following year, and set up a factory. But the world was not yet ready, and after a short production he went bankrupt.

The Mexican War of 1847 was his salvation. Most of his original pistols had gone to Texas, and now the Texans wanted more of them. After this came to the notice of the US Army, Colt was approached for a new design, and an order for 1000 pistols resulted. With no factory, he had to have them made by Eli Whitney, a noted gunmaker and engineer who pioneered the concept of interchangeable parts and mass production. A further order for 1000 set Colt back on his feet, he opened his own factory once more, and from then on never looked back. His 1836 patent in the USA was a 'master patent' insofar as it protected his method of rotating and locking the cylinder, and was capable of being interpreted in a way which virtually protected any method of rotating and locking; so from then until 1857, when the patent expired, Colt had a near-monopoly of revolver manufacture in the USA.

In Europe it was a different story. Colt did not produce in Britain, and allowed his British patent to lapse in 1849, so that there were any number of designs appearing in Britain and on the continent which satisfied the European market. Among these was the Adams revolver, made in London, which differed from the Colt design in two major respects.

The Colt was a single-action revolver; to fire, it was necessary first to cock the hammer by drawing it back with the thumb, and then a light pressure on the trigger would release it to fire the shot. The Colt was also an 'open frame' revolver in that there were three major units - the butt, frame and trigger; the cylinder; and the barrel. The cylinder slid on to an 'arbor' or axis pin on the frame, and the barrel then fitted on the front of the frame and the axis pin, retained in place by a wedge. This was convenient for dismantling to clean or change cylinders, but had a tendency to wear with time.

The Adams revolver had a self-cocking mechanism; to fire, all that was necessary was to pull the trigger, which raised the hammer and then allowed it to drop. The Adams was a 'solid frame' revolver; the butt, frame and barrel were forged in one piece, leaving an aperture into which the cylinder fitted, held by a removable pin.

Colt sold several thousand revolvers to the British Army at the time of the Crimean War, but a young Lieutenant Beaumont of the Royal Engineers saw how the Adams revolver could be improved; he designed a lock mechanism which allowed both systems of operation. The hammer could be thumbed back and a deliberate shot taken with a light trigger pressure; or, if time was pressing, the trigger could be simply pulled through to cock and release the hammer. This became the now-universal 'double action' system, and Adams acquired the rights to this design and applied it to his revolvers. Success, in the shape of a military contract, followed and the double-action pistol gradually began to supplant the single action in Europe. But as this occurred, so the wheel of progress was preparing for another turn; the self-contained metallic cartridge was emerging from its development period.

Left: *A contemporary engraving shows the solid one-piece frame of British Adams-style revolvers.*

Below: *Guerrilla fighter and bandit, George Maddox, with a pair of Remington revolvers.*

1 Flintlock Revolver

LENGTH: 12in (305mm)
WEIGHT: 46oz (1.3kg)
CALIBRE: .4in (10.2mm)
CAPACITY: 8
MV: c.400f/s (122m/s)

The concept of a rotating cylinder containing multiple loaded chambers is an old one, as evidenced by this flintlock weapon made by T. Annely in around 1700. It has a brass barrel and cylinder, the latter with eight chambers. Each chamber has its own primer pan, covered by a sliding brass flap.

When the cock is pulled back, the cylinder rotates until a chamber aligns with the barrel. As the cock flies forward to hit the single steel, a small lever attached to the cock also pushes back the cover of the primer pan, allowing the sparks to ignite the charge. While the basic concept was sound, such weapons were very difficult to make, and the risk of the sparks causing a multiple discharge was always present. This pistol appears to be more in the nature of a technical exercise than a serious military weapon.

2 Collier Flintlock

LENGTH: 14.25in (362mm)
WEIGHT: 35oz (.99kg)
CALIBRE: .473in (12mm)
CAPACITY: 5
MV: c.550f/s (168m/s)

Patented by the American Elisha Collier in 1818, this weapon has a cylinder containing five chambers, with a single primer pan refilled from a small magazine attached to the steel. An effective weapon, it was overshadowed by the advent of the much more reliable percussion revolver.

3 Turner Pepperbox

LENGTH: 9.25in (235mm)
WEIGHT: 32oz (.91kg)
CALIBRE: .476in (12.1mm)
CAPACITY: 6
MV: c.500f/s (152m/s)

The pepperbox was another early revolver concept, this time with multiple barrels rotating around a central axis. This percussion weapon has six barrels in a single block of steel, each with its own nipple. Pulling the trigger raises the hammer and rotates the cylinder ready for firing.

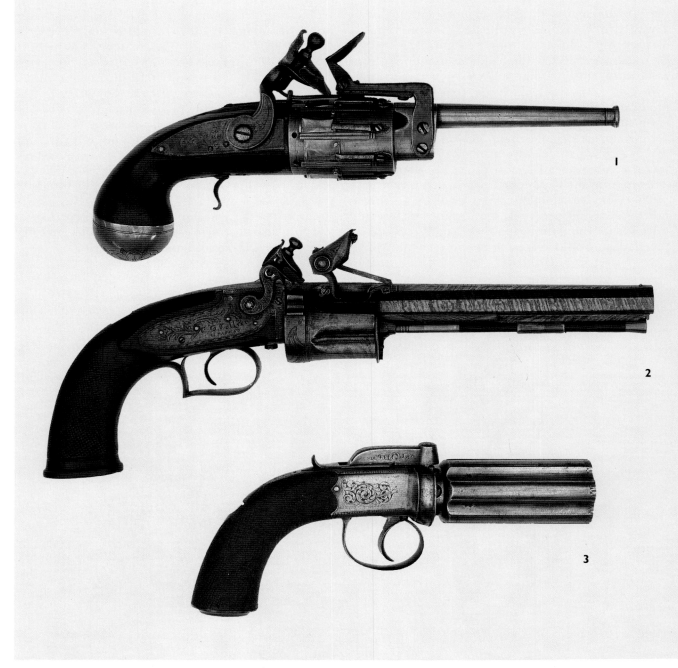

4 Cooper Pepperbox
LENGTH: 7.75in (197mm)
WEIGHT: 26oz (.74kg)
CALIBRE: .4in (10.2mm)
CAPACITY: 6
MV: c.500f/s (152m/s)

Pepperbox pistols were popular as personal defence weapons in Europe and America, but many were also used at sea to defend ships from enemy boarding parties. This English specimen was made by J. Cooper, and is based on the Mariette designs common in Belgium through the 1840s. It has six barrels drilled out of a solid steel block, which is rotated by a pawl and ratchet when the trigger is pulled. The nipples are on the same axis as their respective barrels, protected by flat shielding on each side. When the trigger is pulled, it cocks a flat hammer underneath the weapon, which then flies forward to fire the lowest barrel. A roughly-finished and simple weapon, it represents the cheaper end of the British gunmaking industry. The pepperbox was soon eclipsed by the revolver.

5 Baker Transitional
LENGTH: 11.5in (292mm)
WEIGHT: 35oz (.99kg)
CALIBRE: .44in (11.2mm)
CAPACITY: 6
MV: c.500f/s (152m/s)

This single-action weapon is closely related to the classic percussion revolver, although it is of weaker construction in that the barrel is only held in place by the cylinder axis pin. The nipples are also at right angles to the chambers, increasing the risk of a multiple discharge.

6 Transitional Revolver
LENGTH: 12in (305mm)
WEIGHT: 32oz (.91kg)
CALIBRE: .42in (10.7mm)
CAPACITY: 6
MV: c.500f/s (152m/s)

An interesting transitional revolver of the mid-19th Century in that it has a hinged bayonet attached to the barrel. The double action lock can be cocked and fired by one pull of the trigger. The barrel is fixed only to the cylinder axis pin, while there is no shielding for the nipples.

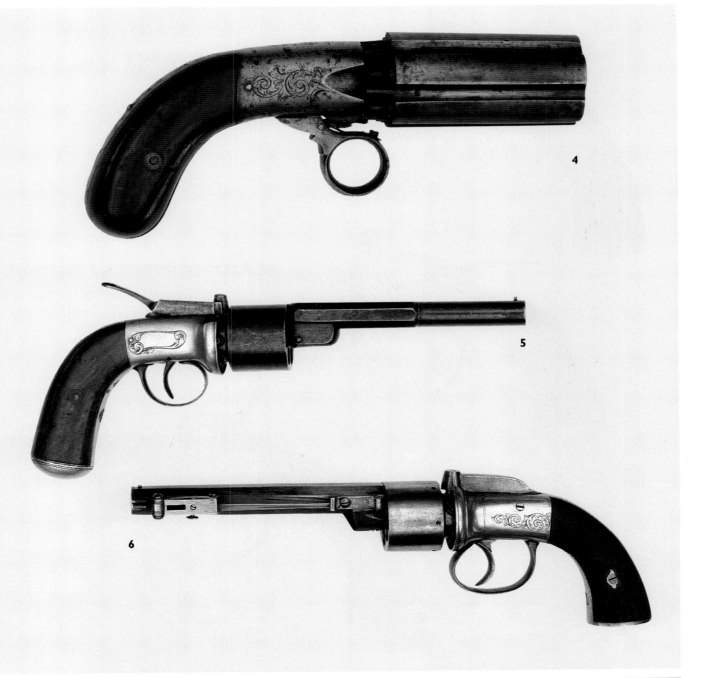

1 Lang Gas-seal
LENGTH: 11in (279mm)
WEIGHT: 32oz (.91kg)
CALIBRE: .42in (10.7mm)
CAPACITY: 6
MV: c.600f/s (183m/s)

This weapon is one of the earliest of a series of British designs which used similar principles to improve the range and power of the percussion revolver. Made by J. Lang of London, it has a six-chambered cylinder which is rotated into place as the hammer is cocked. As the weapon is fired, the movement of the hammer also pushes a plug forward, which forces the cylinder up against the barrel. This provides a good seal and prevents leakage of the propellant gasses and subsequent loss of power. The chambers have a slightly larger diameter than the barrel, ensuring that a ball which is easily loaded into the chamber is a gas-tight fit in the barrel. The barrel has simple adjustable sights, and the hammer is slightly offset to the left to permit their use. This is a reliable and effective weapon.

2 Baker Gas-seal
LENGTH: 13.25in (337mm)
WEIGHT: 49oz (1.39kg)
CALIBRE: .577in (14.6mm)
CAPACITY: 6
MV: c.600f/s (183m/s)

This is a much heavier weapon than the Lang, although it uses similar gas-seal principles. Made in 1852 by T. Baker of London, it has a single-action hammer, with a long spur to allow easy cocking. The barrel is fixed to the frame by the cylinder axis pin and by a lower securing strap.

3 Beattie Gas-seal
LENGTH: 13in (330mm)
WEIGHT: 40oz (1.13kg)
CALIBRE: .42in (10.7mm)
CAPACITY: 6
MV: c.600f/s (183m/s)

Made by J. Beattie of London, this is another weapon using the gas-seal concept to increase power and reduce the danger of a multiple discharge. Such weapons were popular in Britain, even after the appearance of Colt's percussion revolvers at the Great Exhibition of 1851.

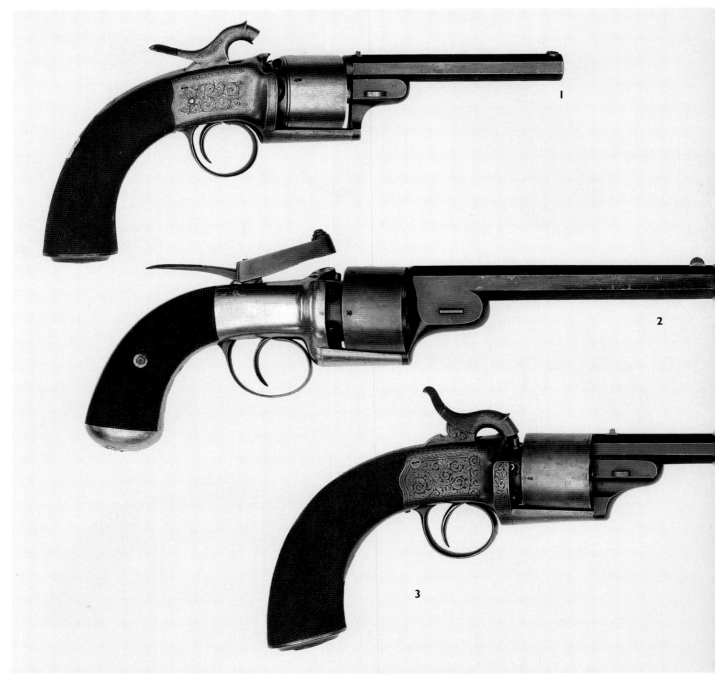

4 Parker Field Gas-seal
LENGTH: 12.5in (317mm)
WEIGHT: 38oz (1.08kg)
CALIBRE: .42in (10.7mm)
CAPACITY: 6
MV: c.600f/s (183m/s)

The fluted six-chambered cylinder gives this gas-seal weapon a distinctive appearance, as does the hinged rammer beneath the barrel. This is used to seat the bullet firmly in each cylinder in turn. As an extra safety measure, the nipples have flat protective shields between them.

5 Kufahl Needle-fire
LENGTH: 9.6in (244mm)
WEIGHT: 22oz (.62kg)
CALIBRE: .3in (7.62mm)
CAPACITY: 6
MV: c.500f/s (152m/s)

The needle fire system used a combustible paper cartridge with a primer that was detonated by a spring-loaded needle driven forwards through the paper. The concept was first invented in 1838 by Johann von Dreyse, and taken up by the Prussian Army who developed a breech-loading rifle using the system. This revolver was patented in Britain by J. Kufahl, and was manufactured from around 1834. The use of a cartridge allowed rapid reloading, further facilitated by removing the axis pin and detaching the cylinder. While an effective weapon, it depended upon a supply of specially made cartridges, while the needle was fragile and liable to break. Even so, it remained in production until 1880, well after the advent of the metallic centre-fire cartridge.

6 Tape-primer Revolver
LENGTH: 10.5in (267mm)
WEIGHT: 24oz (.68kg)
CALIBRE: .32in (8.1mm)
CAPACITY: 6
MV: c.550f/s (168m/s)

This weapon has a manually-rotated cylinder, and has only a single percussion nipple which fires each chamber in turn. Ignition is provided by a paper roll holding primer charges, which is fed onto the nipple from a recess in the butt, rather like the caps used in toy pistols today.

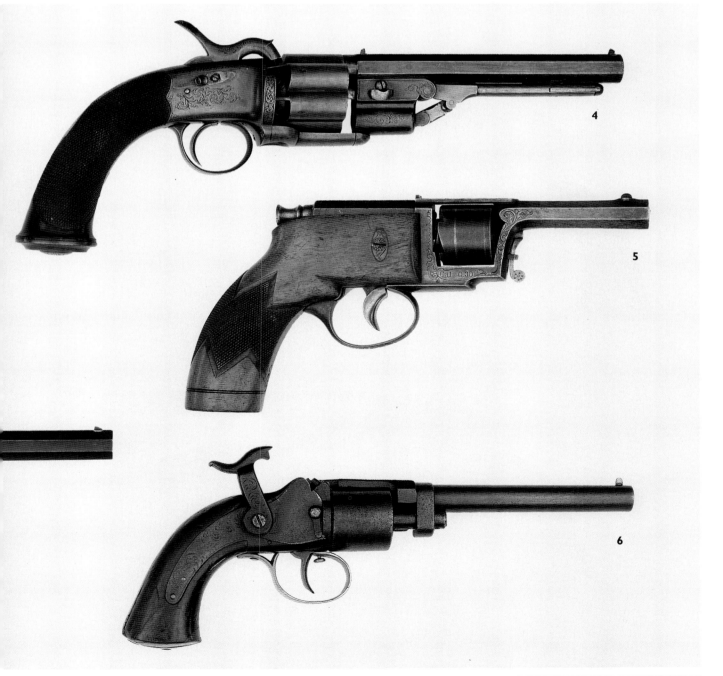

1 Colt Dragoon M 1849

LENGTH: 13.5in (343mm)
WEIGHT: 68oz (1.93kg)
CALIBRE: .44in (11.2mm)
CAPACITY: 6
MV: c.850f/s (259m/s)

In the early part of the 19th Century, Samuel Colt had designed a reasonably successful revolver rifle and a number of other revolver pistols, before designing a cavalry weapon in 1846. Early models used parts from other weapons, but by 1848 the design had been standardised as the Dragoon. Firing a powerful .44in (11.2mm) bullet, it needed to be strongly-built and consequently heavy to withstand the shock and pressure. A powerful rammer beneath the barrel was used to force the bullets into the chamber, which were tight-fitting to prevent gas leakage and ingress of damp. This specimen is the Second Model Dragoon, with the square-backed trigger guard and rectangular cylinder stop-notches. A cavalry weapon, it would normally be carried in saddle holsters.

2 Colt Navy Revolver

LENGTH: 12.9in (328mm)
WEIGHT: 39oz (1.1kg)
CALIBRE: .36in (9.1mm)
CAPACITY: 6
MV: c.700f/s (213m/s)

The Dragoon was too heavy and cumbersome for civilians or even soldiers on foot, so Colt developed a smaller, lighter weapon for more general use. The .36in (9.1mm) Naval Colt was introduced in 1851 and quickly became popular both at home and abroad. The "Navy" identification was because early versions had a naval battle scene engraved on the cylinder. It is virtually a scaled-down Dragoon, with the barrel attached to the strong axis pin and braced against the lower frame. It is a single-action weapon, where the hammer is first cocked by pulling back on its high comb. The gun also has an integral folding rammer, seen here half-way open. Hundreds of thousands of these weapons were made, and many saw extensive service on both sides in the American Civil War.

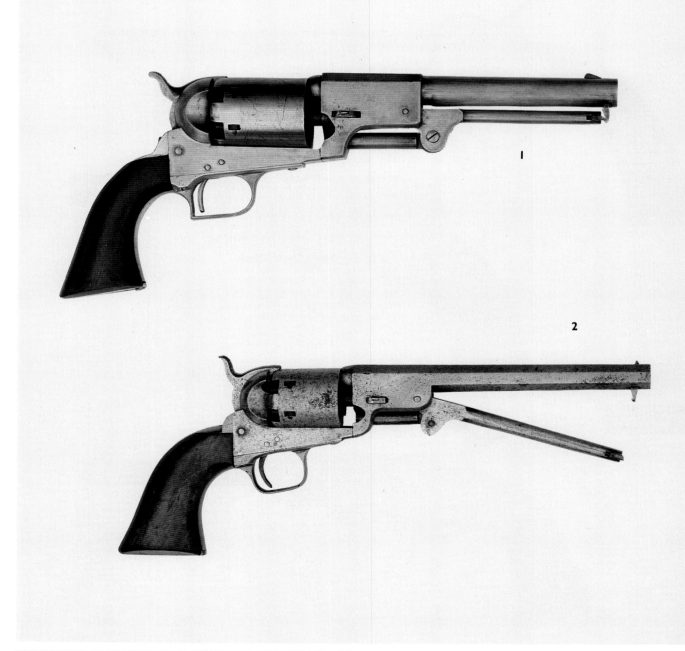

3 Colt New Model Army

LENGTH: 14in (356mm)
WEIGHT: 40oz (1.13kg)
CALIBRE: .44in (11.2mm)
CAPACITY: 6
MV: c.700f/s (213m/s)

This weapon is also known as the Model 1860, and was intended to be a lighter replacement for the Dragoon. Based on the frame of the Colt Navy pattern with a larger cylinder, it has a longer grip and a blended rammer shroud under the barrel. The standard barrel is 8in (203mm) long,

although there were some shorter variants. This specimen has a cut-out in the recoil shield behind the cylinder, which indicates that it was originally equipped with a detachable shoulder stock. Such a combination would turn the revolver into a handy short carbine for mounted soldiers. The Model 1860 was extremely popular during the Civil War, as was a Navy pattern version in .36in (9.1mm) calibre. Samuel Colt died in 1862, leaving this weapon as his finest design.

4 Colt Pocket Revolver

LENGTH: 8.8in (224m)
WEIGHT: c.30oz (.85kg)
CALIBRE: .31in (7.9mm)
CAPACITY: 5
MV: c.500f/s (152m/s)

From 1848, Colt produced a whole range of small calibre "pocket" revolvers, with various lengths of barrel and design of cylinder. This is a five-shot Model 1849 with a 4in (102mm) barrel, a pistol popular with civilians and as a handy secondary weapon for many soldiers.

5 Manhattan Revolver

LENGTH: 11.3in (287m)
WEIGHT: c.30oz (.85kg)
CALIBRE: .31in (7.9mm)
CAPACITY: 5
MV: c.500f/s (152m/s)

Many companies tried to cash in on other people's successful designs by copying them, especially during the American Civil War. This is a copy of Colt's .31in (7.9mm) pocket revolver produced by the Manhattan Firearms Company in large numbers before legal action stopped manufacture.

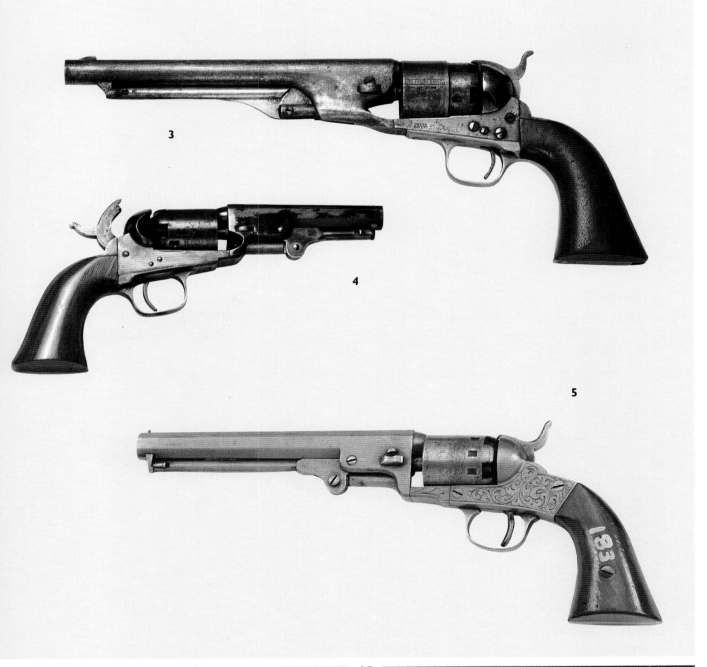

1 Leech & Rigdon
LENGTH: c.14in (356mm)
WEIGHT: c.39oz (1.1kg)
CALIBRE: .36in (9.1mm)
CAPACITY: 6
MV: c.700f/s (213m/s)

Confederate industry was in desperate straights during the Civil War, as most of the gun design and manufacturing resources were in the north. Many people tried to set up manufacturing concerns, and as they normally had no weapons experience, they tended to make copies of exist-ing designs. The Colt Navy model of 1851 formed the basis for many such revolvers, and this spread shows a range of copies of varying standard. In Columbus, Mississippi in late 1862, Leech and Rigdon made a small number of Colt Navy-type weapons, but with a round barrel instead of Colt's octagonal design. These were some of the better-made copies, using high-quality materials and manufactured with a reasonable standard of finish. About 1500 weapons were delivered.

2 Rigdon & Ansley
LENGTH: c.14in (356mm)
WEIGHT: c.39oz (1.1kg)
CALIBRE: .36in (9.1mm)
CAPACITY: 6
MV: c.700f/s (213m/s)

In the spring of 1864, Leech and Rigdon split up, each man going his own way. Rigdon took with him the last few incomplete revolvers, and assembled them in Augusta, Georgia with a new partner, Ansley. The standard of finish was not as high as on the ear-lier weapons.

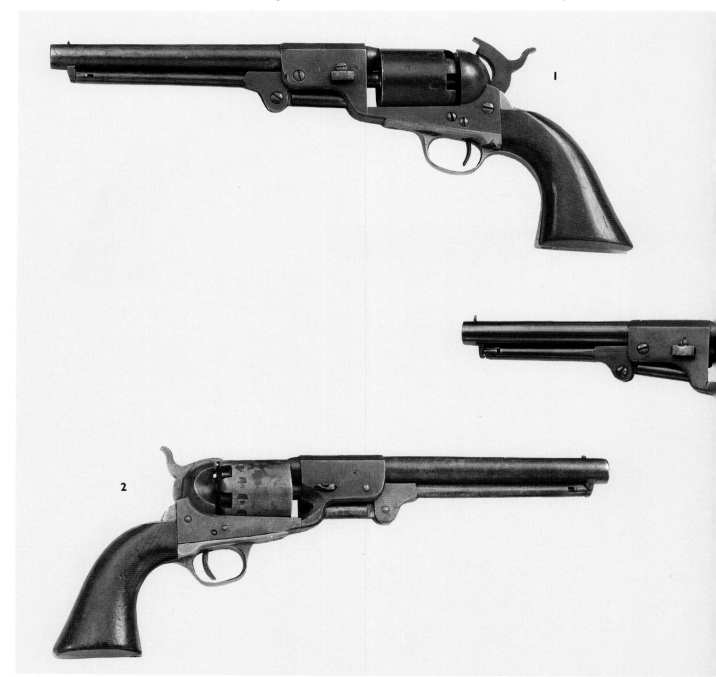

3 Dance & Bro. Navy
LENGTH: c.11.8in (300mm)
WEIGHT: c.37oz (1.05kg)
CALIBRE: .36in (9.1mm)
CAPACITY: 6
MV: c.700f/s (213m/s)

Dance Brothers and Park were based in Columbia, Texas, and in 1862 they made a few hundred Colt-type revolvers. This one is based on the Model 1851 Navy pattern, although it has a round barrel and lacks the recoil shield usually placed behind the cylinder. A wartime emergency weapon.

4 Dance & Bro. Army
LENGTH: c.14.3in (363mm)
WEIGHT: N/a
CALIBRE: .44in (11.2mm)
CAPACITY: 6
MV: c.850f/s (259m/s)

Dance Brothers also made a version of the Colt Dragoon in .44in (11.2mm) calibre. As with its Navy counterpart, it lacked the recoil shield and exploded-cap channel in the breech face. This meant that if a percussion cap burst, fragments would probably hit the firer in the face.

5 Columbus Revolver
LENGTH: 12.8in (325mm)
WEIGHT: c.37oz (1.05kg)
CALIBRE: .36in (9.1mm)
CAPACITY: 6
MV: c.700f/s (213m/s)

The Columbus Firearms Company of Columbus, Georgia made a few hundred Colt Navy copies in 1863. Most had octagonal barrels, although this specimen has a 7in (178mm) Dragoon-style round one. Roughly finished, it is not one of the best of the Confederate copies.

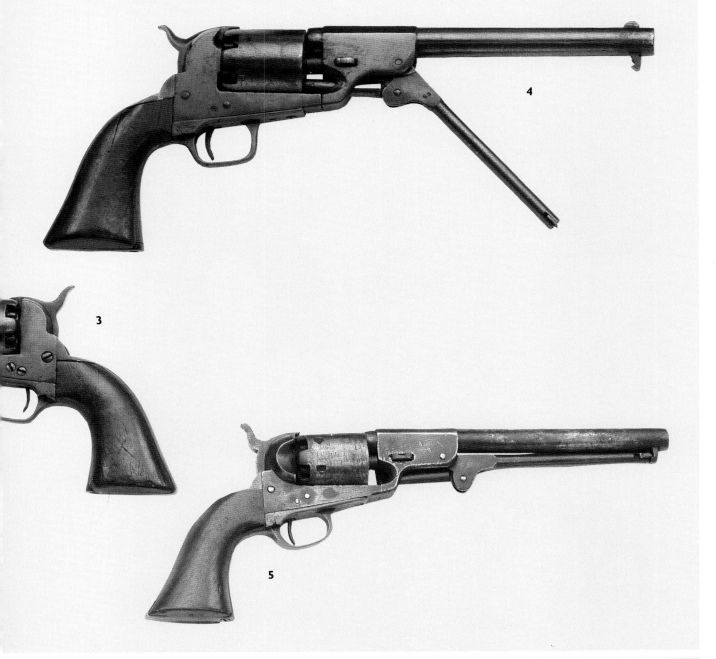

1 Taylor, Sherrard & Co.
LENGTH: c.13.8in (351mm)
WEIGHT: c.68oz (1.93kg)
CALIBRE: .44in (11.2mm)
CAPACITY: 6
MV: c.850f/s (259m/s)

Taylor, Sherrard & Company were based in Lancaster, Texas, and began the production of Colt Dragoon type revolvers in early 1862. This example is closely based on the early model Colt, down to the square edge at the rear of the trigger guard. Only a few were delivered to the Army.

2 Clark, Sherrard & Co.
LENGTH: 13.4in (340mm)
WEIGHT: N/a
CALIBRE: .44in (11.2mm)
CAPACITY: 6
MV: c.700f/s (213m/s)

When the earlier company failed, it was reconstituted as Clark, Sherrard & Company, and began the manufacture of Colt Dragoon copies, but this time with a shorter 7in (178mm) barrel and rounded trigger guard. Hardly any were delivered before the end of the American Civil War.

3 Remington-Beals Army
LENGTH: 13.8in (351mm)
WEIGHT: 46oz (1.3kg)
CALIBRE: .44in (11.2mm)
CAPACITY: 6
MV: c.700f/s (213m/s)

Some of the first revolvers produced by Eliphalet Remington used elements patented by F. Beals, and proved to be reasonably successful with both military and civilian users. This model was first patented in 1858, and a few thousand were manufactured at Remington's factory in New York. Unlike Colt's designs, Remington screwed the barrel into the front of a strong frame, which had both a top and bottom strap. This made for a tough, reliable military weapon. The percussion nipples were well-protected, while the Beal's patent rammer was hinged beneath the octagonal barrel. There is no rear sight, although the barrel has a simple blade at the front. This weapon was the forerunner of Remington's later successful military designs, which challenged the supremacy of Colt.

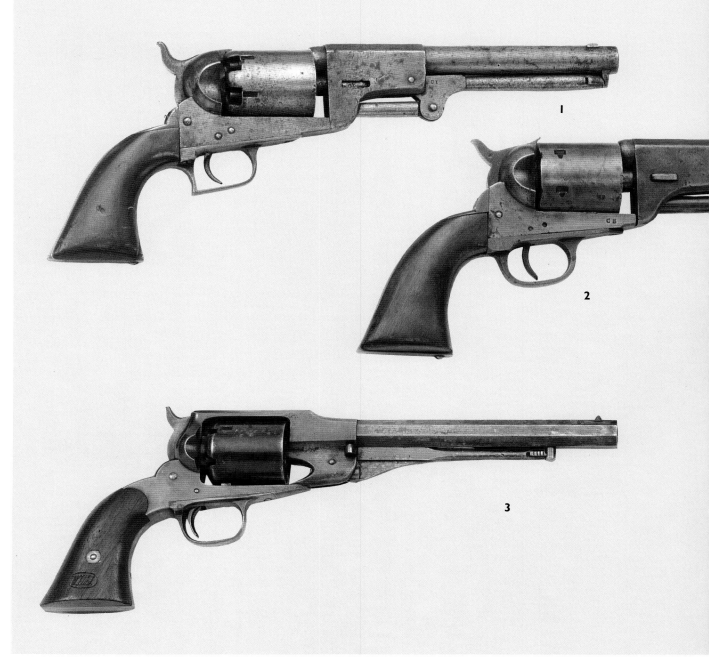

4 Remington-Beals Navy

LENGTH: 12.8in (326mm)
WEIGHT: N/a
CALIBRE: .36in (9.1mm)
CAPACITY: 6
MV: c.700f/s (213m/s)

Remington also manufactured a smaller version of his Army weapon, still using Beal's rammer. Known as the "Navy" type (although few actually went to sea), it fired a smaller calibre .36in (9.1mm) bullet and proved to be much more popular with military and civilian users than its .44in (11.2mm) counterpart. It has a 7.5in (190mm) octagonal barrel, again screwed into a solid frame. Beneath the barrel is the hinged rammer, and beneath that is a smooth web which blends into the bottom strap of the frame. The large trigger guard is brass while there is no decoration or engraving like that often found on Colts. The foresight is a cone-shaped brass pin, while the rearsight is simply a groove cut into the top strap. The lock is a single-action type, which while slow, makes for accurate shooting.

5 Remington Army

LENGTH: 13.75in (349mm)
WEIGHT: 44oz (1.25kg)
CALIBRE: .44in (11.2mm)
CAPACITY: 6
MV: c.700f/s (213m/s)

Remington eventually developed his own superior rammer design, first seen on the Improved Army Model of 1863. This weapon retains the robust one-piece Remington frame, into which the barrel is screwed. A short web prevents the rammer catching on a holster, while a narrow brass trigger guard is screwed onto the frame. The cylinder is plain, and few Remingtons carried the decorative engravings often seen on Colts. The lock mechanism is a simple single-action type, and the whole design makes for a rugged, reliable pistol. Weapons such as this (and the lighter .36in/9.1mm Navy version) were made by the hundred thousand during the Civil War and after, and became the main competitor to Colt for sales to the military and to pioneers in the West.

1 Starr Single-action

LENGTH: 13.5in (343mm)
WEIGHT: 48oz (1.36kg)
CALIBRE: .44in (11.2mm)
CAPACITY: 6
MV: c.700f/s (213m/s)

Ebenezer Starr formed the Starr Arms Company in New York, and in 1856 began the manufacture of a series of revolvers to his own patent. This is the heavy .44in (11.2mm) Army model, sporting a barrel nearly 8in (203mm) long. Unlike Colt, Starr put a top strap on his design, which made for a very strong frame. The cylinder had an integrally-forged axis pin, which reduced the chance of carbon fouling causing a jam. By removing the screw behind the cylinder, the whole front of the gun can be tipped forwards to allow access for cleaning and maintenance. The mechanism is single action, and the cylinder can be locked with a nipple on either side of the hammer, to prevent the chance of accidental discharge if the weapon is dropped. It was used by both sides in the Civil War.

2 Starr Double-action

LENGTH: 11.5in (292mm)
WEIGHT: 51oz (1.44g)
CALIBRE: .44in (11.2mm)
CAPACITY: 6
MV: c.700f/s (213m/s)

Starr's original patent was for double-action (then known as 'self cocking') revolvers in both .36in (9.1mm) and .44in (11.2mm) calibres. They could be cocked using the trigger, then fired as a separate action, or in an emergency simply cocked and fired with one pull of the trigger.

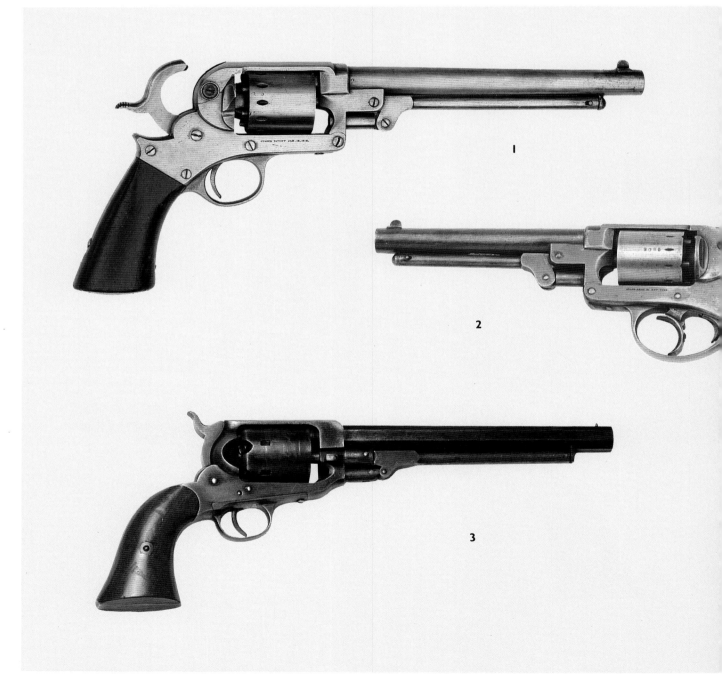

3 Whitney Navy Type
LENGTH: 13.1in (333mm)
WEIGHT: 41oz (1.16g)
CALIBRE: .36in (11.2mm)
CAPACITY: 6
MV: c.700f/s (213m/s)

4 Spiller & Burr
LENGTH: 13.1in (333mm)
WEIGHT: N/a
CALIBRE: .36in (11.2mm)
CAPACITY: 6
MV: c.700f/s (213m/s)

5 Cofer Revolver
LENGTH: 13.1in (333mm)
WEIGHT: N/a
CALIBRE: .36in (11.2mm)
CAPACITY: 6
MV: c.700f/s (213m/s)

Eli Whitney patented a popular and effective .36in (9.1mm) revolver which saw widespread service in the Civil War. It was a well-made, sturdy piece with an integral top strap, a hinged rammer, a 7.6in (193mm) octagonal barrel, and a reliable and simple single-action mechanism.

Like most successful weapons, Whitney's Navy Revolver was widely copied, in this case by the Georgia manufacturer of Spiller and Burr. A few hundred were made for the Confederacy during the Civil War, all with a brass frame of simplified construction, and separate octagonal barrel.

Thomas Cofer of Virginia made a few hundred brass-framed copies of the Whitney, although he simplified the trigger to the sheathed design seen here. The weapon was originally meant to fire Cofer's patented cartridge, but in the main was used with conventional ammunition.

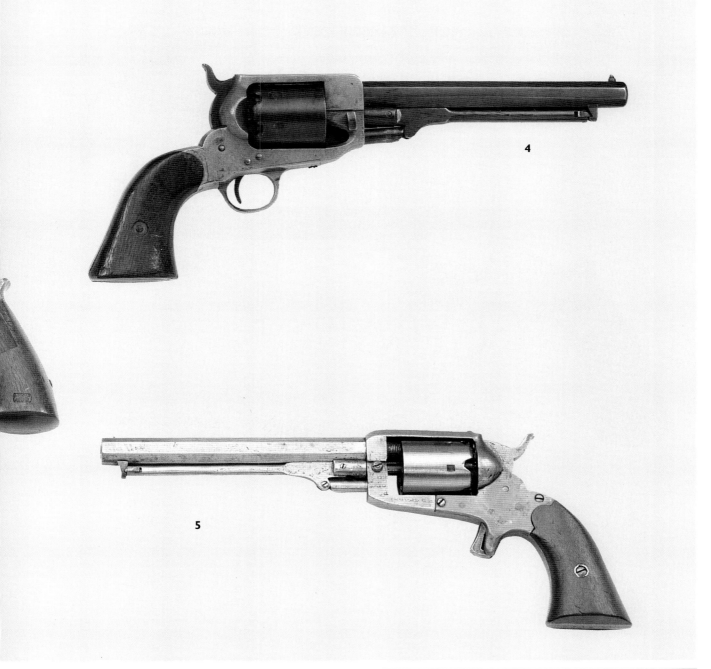

1 Adams Dragoon

LENGTH: 13in (330mm)
WEIGHT: 45oz (1.27g)
CALIBRE: .49in (12.4mm)
CAPACITY: 5
MV: c.700f/s (213m/s)

In 1851 Colt attempted to increase his export chances by displaying his wares at the Great Exhibition in London. Unfortunately for him, Britain had a talented designer in the shape of Robert Adams, who was also exhibiting. His first weapon into production was this long-barrelled self-cock-ing design, sometimes referred to as a Dragoon model. Unlike Colt's products it has a one-piece forged frame of great strength, while the .49in (12.4mm) bullet has prodi-gious man-stopping capability. British officers in far flung corners of the Empire were often faced with determined and powerfully built native opponents. They needed a heavy bullet, and also preferred the rapid firepower of a self-cocking weapon to the preci-sion and long-range accuracy of a single-action Colt.

2 Adams

LENGTH: 11.5in (292mm)
WEIGHT: 30oz (.85g)
CALIBRE: .44in (11.2mm)
CAPACITY: 5
MV: c.550f/s (168m/s)

The Dragoon was too bulky for dismounted men, so Adams soon put this smaller version into production. Its immense strength endeared it to British Army officers, who would have to campaign in places where spare parts and well-equipped armourers were impossible to find.

3 Beaumont-Adams

LENGTH: 11.75in (298mm)
WEIGHT: 38oz (1.08g)
CALIBRE: .44in (11.2mm)
CAPACITY: 5
MV: c.550f/s (168m/s)

The Adams was improved in the late 1850's by the addition of a double action lock to the design of a Lt. F. Beaumont. This meant that the hammer could be raised manually to give a more accurate shot, although in an emergency a firm pull on the trigger still gave rapid, self-cocking fire.

4 Beaumont-Adams

LENGTH: 13in (330mm)
WEIGHT: 47oz (1.33kg)
CALIBRE: .49in (12.4mm)
CAPACITY: 5
MV: c.750f/s (229m/s)

Adams' Dragoon was further developed to stay in competition with Colt. It was given the Beaumont double-action lock, and was also fitted with a hinged rammer, the operating lever of which lay alongside the barrel. This allowed the use of much tighter fitting bullets than before, helping to increase the range and power, while reducing the chance of a round slipping forward. Even so, the heavy Adams was never a particularly good long-range weapon, although its users didn't see this as a significant disadvantage. If an officer needed to fire his revolver, it was usually when things were desperate and the enemy were at close range. In these circumstances stopping power and high rate of fire were what were required. And if all else failed, the heavy Adams would make a useful club.

5 Adams Copy

LENGTH: 13.in (330mm)
WEIGHT: 33oz (.94g)
CALIBRE: .38in (9.6mm)
CAPACITY: 6
MV: c.500f/s (152m/s)

The copying of successful weapons was not limited to America, but was also prevalent in Europe. This is a pirate version of the self-cocking Adams manufactured in Belgium, although it has a Colt-type frame with the barrel screwed to the axis pin and with no top strap.

6 Massachusetts Adams

LENGTH: 11.75in (298mm)
WEIGHT: N/a
CALIBRE: .36in (9.1mm)
CAPACITY: 6
MV: c.500f/s (152m/s)

The Massachusetts Arms Company made a few hundred Beaumont-Adams revolvers under license during the Civil War. Most were modified to fire a .36in (9.1mm) bullet, although there were also some .31in (7.9mm) calibre versions manufactured. They all have a hinged rammer.

1 Webley Longspur

LENGTH: 12.9in (327mm)
WEIGHT: 37oz (1.05kg)
CALIBRE: .44in (11.2mm)
CAPACITY: 5
MV: c.700f/s (213m/s)

The Webley family began making guns in England in the early 19th Century, and the name eventually became synonymous with British service arms. This is one of their earliest designs, patented in 1853 in various models. It has an iron frame, with the 7in (178mm) octagonal barrel attached to the cylinder axis pin and the bottom strap. There is no top strap, and the whole construction is not as solid as the Adams revolvers. It is a single-action weapon, and the long hammer spur gives it its popular name. Like most British revolvers of the period it fires a hefty .44in (11.2mm) bullet, although the cylinder only has five chambers. There is a compound rammer alongside the barrel, while the thumb screw at the front of the frame is used to remove the barrel for cleaning.

2 Longspur Copy

LENGTH: 12.25in (311mm)
WEIGHT: 38oz (1.08kg)
CALIBRE: .42in (10.7mm)
CAPACITY: 6
MV: c.500f/s (152m/s)

This weapon is of unknown origin, although the design is based on the Webley Longspur. It may be a copy by one of the countless small arms manufacturers working in Belgium at this time. It has a similar frame to the Webley, again without a top strap, the barrel being fixed to the axis pin and bottom strap. The small mushroom stud beneath the barrel is slid back to unlock it for removal and cleaning. There is a folding rammer alongside the barrel, of a similar type to those used by Adams. The six-shot cylinder is plainly finished with no stop notches, and is held in place by the rounded nose of the hammer. The lock is of a double action type. There is a curved spur beneath the trigger guard to improve the firer's grip, and the whole pistol is a robust, well-made service weapon.

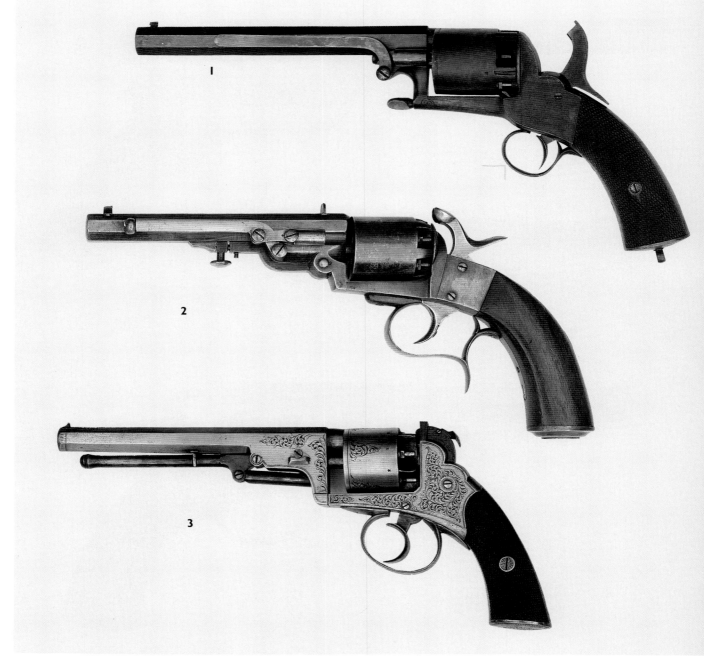

3 Bentley Revolver
LENGTH: 12in (305mm)
WEIGHT: 33oz (.94kg)
CALIBRE: .44in (11.2mm)
CAPACITY: 5
MV: c.600f/s (183m/s)

Joseph Bentley was closely associated with Webley, and their designs bear a close resemblance to each other. This 1853 model has an iron frame, with the barrel attached using a similar method to Colt's system. It has a double-action lock and a safety catch on the hammer.

4 Le Mat 1st Model
LENGTH: 13.25in (337mm)
WEIGHT: 58oz (1.64kg)
CALIBRE: .3in (7.62mm)
CAPACITY: 9/1
MV: c.600f/s (183m/s)

Jean Le Mat was a French Doctor living in New Orleans who patented his unusual design of revolver in 1856. It is a massive and solidly-built weapon with a nine-chamber cylinder and 7in (178mm) upper barrel. The unique feature of Le Mat weapons was the second .67in (16.5mm) smooth-bore barrel along the cylinder axis, which was usually loaded with buckshot. The tip of the hammer can be rotated so that it either hits the upper nipple on the cylinder or the recessed nipple for the centre barrel. The lock is single action, and can be easily accessed by removing the steel plate above the trigger. This version of the Le Mat has a spurred trigger guard to improve grip and a lanyard ring beneath the butt. A folding compound rammer lies alongside the upper barrel.

5 Le Mat 2nd Model
LENGTH: 13.25in (337mm)
WEIGHT: 58oz (1.64kg)
CALIBRE: .3in (7.62mm)
CAPACITY: 9/1
MV: c.600f/s (183m/s)

Le Mat revolvers came in many variations of the same basic design, and this specimen shows some of the differences. It has the rammer on the left, an octagonal upper barrel, and a simple rounded trigger guard. Le Mats were popular weapons with Confederate cavalry officers during the Civil War.

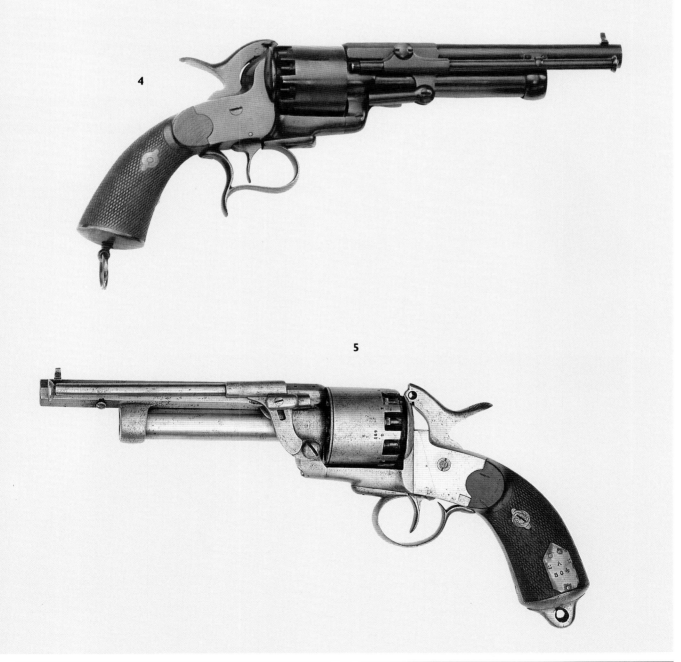

1 Deane-Harding

LENGTH: 12in (305mm)
WEIGHT: 41oz (1.16kg)
CALIBRE: .44in (11.2mm)
CAPACITY: 5
MV: c.550f/s (168m/s)

Deane had been in partnership with Robert Adams, but in 1858 he began the manufacture of this revolver patented by William Harding. It is a double action type intended to compete with the Beaumont-Adams, firing a similar .44in (11.2mm) bullet through a short 5.25in (133mm) barrel.

Instead of the one-piece Adams frame, the barrel and top strap are an integral unit attached to the frame at the bottom strap and in front of the hammer. The barrel assembly can be unlocked and tipped forward for removal and cleaning. A hinged rammer sits beneath the barrel, and the lever is pulled vertically downwards to force the ram into the chamber. This revolver never became a popular weapon, and doubts were often expressed about its reliability. It remained overshadowed by the Adams.

2 Tranter 2nd Model

LENGTH: 11.5in (292mm)
WEIGHT: 29oz (.82kg)
CALIBRE: .44in (11.2mm)
CAPACITY: 5
MV: c.550f/s (168m/s)

An improved variant of Tranter's design is seen here. The rammer, while still a separate item, can be left permanently attached to the gun alongside the barrel. There is also a spring-loaded safety which prevents the hammer dropping until the trigger is fully pulled home.

3 Tranter 1st Model

LENGTH: 11.5in (292mm)
WEIGHT: 31oz (.88kg)
CALIBRE: .44in (11.2mm)
CAPACITY: 5
MV: c.550f/s (168m/s)

William Tranter was a well-established Birmingham gunmaker who developed this double-action revolver. Self-cocking weapons like the early Adams required a heavy pull on the trigger, thus reducing accuracy at range. Tranter's solution was the double trigger design seen here. Pulling

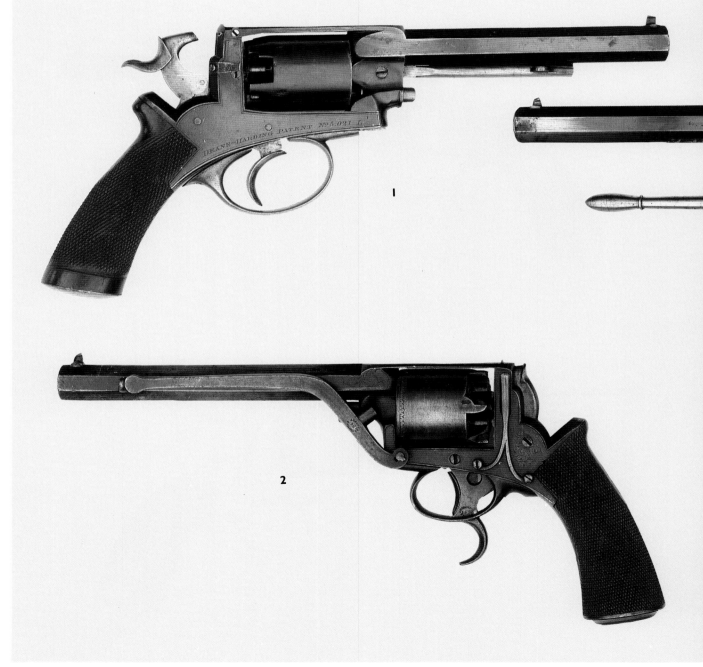

on the lower trigger cocked the hammer, which then required only light pressure on the upper trigger to fire. In an emergency, where rapid fire-power was needed, the firer simply pulled on both triggers simultaneously. The solid one-piece frame is license-built from Adams' design, making for a robust and reliable weapon. The only disadvantage for service users was the separate detachable ram, an item which could easily be dropped at a critical moment, in the heat of the action.

4 Tranter 3rd Model

LENGTH: 11.75in (298mm)
WEIGHT: 36oz (1.02kg)
CALIBRE: .44in (11.2mm)
CAPACITY: 5
MV: c.550f/s (168m/s)

Service users still felt that the separate rammer on the Tranter was a weakness in the design, so he produced this model with a permanently fixed ram. Tranter's system proved to be fast and reliable in action, and his revolvers quickly found favour with many British Army officers.

5 Westley-Richards

LENGTH: 12.25in (311mm)
WEIGHT: 39oz (1.1kg)
CALIBRE: .49in (12.4mm)
CAPACITY: 5
MV: c.550f/s (168m/s)

This is a comparatively rare weapon made by a well-known British maker of the times. The frame has no bottom strap, while the barrel and top strap are an integral unit. There is a hook at the rear of the strap which locks on to the top of the breech, while a sleeve under the barrel slides over the cylinder axis pin. The lock is a double-action one. making use of a combless hammer offset to one side. Such an arrangement means that the nipples are angled to allow the chamber to align with the barrel at the moment of firing. There is an unusual rack and pinion rammer on the left of the barrel. While a well-made weapon, the Westley-Richards appears to be much too flimsy for extended service use, and its unconventional configuaration never gained widespread acceptance.

1 Webley Double-action

LENGTH: 11.5in (292mm)
WEIGHT: 37oz (1.05kg)
CALIBRE: .44in (11.2mm)
CAPACITY: 5
MV: c.550f/s (168m/s)

After the Longspur, Webley went on to manufacture a series of double-action military service revolvers. This one has an octagonal barrel which is forged as an integral unit with the top strap. This piece is firmly attached to the rest of the frame at the top of the breech, on the axis pin, and at the front of the bottom strap. Like most British service weapons of the time, it holds only five large calibre shots, a necessary design compromise between firepower and bulk. The mechanism is double-action, with no safety, although the hammer can be placed at half-cock. The rammer sits under the barrel and is similar to that on Colt revolvers. Webley made a similar double-action revolver with a one-piece frame, into which was screwed the barrel, rather like the Remington.

2 Kerr

LENGTH: 11in (279mm)
WEIGHT: 42oz (1.19kg)
CALIBRE: .44in (11.2mm)
CAPACITY: 5
MV: c.550f/s (168m/s)

James Kerr was the inventor of a rammer used on many of Adam's weapons, and in 1858 he produced this single-action revolver to his own design. Adams had patented the idea of a solid one-piece frame, so Kerr made use of an integral barrel and top strap which was fastened to the frame by two screws. Kerr's idea was that a service revolver would often find itself in remote parts of the globe, where skilled gunsmiths may be hard to find. He therefore fixed the lock mechanism on to a single steel plate which could be removed for access. Simple components, such as a broken mainspring, could than be replaced by anyone with reasonable metal-working skills, such as a village blacksmith. The concept proved popular with British and colonial forces, while some served in the American Civil War.

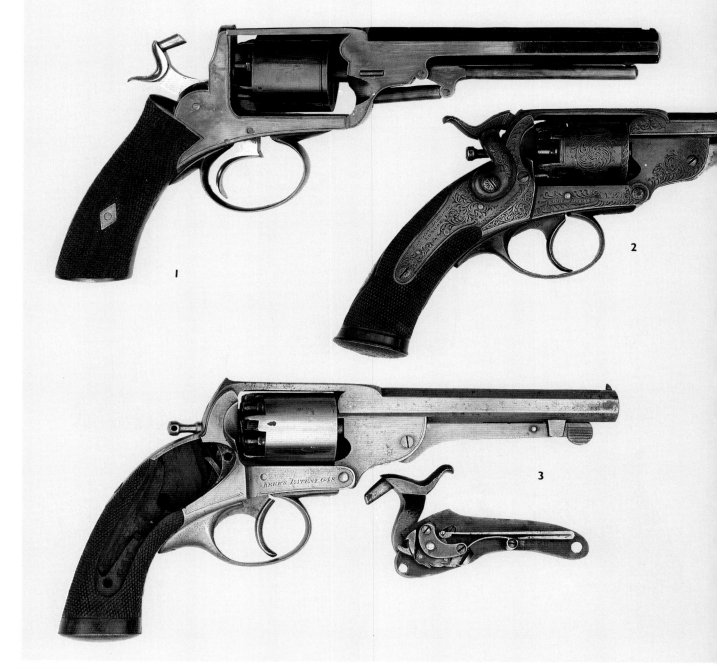

3 Kerr Later Model
LENGTH: 10.6in (269mm)
WEIGHT: 34oz (.96kg)
CALIBRE: .44in (11.2mm)
CAPACITY: 5
MV: c.550f/s (168m/s)

This is a less decorated specimen of the Kerr revolver with minor differences in construction. The lock plate has been removed to show the mechanism. Under the barrel is another design of Kerr patent rammer, while the cylinder axis pin can be seen protruding to the rear.

4 Daw
LENGTH: 10.5in (267mm)
WEIGHT: 26oz (.74kg)
CALIBRE: .38in (9.6mm)
CAPACITY: 5
MV: c.550f/s (168m/s)

This revolver makes use of a 'hesitation' double-action lock, where by slowly pressing the trigger the hammer can be raised to full cock without firing. Further slight pressure drops the hammer and fires the round. In other ways this design resembles those from Colt, with its lack of top strap.

5 Dual-ignition Revolver
LENGTH: 10.8in (274mm)
WEIGHT: 33oz (.94kg)
CALIBRE: .44in (11.2mm)
CAPACITY: 5
MV: c.550f/s (168m/s)

Cartridge revolvers did not make a widespread appearance in Britain until around 1863, and percussion revolvers lingered on for many years after. This Webley-style design is typical of a class of intermediate weapon, in that it can fire either as a percussion or cartridge revolver. It would have come with two interchangeable cylinders, one for each mode of firing. The percussion cylinder is fitted in this specimen (the cartridge cylinder is missing), and so is a folding rammer alongside the barrel. There is a hinged loading gate for use with metal cartridges. The revolver is marked with Webley's name, but it may have been a modification produced by another workshop. The brass cartridge quickly entered widespread use, and dual-ignition revolvers such as this were soon obsolete.

CARTRIDGE REVOLVERS

In the early 19th Century a French gunmaker Bernard Houllier patented a cartridge which consisted of a metal cylinder with a closed base, containing the gunpowder and with the mouth closed by the bullet. Inside the case was a percussion cap, and resting upon this was a sharp pin which extended through the side of the case to protrude for a fraction of an inch. The weapon had a slot in the top of the chamber, allowing the pin to stand proud when the cartridge was loaded. The hammer fell on to the pin, the pin struck the cap, and the bullet was fired. The breech was opened and the empty case removed and thrown away.

Houllier's 'pinfire' cartridge became an immediate success, and pistols, revolvers and shotguns using the system were widely manufactured; indeed pinfire ammunition remained in manufacture in some countries until 1940. It was unpopular with some people because it was unable to stand very high pressures and was thus unsuited to use in rifles, and it was somewhat dangerous to handle since the exposed pins could easily be struck and cause accidental explosions. But for all that, the pinfire system prospered.

Houllier then patented a second idea; in effect, he took the existing percussion cap, opened out the mouth, and put a small bullet into it. This did not appear to have much potential as a military weapon, and Houllier never bothered to pursue the idea, but another French gunmaker, Louis Flobert, perfected it and developed a series of small-calibre 'saloon rifles' which became very popular. More improvements followed, and Flobert's 'bulleted breech cap' turned into the rimfire cartridge, so-called because the priming composition was distributed around the hollow rim. When this cartridge was loaded the rim butted against the rear end of the chamber wall, and the hammer was given a chisel-like firing pin which struck across the rim, crushing it and so igniting the composition inside.

The rimfire cartridge soon crossed the Atlantic where it was seized upon by two gunsmiths, Horace Smith and Daniel Wesson. They had ideas about revolvers but were constrained to wait until Colt's patent expired. They then launched a small revolver, chambered for the .22in (5.56mm) rimfire cartridge; this did well, and since customers demanded something more lethal, they followed it by developing larger rimfire calibres and revolvers to match. Smith and Wesson were just as astute as Colt over the matter of patents; while waiting for Colt's to expire, they had conducted a patent search and had found one which threatened to put them out of business, so they went to the patentee and, for an

Left: *The 'needle fire' system used a long needle to ignite the primer within the cartridge.*

Below left: *French sailors with Lefacheaux pinfire revolvers.*

Below: *A British officer defends himself in the Sudan. It was for just such a situation that British revolvers were designed, making use of a double-action trigger combined with a heavy bullet.*

inconsiderable fee, bought it off him. Unbelievably, this actually protected the principle of boring chambers through a cylinder from one end to the other, and with this it was the turn of Smith & Wesson to monopolise the American revolver market until 1869, at least so far as cartridge revolvers was concerned.

The drawback of the rimfire cartridge was (and still is) that the rim has to be malleable in order to crush, so the metal is too soft to withstand very high pressure; so there can be no high-powered rimfire rifle cartridges. So there was still an incentive to designers to produce a cartridge capable of use in any type of weapon.

This final step was the centre-fire cartridge, in which the cap is placed centrally in the base, allowing the case to be as strong as needed. Unlike the pinfire and the rimfire, the parentage of the centre-fire cartridge is far from easy to unravel, since it is really the sum of several different inventors' efforts and modifications over a period of time.

When the revolver was adapted to the metallic centre-fire cartridge, it brought with it the twin problems of loading and unloading. In the earliest models, this followed the percussion revolver in allowing the cylinder to be quickly removed and replaced with a loaded one, leaving the business of punching out the fired cases and reloading to a more convenient time. Then came 'gate-loading' in which a flap behind the cylinder was hinged open to give access to the just-fired chamber; a rod carried

under the barrel could be pushed back to eject the case, and a fresh round inserted through the 'gate'. An effective method, but slow; wise men still carried a loaded cylinder just in case.

In order to speed things up various methods of 'automatic' or 'collective' ejection were tried; as with several other aspects of firearms design most failed and only two have managed to stand the test of real life; the top break, and the hinged side-opening cylinder.

In the top break, as the name implies, the frame of the revolver is no longer solid, but in two parts which hinge in front of the cylinder. As it hinges down, so a cam forces out a star-like plate in the centre of the cylinder which, catching under the rims of the fired cases, forces them out of the chambers to fall free. Most are arranged so that the stroke of the ejector is slightly greater than the length of an empty case; so that when operated only the empty cases fall out - any bulleted cartridge will remain in its chamber.

The solid frame revolver demands a different approach. In this system, pioneered by Smith and Wesson, the cylinder axis pin is carried on an arm which pivots on the front of the frame. It is locked in place by a thumb catch which, when operated, allows the cylinder to be pushed sideways , swinging out on its arm so as to fully expose the rear face. Once the cylinder has been swung out, the ejector rod can be manually pressed in to force the central star out and eject the cases.

Below: *An American serviceman loads a Smith and Wesson revolver during the Second World War. This large top-opening revolver was overshadowed in service by the Colt M1911 automatic.*

Right: *The Russian Nagant is typical of those designs with a hinged loading gate.*

Below right: *The Webley Mk.I has a hinged frame which breaks open.*

1 German Pinfire
LENGTH: 11in (279mm)
WEIGHT: 27oz (.76kg)
CALIBRE: .43in (11mm)
CAPACITY: 6
MV: c.600f/s (183m/s)

The pinfire system used a brass cartridge holding the propellant and bullet, with the primer in a separate tube or 'pin' extending from the side of the cartridge case. This method became popular in Europe, although it never had great success in Britain or America. Shown here is a finely deco-

rated example of a pinfire revolver, made in Germany in about 1850. The cartridges are loaded via a rear loading gate, and have to be placed such that their pins protrude through the slots cut in the rear edge of the cylinder. When the revolver is cocked and the trigger pulled, the hammer falls on the edge of the cylinder, striking the pin and firing the cartridge. The brass case swells under the pressure of the burning gasses, sealing the breech and preventing leakage, then shrinks back to allow easy removal.

2 German Pinfire
LENGTH: 10.4in (264mm)
WEIGHT: 26oz (.73kg)
CALIBRE: .35in (9mm)
CAPACITY: 6
MV: c.550f/s (168m/s)

Another superbly-made, finely decorated German pinfire revolver from about 1850, this one has a strong one-piece frame with a top strap. The cylinder can be removed easily by pulling back the axis pin; and a loaded one can be put in its place. This weapon also has a double action lock.

3 Lefacheaux Pinfire
LENGTH: 8.4in (213mm)
WEIGHT: 20oz (.56kg)
CALIBRE: .35in (9mm)
CAPACITY: 6
MV: c.600f/s (183m/s)

This weapon was designed by a Frenchman, although it was patented in Britain in 1854. The barrel is attached to the axis pin, rather like on a Colt, and is braced against the lower edge of the frame. There is no trigger guard, although the trigger can be folded forward as a safety measure.

4 Lefacheaux Pinfire

LENGTH: 11.25in (286mm)
WEIGHT: 34oz (.96kg)
CALIBRE: .43in (11mm)
CAPACITY: 6
MV: c.650f/s (198m/s)

This revolver was selected in 1851 for use by the French Navy. It was designed by Eugene Lefacheaux, whose father had been involved in the design of the pinfire system. It is a sturdy and effective weapon, with the heavy round barrel fixed to the cylinder axis pin and screwed to the bottom strap of the frame. In terms of range, power and accuracy, pinfire weapons were a great advance over their percussion predecessors, although they were still slow to reload (the pins had to be placed in exactly the right position). The empty cases also had to be punched out of the cylinder one at a time, using the long rod under the barrel. The pins themselves were fragile and easily broken, so great care had to be taken when handling ammunition. The centre-fire cartridge soon took over.

5 French Pinfire

LENGTH: 9in (229mm)
WEIGHT: 22oz (.62kg)
CALIBRE: .39in (9.9mm)
CAPACITY: 6
MV: c.600f/s (183m/s)

The pinfire system was popular on the continent of Europe, and many small manufacturers in Belgium and France tried their hand. This anonymous weapon is cheaply made, of weak design and poorly assembled. Some weapons of this type saw use during the American Civil War.

6 Belgian Pinfire

LENGTH: 10in (245mm)
WEIGHT: 21oz (.39kg)
CALIBRE: .43in (11mm)
CAPACITY: 6
MV: c.650f/s (198m/s)

Another anonymous pinfire revolver, this time from Belgium, and of better quality than the earlier weapon. It is an effective double-action design of reasonably strong construction, although without a top strap. It would appear to have been intended for paramilitary or police use.

1 Arriaban Pinfire

LENGTH: 11.5in (292mm)
WEIGHT: 34oz (.96kg)
CALIBRE: .43in (11mm)
CAPACITY: 6
MV: c.650f/s (198m/s)

When the Spanish Navy adopted the pinfire revolver, Arriaban and Company made this version of the Lefacheaux design. It is a well-made single-action weapon, with the barrel fixed to the axis pin and the lower frame. The trigger guard has a spur to enhance the firer's grip.

2 Tranter Rimfire

LENGTH: 12in (305mm)
WEIGHT: 50oz (1.4kg)
CALIBRE: .45in (11.4mm)
CAPACITY: 6
MV: c.650f/s (198m/s)

The pinfire system never took off in Britain, manufacturers turning instead to the development of rimfire cartridges, which have the primer on the outside rim of their base. This design by Tranter was first seen in 1863, and like his earlier percussion weapons makes use of Adams' one-piece frame. Unlike his earlier designs, however, this revolver has six chambers in its cylinder rather than five. It retains a patent hinged rammer, although this time it is used to push empty cases out of the cylinder. It is a double-action weapon, although without the Tranter double trigger seen on his percussion revolvers. Like all British service weapons of the period, this revolver fires a heavy, large calibre projectile, guaranteed to permanently stop the fittest, strongest and most determined adversary.

3 Tranter Pocket

LENGTH: 8in (203mm)
WEIGHT: 19oz (.54kg)
CALIBRE: .32in (8.1mm)
CAPACITY: 7
MV: c.550f/s (168m/s)

Tranter also produced a series of pocket revolvers for civilian use, although they were also seen as a back-up weapon for service personnel. This one uses a small rimfire cartridge which would only be effective at point blank range. The cylinder holds seven shots, but no ejector rod is fitted.

4 Allen & Wheelock

LENGTH: 8in (203mm)
WEIGHT: 15oz (.43kg)
CALIBRE: .32in (8.1mm)
CAPACITY: 6
MV: c.500f/s (152m/s)

When Smith and Wesson patented the bored-through cylinder, they spent a good deal of time and effort guarding their patent in the courts. One of the manufacturers which were taken to law were Allen and Wheelock, although they were able to produce this pocket revolver for more than four years before the action was prosecuted. It is another small calibre pocket rimfire weapon, with a single-action side hammer, sheathed trigger and solid frame. The frame has some poorly-executed decorative engravings. Six shots are carried, but the cylinder can not be reloaded while on the frame. Instead, the axis pin has to be withdrawn, the cylinder removed, and the empty cases punched out one by one before reloading. This is a cheaply-made weapon with limited military usefulness.

5 Lagresse

LENGTH: 11.75in (298mm)
WEIGHT: 28oz (.79kg)
CALIBRE: .43in (10.9mm)
CAPACITY: 6
MV: c.550f/s (168m/s)

This unusual and ornate design was produced in Paris in about 1866. It has an octagonal barrel which is screwed to the front of the frame, which also has the cylinder axis pin passing through it. The cylinder has a fully fluted outer surface and has a separate back plate and loading gate, through which are drilled small holes to allow the hammer to hit the cartridges. A groove can be seen cut into the top of the butt to enable the cartridges to be slid into the cylinder. On this specimen there is a noticeable gap between the cylinder and barrel, and the ensuing leakage must have caused a significant loss of power. A hinged rammer is fitted, and is used to push empty cases out of the chambers. The lock is of double-action type. Cumbersome and ornate, it was effective enough.

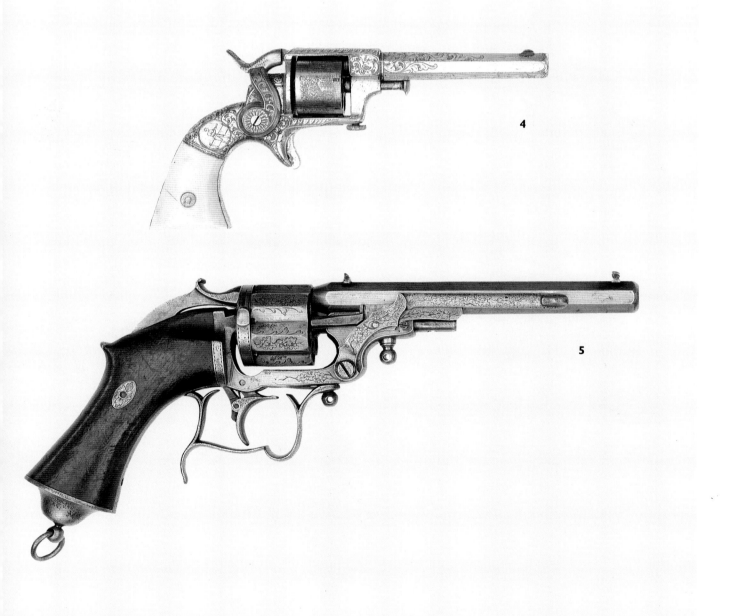

4

5

1 S & W Tip-up (1st)

LENGTH: 7in (178mm)
WEIGHT: 11.5oz (.33kg)
CALIBRE: .22in (5.56mm)
CAPACITY: 7
MV: c.500f/s (1522m/s)

Once Smith and Wesson had bought Rollin White's patent for a cylinder with chambers bored right through, they put into production a pocket revolver using this principle. The Model 1 first appeared in 1857, and this specimen is one of the second series, first seen in 1860. It is a single action weapon with a simple sheathed trigger, firing a small calibre rimfire round, similar to those used by small-bore shooters today. The frame is made from brass and was originally silver-plated. The barrel is hinged at the top of the frame, and can be tipped upwards when the catch at the bottom of the frame is released. The cylinder has to be removed to eject the empty cases and reload. These revolvers quickly became popular with both military and civilian users and many saw service in the Civil War.

2 S & W Tip-up (2nd)

LENGTH: 10in (254mm)
WEIGHT: 21oz (.6kg)
CALIBRE: .32in (8.1mm)
CAPACITY: 6
MV: c.600f/s (183m/s)

In 1861 Smith and Wesson developed the 2nd (or Army) Model of their successful tip-up revolver. It has an iron frame rather than brass, and fires the more powerful .32in (8.1mm) rimfire cartridge. The 2nd Model was made with various barrel lengths, this one being 5in (127mm).

3 S & W Tip-up (3rd)

LENGTH: 6.6in (168mm)
WEIGHT: 9oz (.25kg)
CALIBRE: .22in (5.56mm)
CAPACITY: 7
MV: c.500f/s (152m/s)

After the Civil War, Smith and Wesson produced this iron version of their successful .22in (5.6mm) revolver. It has an attractive plated finish and a curved 'bird-beak' butt. It was intended in the main for civilian users in the more settled eastern states, who didn't want to carry a bulky belt-gun.

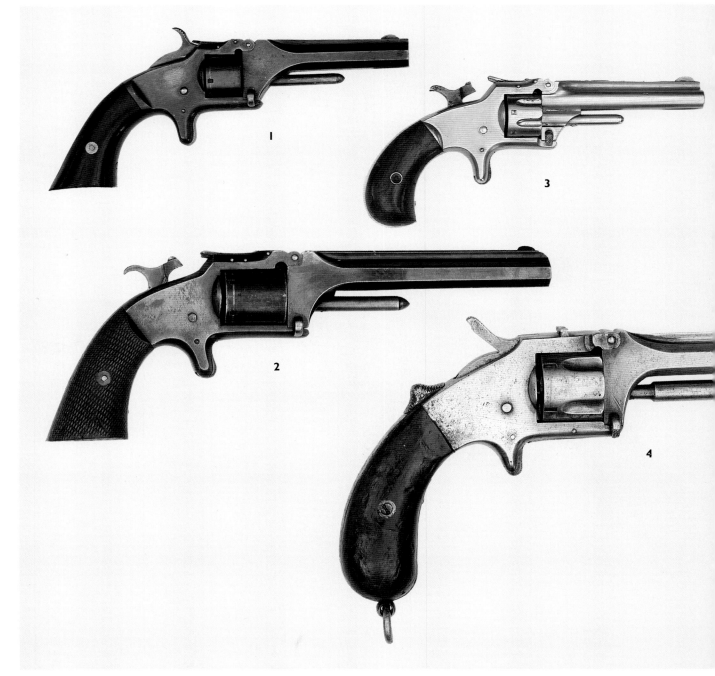

4 S & W Copy
LENGTH: 10.75in (273mm)
WEIGHT: 32oz (.9kg)
CALIBRE: .44in (11.2mm)
CAPACITY: 5
MV: c.600f/s (183m/s)

Smith and Wesson's patent only extended to the United States, so many European manufacturers were able to produce revolvers with bored-through cylinders. This is a blatant copy of the tip-up revolver, although it is much heavier and fires a powerful centre-fire cartridge.

5 Adams Centre-fire
LENGTH: 11.5in (292mm)
WEIGHT: 33oz (.94g)
CALIBRE: .44in (11.2mm)
CAPACITY: 5
MV: c.550f/s (168m/s)

The rimfire system was too fragile for use on heavy cartridges, and was soon replaced in most cases by the centre-fire concept. With the primer at the base of the case, much more powerful rounds than before could be shot with safety, and centre-fire quickly became the standard for military users in Britain and America. Shooters who had well-proven percussion weapons were often reluctant to part from them, so many guns were converted to the new system. This a service percussion Adams, which has had its cylinder replaced by a bored-through one. A sprung loading gate has also been attached behind the cylinder, and a similarly shaped blanking plate has been fitted to the other side. A simple ejector rod is held in a sleeve, brazed to the frame.

6 Devisme
LENGTH: 12.5in (317mm)
WEIGHT: 32oz (.91kg)
CALIBRE: .41in (10.4mm)
CAPACITY: 6
MV: c.550f/s (168m/s)

Devisme was a French gun-maker who experimented with centre-fire cartridges at an early date. This model was demonstrated in 1867, and is a single-action type with a fully fluted cylinder. The top strap is unlocked and the barrel tipped down to gain access to the cylinder.

1 Thomas

LENGTH: 10.75in (273mm)
WEIGHT: 31oz (.88kg)
CALIBRE: .45in (11.4mm)
CAPACITY: 5
MV: c.600f/s (183m/s)

This British design appeared in 1869, and was an early attempt to speed up the reloading process on a cartridge revolver. It is a service-calibre double-action weapon, with a heavy octagonal barrel. This can be unlocked and rotated through 180°, then pulled forwards with the cylinder attached. As this is done, a star-shaped extractor which is fixed to the breech catches the rims of the cases and holds them until the cylinder is pulled clear. The empty cases are then shaken clear and the barrel and cylinder locked back in place. New cartridges are loaded in the normal way, past the hinged gate seen behind the cylinder. The system worked well enough, but was never a commercial success, soon being overtaken by better and more reliable designs. Only a few of these weapons saw service.

2 British Tip-up

LENGTH: 8.5in (216mm)
WEIGHT: 21oz (.6kg)
CALIBRE: .38in (9.6mm)
CAPACITY: 6
MV: c.600f/s (183m/s)

This anonymous British design has the barrel hinged at the top of the frame, allowing it to swing upwards for reloading. The cylinder and axis pin goes with it, then the thick pin under the barrel is used to push down a star-shaped extractor which lifts out the empty centre-fire cases for reloading.

3 Webley No.1

LENGTH: 9.5in (241mm)
WEIGHT: 42oz (1.19kg)
CALIBRE: .577in (14.6mm)
CAPACITY: 6
MV: c.600f/s (183m/s)

This huge weapon was designed to fire the spiral wound Boxer cartridge, of the same calibre as the British service rifle. It has a one-piece frame of immense strength, together with an integral barrel. To reload, the cylinder and its backplate have to be completely removed.

4 Galand & Sommerville

LENGTH: 10in (254mm)
WEIGHT: 35oz (.99kg)
CALIBRE: .45in (11.4mm)
CAPACITY: 6
MV: c.600f/s (183m/s)

This weapon was a joint venture between Galand of Belgium and Sommerville of England, and was made in both countries in 1868. If the lever under the barrel is operated, it pulls the barrel and cylinder forward away from the frame, causing a star extractor to remove the empty cases.

5 Bland-Pryse

LENGTH: 11.5in (292mm)
WEIGHT: 46oz (1.3kg)
CALIBRE: .577in (14.6mm)
CAPACITY: 6
MV: c.650f/s (198m/s)

Charles Pryse patented the top-breaking revolver in Britain in 1876, and in 1877 weapons to this design were being produced in Britain by various manufacturers, noticeably Webley. This specimen is unidentified, although it is undoubtedly a Bland-Pryse type. It is solidly made, with

the barrel and top strap as one piece. The barrel is locked in place just behind the top of the cylinder, while there is a hinge under the front of the frame. There are two catches on either side of the frame, behind the cylinder, and if they are pressed the barrel is unlocked, to be tipped forwards and downwards, complete with the cylinder. A star extractor at the rear of the cylinder ejects the spent cases. The weapon is chambered for a massive .577in (14.6mm) cartridge guaranteed to stop anyone.

6 Webley Bulldog

LENGTH: 5.5in (140mm)
WEIGHT: 11oz (.31kg)
CALIBRE: .32in (8.1mm)
CAPACITY: 5
MV: c.500f/s (152m/s)

The 'British Bulldog' range was a series of Webley revolvers produced in the 1880s. This is one of the smaller models, chambered for a .32in (8.1mm) centre-fire cartridge. It has a solid one-piece frame and has a double-action lock. This was a handy and popular series.

1 Le Mat

LENGTH: 10.2in (259mm)
WEIGHT: 49oz (1.39kg)
CALIBRE: .44in (11.2mm)
CAPACITY: 9/1
MV: c.600f/s (183m/s)

Le Mat's unusual design of percussion revolver has already been described (page 45), and similar principles are used by this monster. No less than nine man-stopping .44in (11.2mm) cartridges are carried in the cylinder, fired by the single-action lock. There is also a single smooth-bore .65in (16.5mm) barrel along the cylinder axis which can be loaded with buckshot. This barrel has its own hinged breech block behind the cylinder, which has to be swung out to the side to reload. The tip of the hammer has a hinged block, which can be rotated so that the centre barrel is fired rather than the top chamber of the cylinder. This revolver appears to have been used by guards at French penal colonies, and was probably regarded as too cumbersome for military service.

2 Tranter Centre-fire

LENGTH: 10.5in (267mm)
WEIGHT: 35oz (.99kg)
CALIBRE: .45in (11.4mm)
CAPACITY: 6
MV: c.650f/s (198m/s)

In 1868, William Tranter produced this service revolver which fired a .45in (11.4mm) version of the spiral wound Boxer cartridge. Originally designed for British infantry rifles, the Boxer system had a cast iron base to the cartridge, with a hole drilled for the primer cap. The sides of the case were made from brass foil, wound round in a spiral and fixed to the base. Still based on the Adams frame, this revolver has an integral octagonal barrel and plain six-shot cylinder. It has a sprung loading gate at the rear of the cylinder, while the ejector rod under the barrel has to be swung out to punch the empty cases out of the cylinder one-by-one. It is a solid, workmanlike design, with a detachable plate above the butt allowing easy access to the lock and mainspring for field maintenance.

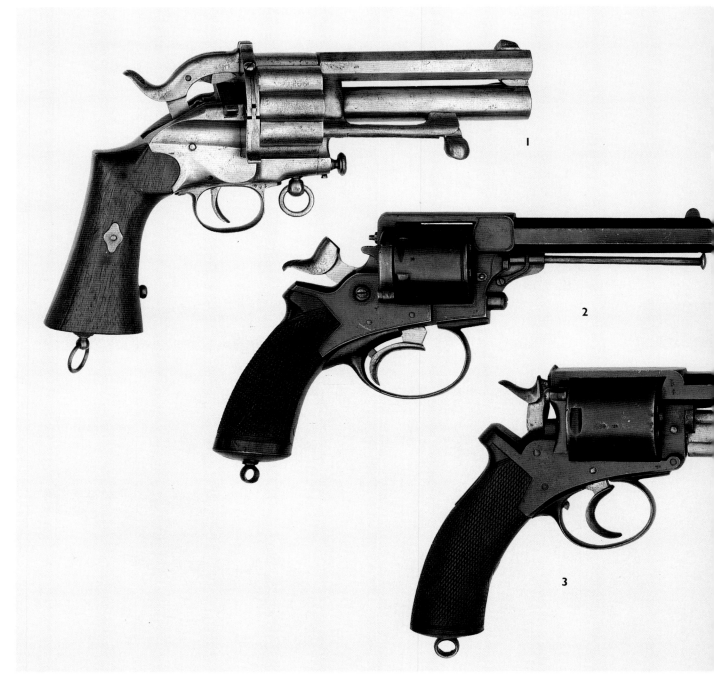

3 Adams Copy

LENGTH: 11in (279mm)
WEIGHT: 35oz (.99kg)
CALIBRE: .42in (10.7mm)
CAPACITY: 6
MV: c.600f/s (183m/s)

Adams perfected a centre-fire revolver in 1868, which was widely copied in Europe. This is a Belgian copy, with an Adams-style cylinder, loading gate and loading groove cut into the frame. Unlike the British weapon it has a two-piece frame, the barrel being integral to the top strap.

4 Mauser Zig-zag

LENGTH: 11.75in (298mm)
WEIGHT: 42oz (1.19kg)
CALIBRE: .43in (10.9mm)
CAPACITY: 6
MV: c.650f/s (198m/s)

This revolver was considered by the German Army in 1878. Designed by Peter Paul Mauser, it has a zig-zag groove cut into the outside of the cylinder, into which a stud fits. This stud is driven pushed forward as the trigger is pulled, causing the cylinder to rotate into position. There is a release catch on the left side of the frame which allows the toggle in front of the trigger guard to be pulled. This unlocks the barrel and cylinder assembly, which is hinged so that it tips upwards beyond the vertical for unloading. This motion causes a star-shaped ejector to remove the empty cases from the cylinder. New cartridges need to be loaded while the cylinder is still vertical. This weapon was rejected as too complex, although Mauser himself went on to produce many other designs.

5 British Tip-up

LENGTH: 10.5in (267mm)
WEIGHT: 35oz (.99kg)
CALIBRE: .50in (12.7mm)
CAPACITY: 6
MV: c.600f/s (183m/s)

This unidentified British weapon breaks open in a similar way to Mauser's design, although it uses a more conventional pawl and ratchet system to advance the cylinder. Reloading the cylinder when the barrel is vertical can be awkward when in a hurry, and it is easy to drop a cartridge.

4

5

1 Pryse-type
LENGTH: 7.5in (190mm)
WEIGHT: 25oz (.71kg)
CALIBRE: .45in (11.4mm)
CAPACITY: 5
MV: c.650f/s (198m/s)

This British weapon is similar to those produced by Webley to Charles Pryse's top-opening patent. The barrel is hinged at the front of the frame, and is tipped forward, together with the cylinder, for reloading. It is a compact and reasonably light revolver, firing a powerful cartridge.

2 Pryse-type
LENGTH: 8.5in (216mm)
WEIGHT: 25oz (.71kg)
CALIBRE: .45in (11.4mm)
CAPACITY: 5
MV: c.650f/s (198m/s)

This Pryse-type revolver is believed to be of Webley manufacture. It employs a type of safety device known as the rebounding hammer, where the hammer is normally kept locked a short distance from the firing pin to prevent an accidental discharge if knocked or dropped.

3 Webley-Pryse No.4
LENGTH: 10.75in (273mm)
WEIGHT: 36oz (1.02kg)
CALIBRE: .476in (12.1mm)
CAPACITY: 6
MV: c.650f/s (198m/s)

This is one of Webley's early Pryse-type revolvers, and was popular with British serving officers. The vertical catch behind the cylinder is used to unlock the barrel, which swings downwards along with the cylinder for reloading. The integral star ejector extracts the empty cases as the cylinder moves. It also has a double-action mechanism with the rebounding hammer safety device. When the trigger is pulled, the hammer impacts the firing pin, before lifting back some .15in (4mm) as the trigger is released. It is locked here, while the cylinder is also locked in place by a trigger stop. These mechanisms reduce the risk of accidental discharge by any sharp impact on the hammer, such as could be caused by dropping the weapon on a hard surface. A popular service weapon.

4 French Model 1873

LENGTH: 9.5in (241mm)
WEIGHT: 38oz (1.08kg)
CALIBRE: .45in (11.4mm)
CAPACITY: 6
MV: c.650f/s (198m/s)

This hefty revolver was manufactured at the St Etienne armoury, and was the first centre-fire weapon to be adopted by the French Army. It is a solid, heavy and robust design with a one-piece frame, the large screw under the barrel being used to hold the Colt-style ejector rod in place. It has a conventional double-action lock, and this specimen has the hammer at the half-cock position, which locks the hammer and cylinder for safe carriage and handling. The loading gate is on the right of the frame, and can be seen hinged open in the photograph. On the left side of the frame there is a removable inspection plate for access to the lock mechanism and spring. The Model 1873 quickly became popular as a reliable and effective service weapon in all places where the French Army fought.

5 German Commission

LENGTH: 10in (254mm)
WEIGHT: 35oz (.99kg)
CALIBRE: .455in (11.5mm)
CAPACITY: 6
MV: c.650f/s (198m/s)

This 1883 design was a product of one of the commissions tasked with organising the re-equipment of the German Army in 1879. It has a solid, one piece frame, into which the barrel is screwed. It is a simple weapon, with a double-action lock and a separate safety catch on the left side of the frame. There is a hinged loading gate behind the cylinder on the right side of the frame. The diameter of the chambers vary along their length so that the bullet is gripped as securely as its case. There is no form of integral extraction device, so to remove empty cases the firer would either have to find a stick of suitable diameter, or completely remove the cylinder and use the axis pin. This was a conservative and uninspired design, typical of those produced by government committee.

1 Gasser
LENGTH: 14.75in (375mm)
WEIGHT: 52oz (1.74kg)
CALIBRE: 11mm (.433in)
CAPACITY: 6
MV: c.900f/s (274m/s)

Gasser were a well known Austrian firm who made large quantities of revolvers for Balkan armies in the 1870s and 1880s. This huge cavalry revolver has a Colt-style open frame, with the barrel attached to the axis pin. It is chambered for the powerful Werndl carbine cartridge.

2 Montenegrin Gasser
LENGTH: 10.4in (264mm)
WEIGHT: 33oz (.94kg)
CALIBRE: .42in (10.7mm)
CAPACITY: 5
MV: c.550f/s (168m/s)

Gasser designs were copied in many Balkan countries, and are often referred to as Montenegrin Gassers. This example has a solid one-piece frame, although it retains the Gasser safety catch just above the trigger. It should have an extraction rod under the barrel but this is missing.

3 Colt Single-action Army
LENGTH: 11in (279mm)
WEIGHT: 35oz (.99kg)
CALIBRE: .45in (11.4mm)
CAPACITY: 6
MV: c.650f/s (198m/s)

Colt had used patent law to retain domination of the early revolver market, but when brass cartridges were introduced they faced a Smith and Wesson monopoly on bored-through cylinders. When that patent ran out, Colt were ready with this classic centre-fire cartridge revolver. Launched in 1873, it became known as the Single-action Army revolver and proved popular with military users. It was made to fire a number of cartridges and in three different barrel lengths. This specimen has the 5.5in (140mm) barrel and fires a .45in (11.4mm) cartridge. It has a solid frame with a top strap, into which the barrel is screwed. A hinged loading gate can be seen at the rear of the cylinder, while an ejection rod sits under the barrel. This revolver is sometimes known as the Model 1873.

4 Colt Single-action Army

LENGTH: 13in (330mm)
WEIGHT: 38oz (1.08kg)
CALIBRE: .44in (11.2mm)
CAPACITY: 6
MV: c.650f/s (198m/s)

This Colt single-action revolver, has a 7.5in (190mm) barrel and is chambered for the .44in (11.2mm) cartridge. Sometimes known as the Cavalry model, the longer-barrelled weapon proved to be just as popular as the others in the series. The versions with the 5.5in (140mm) barrel were sometimes known as Artillery models, while the 4.75in (121mm) guns were referred to as Civilian revolvers. 'Peacemaker' is another name associated with these weapons, which helped to restore Colt's dominance of the American market, although they were never as widespread as Hollywood might suggest. The cartridge fired by this example is the same as that used by the Winchester 1873 Model rifle, which simplified ammunition supply in remote frontier areas of the West.

5 Rast & Gasser

LENGTH: 8.75in (222mm)
WEIGHT: 28oz (.79kg)
CALIBRE: .31in (81mm)
CAPACITY: 8
MV: c.750f/s (229m/s)

This solid-framed double-action revolver entered service with the Austrian Army in 1898. The loading gate can be seen behind the cylinder, and is hinged down and to the rear to reload. It carries eight rounds, although they have poor stopping power for a service arm.

6 Double-barrelled

LENGTH: 7.5in (190mm)
WEIGHT: 18oz (.51kg)
CALIBRE: .22in (5.6mm)
CAPACITY: 12
MV: c.650f/s (198m/s)

A Belgian design, this unusual weapon has two barrels side by side, which are fired simultaneously by the hammer. Presumably this was to increase the stopping power of the light, small calibre cartridges, although a larger calibre weapon would been more useful and easier to handle.

1 Remington

LENGTH: 13in (330mm)
WEIGHT: 43oz (1.22kg)
CALIBRE: .44in (11.2mm)
CAPACITY: 6
MV: c.700f/s (213m/s)

In 1875 Remington produced their first cartridge revolver, which bore a strong resemblance to their earlier percussion models. The photograph shows the sturdy construction and classic lines of this weapon, which was chambered to fire a .44in (11.2mm) cartridge. It has a one-piece frame with integral top strap, into which is screwed the round barrel. There is a hinged loading gate behind the cylinder, while a Colt-style ejector rod is under the barrel. Under the ejector rod there is a steel web, which makes it easier to slide the revolver in and out of a holster. It is a tough, reliable and accurate weapon, which was offered on more than one occasion to the US Army, but was rejected in favour of the Colt. An improved model was introduced in 1891, but it was unable to challenge Colt.

2 S & W New Model No.3

LENGTH: 12in (305mm)
WEIGHT: 44oz (1.25kg)
CALIBRE: .32in (8.1mm)
CAPACITY: 6
MV: c.800f/s (244m/s)

It was not until 1870 that Smith and Wesson began to make service-calibre arms. Their New Model No.3 was sold in large numbers to the Russian Army in 1871, and was also developed in a number of forms for the American market. There were double-action variants and also weapons chambered for larger calibres. This is the 1887 single-action version chambered for .32in (8.1mm). It is a strongly-made weapon, which breaks open behind the cylinder. To reload, the catch in front of the hammer is released, then the barrel and cylinder tipped forward and down. At the same time a star-ejector flips the empty cases out of the cylinder. While an effective enough weapon, the New Model No.3 never successfully competed with Colt and Remington in America.

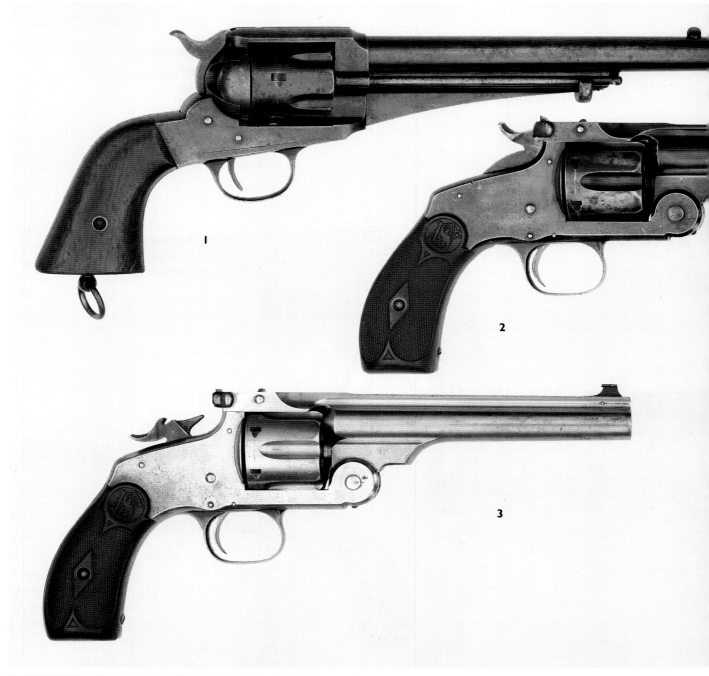

3 S & W New Model No.3
LENGTH: 11.5in (292mm)
WEIGHT: 40oz (1.13kg)
CALIBRE: .44in (11.2mm)
CAPACITY: 6
MV: c.750f/s (229m/s)

Another variant of the No.3 revolver, this one has a double-action lock with rebounding hammer, and is chambered for the Russian .44in (11.2mm) cartridge. American users were wary of such powerful cartridges in a break-open arm, and never really took to this weapon.

4 S & W Safety Model
LENGTH: 6.75in (171mm)
WEIGHT: 13oz (.37kg)
CALIBRE: .32in (8.1mm)
CAPACITY: 6
MV: c.800f/s (244m/s)

This pocket revolver has a fully enclosed hammer to prevent it snagging on clothes or equipment. The action is self-cocking only, and there is a safety lever at the back of the butt which has to be gripped before the trigger can be pulled. This is a safe and reliable self-defence weapon.

5 S & W Copy
LENGTH: 12.5in (317mm)
WEIGHT: 36oz (1.02kg)
CALIBRE: .44in (11.2mm)
CAPACITY: 6
MV: c.700f/s (214m/s)

This a poorly-made copy of the Smith and Wesson Model No.3 which was produced for the Russian Army. It has a double-action lock, although it lacks the rebounding hammer and other safety features of the original design It was made in Belgium by an anonymous manufacturer.

6 S & W Copy
LENGTH: 8in (203mm)
WEIGHT: 22oz (.62kg)
CALIBRE: .38in (9.6mm)
CAPACITY: 6
MV: c.740f/s (226m/s)

A Belgian copy of a double-action Smith and Wesson, this is of reasonable quality and effectiveness. It combines reasonable stopping power with low weight and compact dimensions, and would have been used for self-defence or even as a secondary weapon by military personnel.

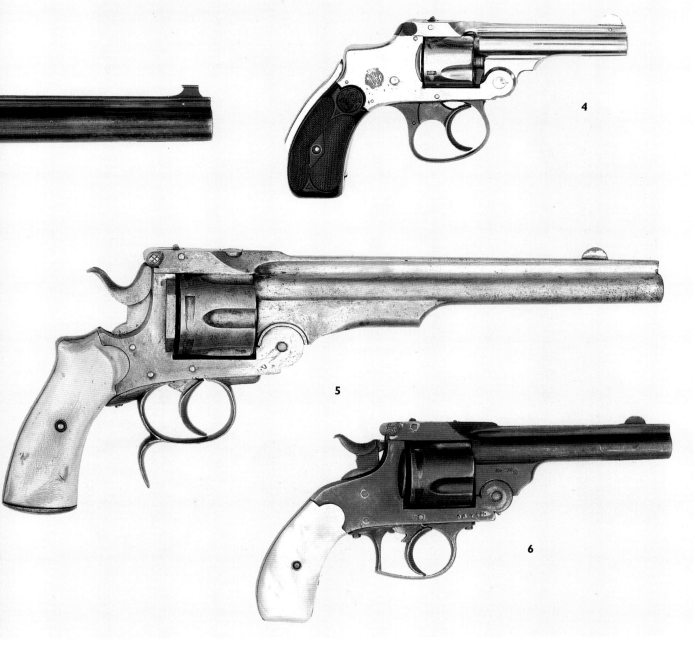

1 S & W Hammerless

LENGTH: 7.5in (190mm)
WEIGHT: 18oz (.51kg)
CALIBRE: .38in (9.6mm)
CAPACITY: 5
MV: c.625f/s (190m/s)

This is a similar shrouded hammer design to the Smith and Wesson safety model, although it fires a more powerful cartridge. It also uses a hesitation lock, where a first strong pull is needed to cock the hammer, but only light trigger pressure is required to fire it. There is a safety lever behind the butt.

2 S & W Double-action

LENGTH: 7.5in (190mm)
WEIGHT: 18oz (.51kg)
CALIBRE: .38in (9.6mm)
CAPACITY: 5
MV: c.625f/s (190m/s)

This is a later version of the Smith and Wesson New Model, introduced in 1895. It is a double-action weapon which breaks open behind the cylinder for reloading. It was made in a number of calibres and sizes, and this is the .38in (9.6m) version with a short 3.25in (83mm) barrel.

3 Iver Johnson

LENGTH: 6.5in (165mm)
WEIGHT: 14oz (.39kg)
CALIBRE: .32in (8.1mm)
CAPACITY: 5
MV: c.550f/s (168m/s)

Iver Johnson first began producing cheap firearms under a variety of trade names in 1871, and later set up a factory in Massachusetts to make a series of revolvers. This double-action model was made in 1891, and is a reasonably safe and effective self-defence weapon while remaining rela-tively cheap. In appearance it owes something to the Smith and Wesson No.3, as it also breaks behind the cylinder to reload. The cylinder and barrel are tipped forward and down, causing the star-shaped ejector behind the cylinder to extract the empty cases. The 3in (76mm) barrel is extremely short, and is strongly made with a solid rib along the top, into which is slotted the foresight. The rearsight is a simple notch cut into the top extension of the standing breech, which also locks the frame.

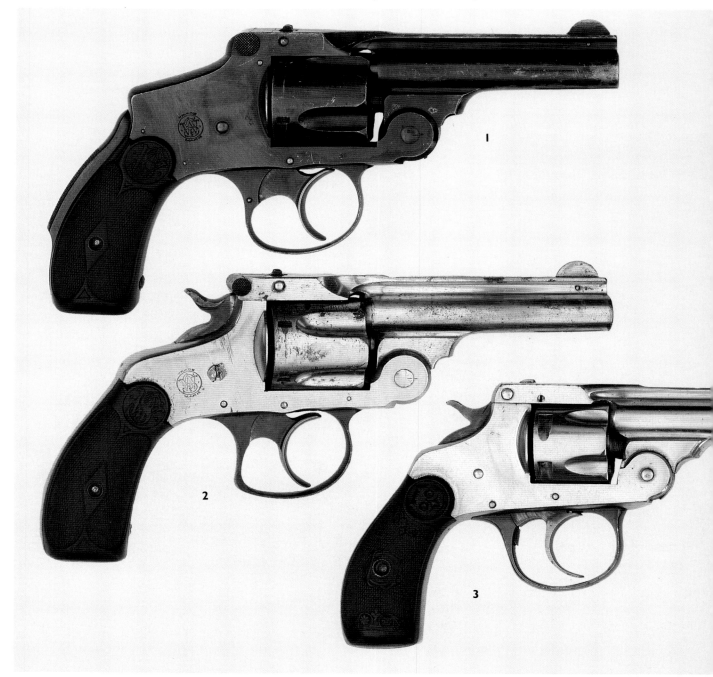

4 Iver Johnson

LENGTH: 7.5in (190mm)
WEIGHT: 15oz (.42kg)
CALIBRE: .32in (8.1mm)
CAPACITY: 5
MV: c.550f/s (168m/s)

This is a later model of the Iver Johnson series of revolvers, and strikes a reasonable balance between cheapness and effectiveness. It is well made, having a nickel-plated frame which breaks open at the top to allow access to the cylinder for reloading. The catch is a different design from the ear-lier models, and uses two parallel projections on the standing breech which slot into corresponding apertures on the top strap. This revolver is fitted with an unusual safety device patented by Johnson in the 1890s. Instead of the hammer striking the firing pin on the standing breech, it hits a flat bar which transfers the impact energy to the pin. This bar only rises into position if the trigger is pulled properly, and if it is down the hammer fouls the top of the breech and can not reach the firing pin.

5 Harrington & Richardson

LENGTH: 8.75in (222mm)
WEIGHT: 23oz (.65kg)
CALIBRE: .38in (9.6mm)
CAPACITY: 6
MV: c.625f/s (190m/s)

Gilbert Harrington and William Richardson formed a company in Massachusetts in 1874, with the intention of producing reliable revolvers at a reasonable price for military and civilian users. In the 1890s they developed a series of break-open 'Automatic Ejector' weapons in a variety of calibres and sizes. This one is chambered for a .38in (9.6mm) cartridge and has a 4in (102mm) barrel. It uses a similar design of locking catch to the Smith and Wesson revolvers, with the barrel and cylinder tipping forwards and downwards for reloading. While of compact dimensions it has a large butt to give good grip, and fires a cartridge with good man-stopping capabilities, making the Defender a more effective weapon that many of its pocket revolver contemporaries.

4

5

1 Galand Revolver

LENGTH: 13in (330mm)
WEIGHT: 46oz (1.3kg)
CALIBRE: 11mm (.433in)
CAPACITY: 6
MV: c.700f/s (213m/s)

After his collaboration with Sommerville (see page 58,) Charles Galand went on to produce his own series of revolver designs. This double action weapon is unusual in that is fitted with a flimsy and somewhat cumbersome skeleton stock which folds along the right side of the weapon. The trigger guard is actually an extension of a longer lever hinged under the front of the barrel. It is released by a catch behind the trigger, after which it is pulled downwards and to the front. This movement pulls the barrel and cylinder forward along the axis pin, which also causes the rear-mounted star-ejector to hold back the empty cases until they are clear of the cylinder, when they can be shaken free. New cartridges have to be loaded through a conventional gate once the weapon has been closed up.

2 Tranter Double-action

LENGTH: 10.25in (260mm)
WEIGHT: 26oz (.74kg)
CALIBRE: .38in (9.6mm)
CAPACITY: 5
MV: c.600f/s (183m/s)

Rimfire cartridges stayed in use for quite some time, as witnessed by this conversion to a Tranter percussion revolver. A new cylinder, loading gate and hammer have all been fitted to the solid one-piece frame, giving a trusted and reliable weapon a new lease of life as a cartridge revolver.

3 Pryse Copy

LENGTH: 8.5in (216mm)
WEIGHT: 29oz (.82kg)
CALIBRE: .455in (11.5mm)
CAPACITY: 5
MV: c.600f/s (183m/s)

This is yet another copy of the Webley-Pryse revolver, this time made in Britain. It faithfully follows the Pryse design of locking catch which permits the frame to break open at the top and the barrel to hinge forward for reloading. It retains the rebounding hammer safety feature.

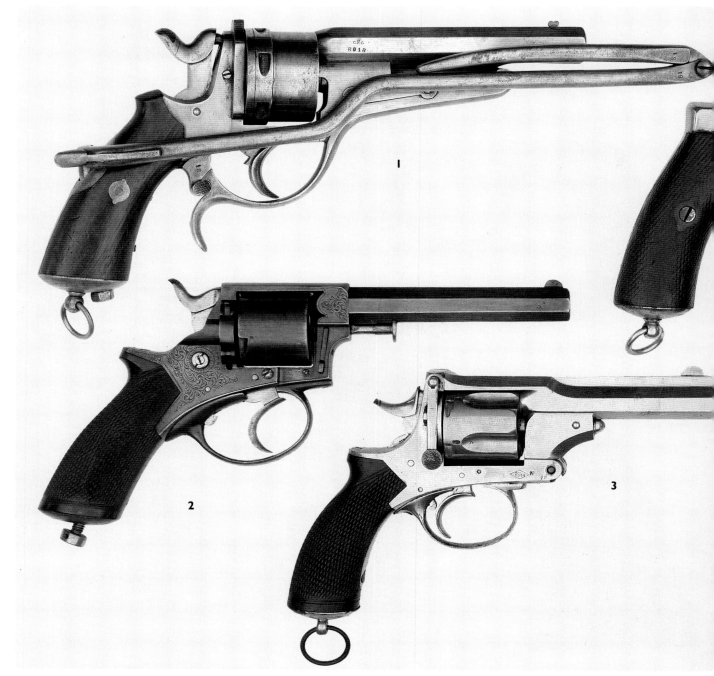

4 Chamelot-Delvigne

LENGTH: 11.2in (284mm)
WEIGHT: 40oz (1.13kg)
CALIBRE: .41in (10.4mm)
CAPACITY: 6
MV: c.625f/s (190m/s)

The Chamelot-Delvigne lock was a robust double-action system first manufactured by Pirlot Freres of Liege, Belgium. It quickly became widespread in Europe, and many service arms were made using the same principles. This is an Italian version of the Chamelot-Delvigne Model 1872, made at the Glisenti factory sometime in the 1880s. Chambered for a .41in (10.4mm) cartridge, it has a 6.25in (159mm) barrel which gives reasonable accuracy and stopping power. It has a solid one-piece frame, with the barrel screwed into it. There is a loading gate on the right side of the frame, which hinges down and to the rear, while an ejector rod is in the sleeve under the barrel. The butt has plain wooden side plates, and the whole revolver is a plain but reliable design.

5 Chamelot-Delvigne

LENGTH: 9.5in (241mm)
WEIGHT: 38oz (1.08kg)
CALIBRE: .45in (11.4mm)
CAPACITY: 6
MV: c.600f/s (183m/s)

This Belgian revolver is of Chamelot-Delvigne type, although its origins are unknown. It has the one-piece solid frame and screwed in barrel, together with the hinged loading gate and sleeved ejector rod. Unusually for a revolver, the foresight can be adjusted laterally.

6 Lebel Model 1892

LENGTH: 10in (254mm)
WEIGHT: 28oz (.79kg)
CALIBRE: 8mm (.315in)
CAPACITY: 6
MV: c.700f/s (213m/s)

Introduced in 1892, this revolver stayed in French service until the Second World War. It has a solid frame, and the cylinder can be swung out to the right on its own separate frame. It was held in place by a hinged lever on the right of the frame, shown here pulled back.

1 Enfield Mk. II

LENGTH: 11.5in (292mm)
WEIGHT: 40oz (1.13kg)
CALIBRE: .476in (12.1mm)
CAPACITY: 6
MV: c.700f/s (213m/s)

Experience of colonial warfare in the 1870s had suggested to the British army that the standard Adams revolver firing a .45in (11.4mm) cartridge was not powerful enough to stop a man in all circumstances. Their response was to develop a new round of .476in (12.1mm) calibre, and a revolver designed by an American, Owen Jones. Made by the Royal Small Arms Factory at Enfield, the Mk. I was introduced in 1880, with the Mk. II superseding it in 1882. Unlike the Adams, it has a two-piece frame, with the barrel locked by a spring catch in front of the hammer. When the revolver is opened, the barrel tips downwards, but unlike the Webley designs, the cylinder is just drawn forwards along the axis pin. The cases are pulled clear by the star ejector fixed to the standing breech.

2 Bodeo Model 1889

LENGTH: 10.5in (267mm)
WEIGHT: 32oz (.91kg)
CALIBRE: .41in (10.4mm)
CAPACITY: 6
MV: c.650f/s (198m/s)

This weapon became the standard Italian service revolver in 1891, and examples were still in use at the end of the Second World War. It is a simple and robust arm with a solid frame, into which the tapered octagonal barrel is screwed. The hammer is locked whenever the loading gate is opened.

3 Meiji Type 26

LENGTH: 9.25in (235mm)
WEIGHT: 32oz (.91kg)
CALIBRE: .35in (9mm)
CAPACITY: 6
MV: c.600f/s (183m/s)

This Japanese revolver was designed in 1893, or year 26 of the Meiji Era, hence the designation. It is a strongly-built weapon in the style of a Smith and Wesson, although some of the workmanship and materials are of poor quality. It has a self-cocking mechanism with a heavy trigger pull.

4 Nagant Model 1895

LENGTH: 7.68in (193mm)
WEIGHT: 28oz (.79kg)
CALIBRE: 7.62mm (.30in)
CAPACITY: 7
MV: c.1000f/s (305m/s)

This revolver was designed by the Belgian Leon Nagant, and in 1895 it was adopted as the standard Russian service weapon. In 1901 the Russians began licensed production at the Tula Arsenal, and over the next 30 years several million weapons were manufactured in a number of versions.

Nagant's intention was to improve the power of a revolver by designing a system to prevent gas leakage between the cylinder and barrel. When the hammer is cocked, a cam pushes the cylinder forward on its axis until the chamber encloses the tapered rear of the barrel. This seal is further enhanced by the lip of the cartridge case protruding into the barrel. Whether this complexity was justified is open to question, but the fact remains that the Nagant was a tough, reliable and effective weapon.

5 Eibar Revolver

LENGTH: 11in (279mm)
WEIGHT: 36oz (1kg)
CALIBRE: 11mm (.433in)
CAPACITY: 6
MV: c.700f/s (213m/s)

This is a Spanish copy of the Smith and Wesson revolver, made by Aranzabal and popular in Spain and South America. It dates from around 1890, and breaks at the top of the frame to tip the barrel and cylinder down to reload. It is strongly made, although the work is poor in places.

6 Trocaola Revolver

LENGTH: 10in (254mm)
WEIGHT: 40oz (1.13kg)
CALIBRE: 455in (11.5in)
CAPACITY: 6
MV: c.650f/s (198m/s)

Another Spanish copy of the Smith and Wesson, although of much better quality. It was first made in 1900, and in 1915 the British Army bought large quantities to supplement home production of revolvers. This is one of these, and is marked with the British military service designation.

1 Webley R.I.C. No. 1
LENGTH: 9.25in (235mm)
WEIGHT: 30oz (.85kg)
CALIBRE: .45in (11.4mm)
CAPACITY: 6
MV: c.650f/s (198m/s)

This design was first manufactured in 1867, but it was its adoption by the Royal Irish Constabulary in 1868 that gave it its popular name. It is a compact but powerful weapon, with the 4.5in (114mm) barrel screwed into a solid one-piece frame. The barrel is round, although it is raised on its top surface to form a strengthening rib. A foresight is slotted into this, and the rear-sight is a simple groove cut into the top strap. A loading gate is hinged on the right of the cylinder, while under the barrel there is a pivoting extractor rod. The mechanism is double-action, and can be locked at half cock as a safety measure. The butt plates are walnut, while there is a lanyard ring underneath. Revolvers of this type were produced in a number of barrel lengths and calibres.

2 Webley R.I.C. No. 2
LENGTH: 8.25in (210mm)
WEIGHT: 27oz (.76kg)
CALIBRE: .45in (11.4mm)
CAPACITY: 6
MV: c.650f/s (198m/s)

Here is an example of the second model of the R.I.C. revolver, this time with a 3.5in (89mm) barrel. The barrel itself has a tapered flange above it, while the butt has a new shape and rubber side plates. This specimen saw military service during the Second Afghan War of 1878-88.

3 British R.I.C. Copy
LENGTH: 8.75in (222mm)
WEIGHT: 30oz (.85kg)
CALIBRE: .45in (11.4mm)
CAPACITY: 5
MV: c.650f/s (198m/s)

The R.I.C. revolver became one of the most popular weapons produced by Webley, and was therefore copied by many manufacturers. This is a British version, although it has a one-piece frame and integral barrel, unlike the Webleys. The cylinder only holds five shots and is part fluted.

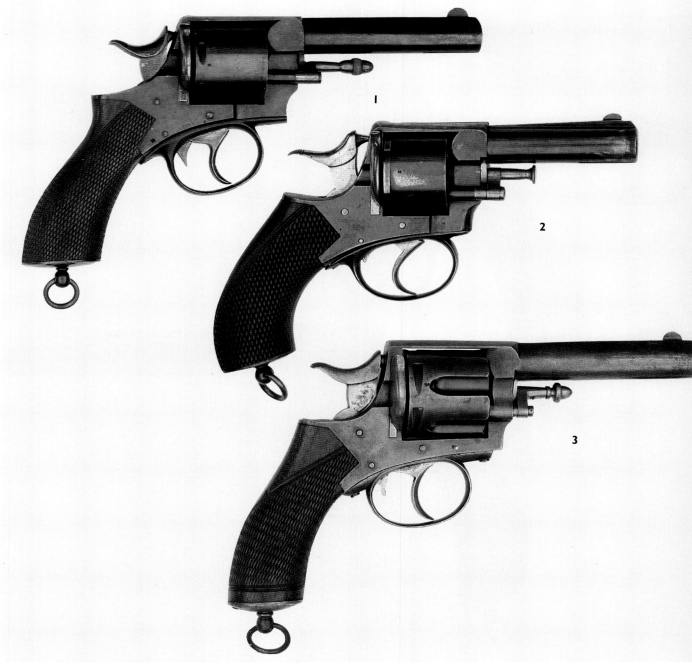

4 Belgian R.I.C. Copy

LENGTH: 8in (203mm)
WEIGHT: 28oz (.79kg)
CALIBRE: .45in (11.4mm)
CAPACITY: 5
MV: c.600f/s (183m/s)

Copies of the R.I.C. revolver were not confined to Britain, and this example is from Belgium. It closely resembles the second model, and has a one-piece frame into which the octagonal barrel is screwed. This appears to be one of the better made R.I.C. copies, made from quality materials.

5 Webley-Wilkinson

LENGTH: 11in (279mm)
WEIGHT: 38oz (1.08kg)
CALIBRE: .455in (11.5mm)
CAPACITY: 6
MV: c.650f/s (198m/s)

This Webley service revolver was first produced in 1892, and is very similar to the Webley-Pryse models described earlier. The main difference is in the way it is locked behind the cylinder. The barrel top strap extends over the raised part of the standing breech, and is held in place by a spring-loaded latch. This latch is operated by a lever on the left side of the frame, and is a strong and reliable system. If the weapon is not properly closed, the latch fouls the upper part of the hammer and the weapon can not be fired. When the revolver is broken open, it hinges downwards to eject the empty cases and allow reloading. While a Webley design, this revolver was 'rebadged' by the famous Wilkinson Sword Company of London, who sold them along with their swords to British officers.

6 Webley-Kaufmann

LENGTH: 11in (279mm)
WEIGHT: 38oz (1.08kg)
CALIBRE: .455in (11.5mm)
CAPACITY: 6
MV: c.650f/s (198m/s)

This double-action revolver is a development of the Webley-Pryse series, and is of the familiar break open type. It uses yet another type of locking system, where the top strap fits into a slot on the breech, and the two are pinned through a small hole by a spring-loaded bolt which is pushed outwards.

1 Webley New Model
LENGTH: 10.5in (267mm)
WEIGHT: 38oz (1.08kg)
CALIBRE: .45in (11.4mm)
CAPACITY: 6
MV: c.700f/s (2135m/s)

When Colt produced a solid-framed revolver in 1877, Webley were quick to follow with their own design. Chambered for use with .45in (11.4mm) it would also fire .455in (11.5mm) and .476in (12.1mm) calibre cartridges (as would most other Webleys of the period).

2 Webley-Government
LENGTH: 11.25in (286mm)
WEIGHT: 40oz (1.13kg)
CALIBRE: .455in (11.5mm)
CAPACITY: 6
MV: c.650f/s (198m/s)

Developed from the Webley-Kaufmann in about 1885, this break-open revolver is locked by a stirrup catch over the top strap and breech. If this catch is not properly closed, it fouls the hammer and prevents firing. There was a long dispute with Edwinson Green over ownership of the idea.

3 Webley Mk. I
LENGTH: 8.5in (216mm)
WEIGHT: 34oz (.96kg)
CALIBRE: .455in (11.5mm)
CAPACITY: 6
MV: c.600f/s (183m/s)

The Enfield Mk. II (see page 72) was adopted for British service in 1880, but extensive field experience showed up flaws in the design. After further trials in 1887, a new weapon was chosen, known as the Webley Service Model Mk. I. This was chambered for the .455in (11.5mm) cartridge, and is a relatively compact revolver with a 4in (102mm) barrel. It breaks open in the normal Webley manner, and is locked by the stirrup-catch system claimed to have been invented by Edwinson Green. It is of extremely strong construction, with a tapered rib above the octagonal barrel. The small horizontal projection in front of the cylinder is a guide which prevents the weapon snagging on a holster. The butt grips are made from Vulcanite, and there is a lanyard ring below.

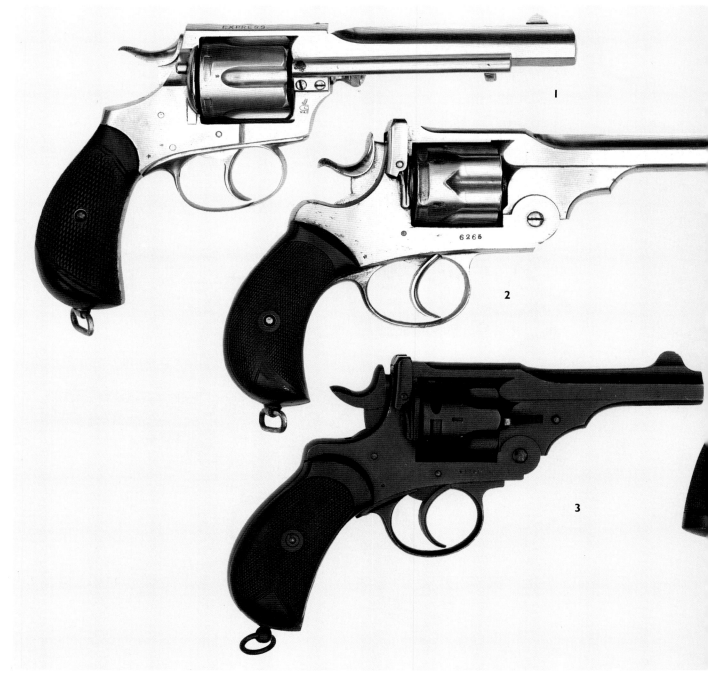

4 Webley Mk. IV
LENGTH: 11in (279mm)
WEIGHT: 37oz (1.05kg)
CALIBRE: .455in (11.5mm)
CAPACITY: 6
MV: c.650f/s (198m/s)

The Mk. IV was introduced in 1899, and quickly became known as the Boer War model. Changes from the earlier weapons were minimal, and it was made in a number of different barrel lengths. This gun has the short 3in (76mm) barrel, and has suffered an internal explosion.

5 Tranter Army
LENGTH: 11.75in (298mm)
WEIGHT: 36oz (1.02kg)
CALIBRE: .45in (11.4mm)
CAPACITY: 6
MV: c.650f/s (198m/s)

In 1879, William Tranter also saw the potential of break-open revolvers, and finally moved away from the solid Adams frame to this two-piece design. Bearing a strong resemblance to Tranter's earlier revolvers, this service-calibre weapon is another with an integral barrel and top strap, and opens to reload in a similar way to the Webleys and Smith and Wessons. The top strap has a rectangular aperture which fits over a projection on the standing breech, and the two are locked together by a sprung hook on the left of the frame. When the double-action hammer is down, a slot in its face also locks a protruding surface on the top strap. When the weapon is opened, a star-ejector removes the empty cartridge cases. The cylinder is fluted to reduce weight, and is easily removed.

6 Webley Mk. III
LENGTH: 8.25in (210mm)
WEIGHT: 19oz (.54kg)
CALIBRE: .38in (9.6mm)
CAPACITY: 6
MV: c.600f/s (183m/s)

Webley later developed a Mk. II and Mk. III for service use, but this is in fact a police and civilian Mk. III pocket revolver chambered for .38in (9.6mm) and scaled down from the military weapon. It is an effective close-quarters weapon, although the butt is somewhat small.

1 Colt Double-action
LENGTH: 10.25in (260mm)
WEIGHT: 36oz (1.02kg)
CALIBRE: .476in (12.1mm)
CAPACITY: 6
MV: c.750f/s (229m/s)

This 1887 solid-frame revolver was the first Colt to have a double-action mechanism. It was made in various calibres and sizes, and this model is chambered for the British .476in (12.1mm) service round. Unusually for a Colt, it was criticised for poor balance and mechanical unreliability.

2 Colt New Navy
LENGTH: 11.25in (286mm)
WEIGHT: 34oz (.96kg)
CALIBRE: .38in (9.6mm)
CAPACITY: 6
MV: c.780f/s (238m/s)

Adopted by the US Navy in 1892, this weapon was also used by the Army and Marine Corps, although they found that its .38in (9.6mm) round lacked stopping power and soon changed to the later New Service model. It is a double action weapon with a solid frame and screwed on barrel.

The cylinder is on the Colt patent yoke, and is swung out to the left for rapid reloading. A manually operated extractor ejects the empty cases, then new rounds can easily be loaded. The thumbcatch used to release the cylinder can be seen just under the hammer in the photograph. This specimen has a 6in (152mm) barrel, although the gun was also available in 3in (76mm) and 4.5in (114mm) lengths. There were also versions in .41in (10.4mm) calibre. It is a sturdy and reliable revolver.

3 Colt Army Special
LENGTH: 11.25in (286mm)
WEIGHT: 35oz (.99kg)
CALIBRE: .38in (9.6mm)
CAPACITY: 6
MV: c.1000f/s (305m/s)

The US Army had found the New Navy revolver lacking in stopping power, and attempted to upgrade it by chambering it for the .38in (9.6mm) Special, a longer and much more powerful round than the standard. This is the 1908 model, with a revised cylinder and reshaped trigger guard.

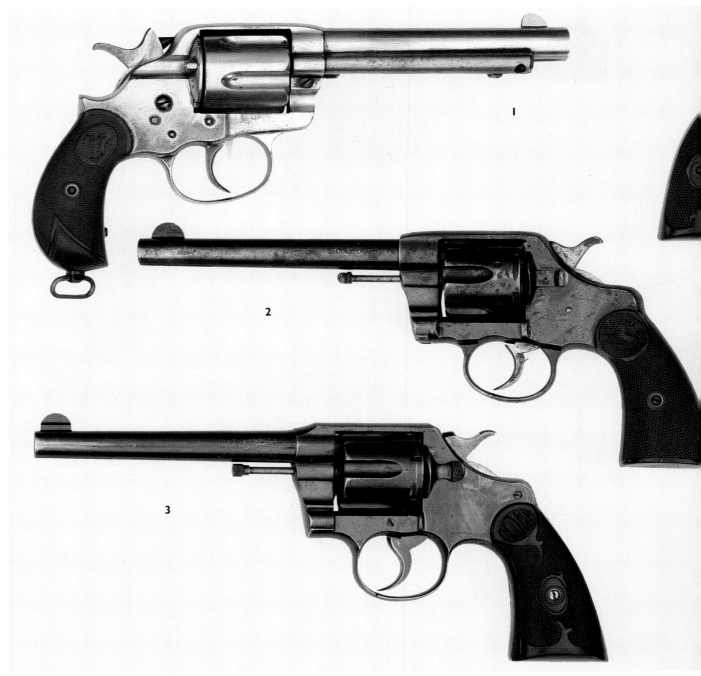

4 Colt Police Positive
LENGTH: 10.25in (260mm)
WEIGHT: 24oz (.68kg)
CALIBRE: .22in (5.6mm)
CAPACITY: 6
MV: c.700f/s (213m/s)

Colt produced versions of the New Service models for police use in .32in (8.1mm) and .38in (9.6m) calibres. They proved immediately successful, and users soon asked for small calibre versions for indoor training and target shooting. This is a Police Positive chambered for .22in (5.6mm).

5 Colt New Service
LENGTH: 10.75in (273mm)
WEIGHT: 40oz (1.13kg)
CALIBRE: .455in (11.5mm)
CAPACITY: 6
MV: c.650f/s (198m/s)

This is another of the new series of double-action Colts produced at the end of the 19th Century, and is the largest and most robust of them all. It managed to combine speed of loading with the strength of a solid frame by using a swing-out cylinder on Colt's special yoke. It was produced in six sizes, and this one has a 5.5in (140mm) barrel with a blade foresight and grooved rear-sight, together with a large comfortable rubber-gripped butt. It is a big solid gun, which replaced the New Navy Colt in US Army service, and was the standard officer's sidearm from 1907 until the advent of the M1911 automatic pistol. This specimen is chambered for the .455in (11.5mm) British service cartridge, and is one of those supplied to the United Kingdom during the First World War.

6 Colt Target
LENGTH: 12.75in (324mm)
WEIGHT: 43oz (1.2kg)
CALIBRE: .455in (11.5mm)
CAPACITY: 6
MV: c.650f/s (198m/s)

This is a specialised target revolver, chambered for British military ammunition and probably owned by an army officer pistol enthusiast. It has a long 7.5in (190m) barrel and an adjustable rearsight, while the lock mechanism has been finely adjusted for precision shooting.

1 Kynoch Revolver

LENGTH: 11.5in (292mm)
WEIGHT: 42oz (1.19kg)
CALIBRE: .455in (11.5mm)
CAPACITY: 6
MV: c.650f/s (198m/s)

This is a heavy service calibre revolver patented in Britain in 1885 and manufactured by George Kynoch of Birmingham. It was originally intended to compete for service orders after the failure of the Enfield Mk. II, but the Webley was chosen instead. This is an interesting weapon, however, in that it makes use of a double trigger system based on that invented by William Tranter for his percussion revolvers. By pulling on the lower trigger, the hammer is raised to the cocked position. Only light pressure is required on the upper trigger to fire the weapon. In an emergency both triggers are pulled simultaneously to give fast, if inaccurate shooting. The hammer is shielded by the frame, and can not be cocked by hand. The frame is a two-piece break-open type.

2 Webley-Fosbery

LENGTH: 11.5in (292mm)
WEIGHT: 38oz (1.08kg)
CALIBRE: .455in (11.5mm)
CAPACITY: 6
MV: c.650f/s (198m/s)

After winning the Victoria Cross in India, Colonel George Fosbery retired from the British Army to concentrate on weapons design. This revolver was made in 1901 by Webley to his specification, and at first glance appears to be a normal double-action service weapon. Closer inspection reveals that the cylinder and barrel are able to slide backwards along guides on the butt and frame. This movement automatically turns the cylinder to the next position while recocking the hammer, ensuring that light trigger pressure is all that is needed for subsequent shots. Impressive under range conditions, it was less successful in action. The recoil system is easily clogged by mud and dirt, while if the firer's arm is not held absolutely rigid, the recoil may not be enough to operate the mechanism.

3 S & W Gold Seal

LENGTH: 11.75in (298mm)
WEIGHT: 38oz (1.08kg)
CALIBRE: .455in (11.5mm)
CAPACITY: 6
MV: c.650f/s (198m/s)

Smith and Wesson revolvers faced customer resistance in the United States, where shooters were suspicious of break-open revolvers firing powerful cartridges. To overcome this distrust, the company eventually produced a solid-framed revolver by around 1897, and this model first appeared in 1908. Known as the 'Hand Ejector', 'New Century' or 'Gold Seal' model, it has a solid frame with a round screwed-in barrel. The lock is a very smooth double-action one, enabling fast, accurate shooting. A catch on the left side of the frame unlocks the cylinder, which swings out to the left on a separate yoke, rather like that on the contemporary Colts. Pushing in a pin on the front of the cylinder then operates the star-ejector and flips the empty cases out of the weapon.

4 S & W Model 1917

LENGTH: 9.6in (244mm)
WEIGHT: 34oz (.96kg)
CALIBRE: .45in (11.4mm)
CAPACITY: 6
MV: c.700f/s (213m/s)

When America entered the First World War, Smith and Wesson produced this version of their solid-framed revolver to meet the sudden need for sidearms. The Colt M1911 automatic was the standard service pistol so the revolver was chambered to take the same .45in (11.4mm) ACP round.

5 S & W British Service

LENGTH: 10in (254mm)
WEIGHT: 29oz (.82kg)
CALIBRE: .38in (9.6mm)
CAPACITY: 6
MV: c.650f/s (198m/s)

In 1940, Britain faced Germany alone, and was desperate need of military equipment of all kinds. Among the weapons supplied by the United States were thousands of solid framed Smith and Wesson revolvers, chambered for .38in (9.6mm) standard service ammunition.

1 Webley & Scott Mk V
LENGTH: 11in (279mm)
WEIGHT: 38oz (1.08kg)
CALIBRE: .455in (11.5mm)
CAPACITY: 6
MV: c.650f/s (198m/s)

The Webley Mk. IV saw service in the Boer War, but in 1913 it was replaced by the Mk. V. Similar in most respects to the earlier weapons, it fires the .455in (11.5mm) cartridge using a double action lock. It breaks open using the normal Webley stirrup catch, while the cylinder is easily removed.

2 Webley & Scott Mk VI
LENGTH: 11in (279mm)
WEIGHT: 37oz (1.05kg)
CALIBRE: .455in (11.5mm)
CAPACITY: 6
MV: c.650f/s (198m/s)

This was the final, and best known of the Webley series of British service arms, and incorporated the experience from all the earlier models. Introduced in 1915, it saw widespread service in both World Wars, being manufactured in huge quantities. The revolver breaks open at the top of the frame, and is locked by the standard Webley stirrup catch. A robust and reliable weapon, it stood well up to the rigours of trench warfare. Some officers used a privately purchased extension stock, while there was even a short detachable bayonet designed for it. The Mk VI was officially replaced in 1932, after the army switched to .38in (9.6mm) for its handguns, although many officers kept them for years afterwards. Never the most accurate of revolvers, it was tough and dependable in combat.

3 Webley & Scott Mk VI
LENGTH: 11in (279mm)
WEIGHT: 38oz (1.08kg)
CALIBRE: .22in (5.56mm)
CAPACITY: 6
MV: c.600f/s (183m/s)

Learning to shot a pistol well with full-powered ammunition is an expensive and difficult task. To reduce costs and permit safe indoor training, many forces use small-calibre versions of standard weapons. This is a Mk VI Webley chambered for .22in (5.56mm) ammunition.

4 Enfield No.2 Mk I

LENGTH: 10in (254mm)
WEIGHT: 29oz (.82kg)
CALIBRE: .38in (9.6mm)
CAPACITY: 6
MV: c.700f/s (213m/s)

After the First World War the British Army decided that it didn't really need a pistol bullet as powerful as the .455 in (11.5mm) round of the Webley Mk VI, and settled instead on a .38in (9.6mm) cartridge. This would make for a lighter weapon with a less fearsome recoil, and would make training and general weapon handling easier. Many of Webley's patents had by now lapsed, so the Government decided to build the new revolver at their own factory at Enfield. The ensuing Enfield No. 2 Mk. I closely resembles the Webley Mk VI, although it is significantly lighter and smaller. It breaks at the top of the frame, and is locked by a Webley stirrup catch, while the barrel is octagonal and has a screw-on blade foresight. The lock is of double-action type with a rebounding hammer.

5 Enfield No.2 Mk I*

LENGTH: 10in (254mm)
WEIGHT: 27oz (.76kg)
CALIBRE: .38in (9.6mm)
CAPACITY: 6
MV: c.700f/s (213m/s)

Once the Enfield was in service, it was found that the hammer could catch on fittings and equipment in the confined space of a tank or other vehicle. The Mk. I* was introduced to overcome this, and had a combless hammer which could only be cocked by pulling the trigger.

6 Webley Mk IV

LENGTH: 11.25in (286mm)
WEIGHT: 34oz (.96kg)
CALIBRE: .38in (9.6mm)
CAPACITY: 6
MV: c.780f/s (238m/s)

Even when they lost the British service business to the Enfield, Webley developed their own .38in (9.6mm) revolver. It was so like the Enfield in usage and appearance, that when supplies of revolvers ran short in the Second World War, thousands were ordered by the army.

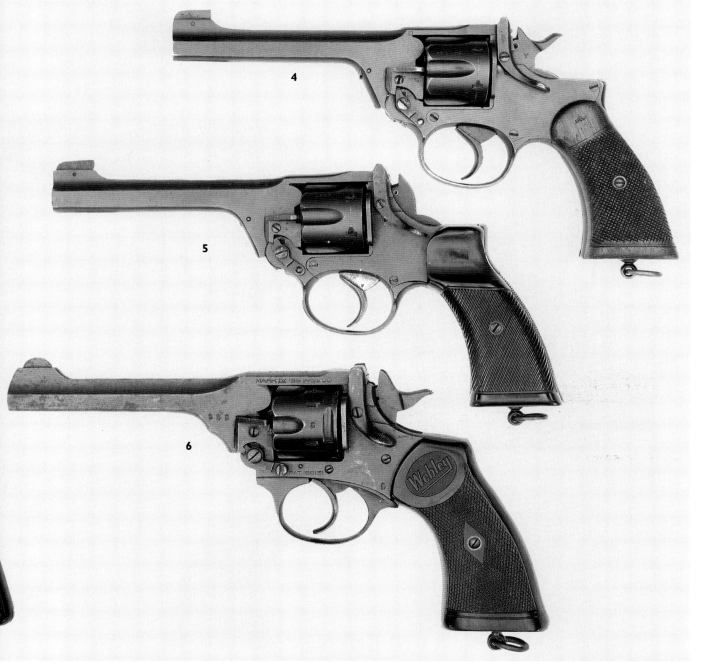

1 Colt Official Police
LENGTH: 10.25in (260mm)
WEIGHT: 34oz (.96kg)
CALIBRE: .38in (9.6mm)
CAPACITY: 6
MV: c.700f/s (213m/s)

In 1926 the Colt military models were renamed the Colt Official Police revolvers, mainly because law enforcement agencies were staying with revolvers while the army had switched to automatics. This one is in .38in (9.6mm) calibre, although most were in .41in (10.4mm).

2 S & W Military
LENGTH: 8in (203mm)
WEIGHT: 28oz (.79kg)
CALIBRE: .38in (9.6mm)
CAPACITY: 6
MV: c.600f/s (183m/s)

This strange revolver is actually a Smith and Wesson solid-framed Police model with the barrel cut down and a ribbed foresight added. This was probably done to aid concealment, as it makes the weapon useless at all but the shortest ranges. The value of such a modification is questionable.

3 Taurus Magnum M86
LENGTH: 9.25in (235mm)
WEIGHT: 35oz (.99kg)
CALIBRE: .357in (9.06mm)
CAPACITY: 6
MV: c.1400f/s (427m/s)

The modern revolver is rarely used by military personnel, although many police forces still carry these weapons. It has retained some popularity, however, in the light of the development of enlarged Magnum cartridges. These are significantly more powerful than their normal counterparts, and demand a strong, well-built pistol to fire them. Most firers will only trust a solid-framed revolver with such a round, and this is a good example. It fires the .357in (9.06mm) Magnum cartridge, which is .1in (2.54mm) longer than the .38in (9.6mm) Special. Made by Taurus of Brazil, it has a fixed foresight, but the range of the ammunition makes an adjustable rearsight viable. It strong and well-made, and the cylinder swings out to the left on its own yoke for reloading.

4 Colt Python
LENGTH: 11.5in (292mm)
WEIGHT: 43.5oz (1.23kg)
CALIBRE: .357in (9.06mm)
CAPACITY: 6
MV: c.1400f/s (427m/s)

The Python is claimed by many to be the best revolver in the world, and is another chambered for the mighty .357in (9.06mm) Magnum cartridge. It has an extremely solid one-piece frame, and the heavy barrel has an extended top rib to aid instinctive sighting. For more measured aiming there is a blade foresight, while the rearsight is adjustable both laterally and in elevation. Many police departments worried by the heavy firepower deployed by modern criminals are trading up to Magnum revolvers, but military use is restricted largely to special forces units. Anti-terrorist forces need to be able to kill their target with the first shot, and are able to train firers to overcome the not inconsiderable blast, noise and recoil. The intimidation value of such a beast is also considerable.

5 S & W Model 686
LENGTH: 11.5in (292mm)
WEIGHT: 46oz (1.30kg)
CALIBRE: .357in (9.06mm)
CAPACITY: 6
MV: c.1400f/s (427m/s)

A competitor to the Python, although at nearly half the price, is the Smith and Wesson series of .357in (9.06mm) Magnum revolvers. This is the Model 686, which is built around a massive stainless steel one-piece frame. The cylinder can be swung out to the left for reloading, which can be speeded up by using one of the pre-filled loading aids available. It has an adjustable rearsight, while the foresight is a simple blade. The barrel has an extended rib above it, while there is another strengthening rib and sheath for the ejection rod beneath. The Smith and Wesson is popular with target shooters, and those who hunt dangerous game, while it is also used by military special forces teams, police forces and hostage rescue units. The gun shown here has a standard 6in (152m) barrel.

AUTOMATIC PISTOLS

The introduction of bolt action rifles in the latter 1880s led a number of designers to apply a similar operating principle to a hand gun. The usual method was to place a lever, ending in a ring, beneath the weapon; the firer put his forefinger into this ring and pushed forward and the lever opened the bolt-action breech. He then pulled back and the bolt closed, feeding a cartridge from a magazine. The final movement of the lever either fired the cartridge or brought his finger alongside a trigger so that he could fire without having to remove his finger from the operating lever.

These mechanical repeating pistols worked well when they were new, well lubricated, and provided with carefully selected ammunition. Once old, dirty and with run-of-the-mill ammunition, they tended to jam or stick and generally lost their attraction. But before the repeaters could really get into the

market-place, Hiram Maxim appeared with the automatic machine gun, and this led designers to the conclusion that the same operating principles might probably be applied to a hand gun. They could; and with the arrival of the automatic pistol the mechanical repeater vanished into history.

The reason for mentioning the repeater is that it was just such a pistol which formed the link between the automatic pistol and its predecessors. Josef Laumann of Vienna patented a repeater in 1890, a design of the usual bolt-action-and-lever type. In 1891 he modified it slightly, but then he appears to have had an inspiration and in 1892 took out a fresh patent which changed the method of operation. Instead of using a finger-lever to open the bolt, he allowed the pressure inside the cartridge to blow the case back against the bolt and thus force the bolt backwards; he left part of his lever

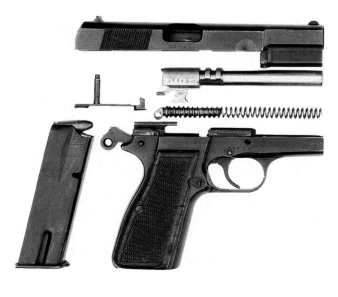

Left: *A portrait of two Boer commanders in 1901, with one of them sporting a Mauser Model 1896. Both sides in the South African War used this weapon, which when combined with its wooden stock/holster, turned into a handy self-loading carbine. This war was notable for the effectiveness of extremely long-range rifle fire.*

Below: *A dismantled FN GP35 shows the design and construction of a Browning-type automatic pistol. Above the frame assembly is the guide rod, which also holds the recoil spring. Above this is the barrel, with its cam slot beneath and two locking lugs above, and then the slide. The spring-loaded magazine is to the left.*

mechanism in order to slow down this opening movement, so inaugurating the first 'delayed blowback' pistol. His design went on the market as the Schonberger pistol in 1892, named for the superintendent of the Steyr factory which made it.

It would be as well, at this point, to clear up a terminological inexactitude; the general run of automatic pistols are not automatic. The strict definition of 'automatic' as applied to weapons is 'an arm which, when the trigger is pressed, will fire and will continue to fire until the trigger is released or the supply of ammunition ceases.' Some of the earliest automatic pistols were, indeed, built to this specification; but it was soon discovered that a fully-automatic pistol is virtually uncontrollable, spewing out its entire magazine in a split second and jumping wildly away from the target in the process. And so the 'disconnector' appeared, a device which disconnects the trigger from the rest of the weapon as soon as a shot has been fired and does not reconnect it until the firer releases his pressure and allows the trigger to return to the rest position. So an 'automatic' pistol is really a self-loading pistol; there are pistols which fire in the full-automatic mode, but they are highly specialised and rare weapons which take some handling.

In 1893 the Borchardt pistol appeared; this adapted the toggle lock of the Maxim machine gun to a hand weapon, and in due course it was re-worked to become the Parabellum, more familiarly known by the re-worker's name of Luger. In the following year Theodor Bergmann produced the first of a series of blowback pistols, and in 1895 came the Mauser, another famous name and equally famous shape. With these to break the ice, designs now came thick and fast, and military recognition was rapid. The Swiss adopted the Luger in 1900, the Austro-Hungarians a Roth pistol in 1907, the German Army their version of the Luger in 1908 and in 1911 the US Army adopted a near-immortal design by John Moses Browning which became the Colt Model 1911. Browning also sold the designs of a number of blowback pistols to the Fabrique Nationale d'Armes of Liege, Belgium, who put them on the market under the Browning name. By the time war broke out in 1914 Fabrique Nationale were well into their second million Browning automatic pistols.

The blowback pistol is the normal method of operation for pocket pistols of low power - 7.65mm (.301in) or less, and 9mm (.354in) Short. Delayed blowback still appears here and there where a more powerful cartridge is required. But where power is needed, then a locked breech must be used, and here the Browning system of disengaging the barrel from the recoiling slide by means of a link or a cam has reigned supreme for almost 90 years. The rotating barrel still appears - from Steyr-Mannlicher (who pioneered it in 1907) and from Colt; there is the wedge-locking system pioneered by Walther and now used by Beretta, and there are a handful of gas-actuated and other systems in use. But the rich diversity of shapes and systems which abounded in the 1930s is gone, sacrificed on the altar of production facility. A modern computer-controlled machine tool can produce a pistol frame to an accuracy of 5 microns and do it day in and day out; but only if the design meets certain parameters of simplicity. There is no room in today's cost-conscious and competitive world for the elegant complexities of Borchardt's toggle lock or Roth's long recoil system. Which is perhaps a pity.

Left: *A French Master Sergeant cleans his Colt M1911. This heavy, reliable automatic is one of the all-time classic pistols.*

Below: *A youthful German marches his American prisoners into captivity. He is armed with a Walther P38.*

1 Borchardt Pistol

LENGTH: 13.75in (349mm)
WEIGHT: 46oz (1.3kg)
CALIBRE: 7.65mm (.301in)
CAPACITY: 8
MV: c.1100f/s (335m/s)

Designed by Hugo Borchardt, this large and heavy pistol first appeared in 1893, and with its detachable stock/ holster saw moderate success as a cavalry carbine. It uses similar principles to Maxim's machine gun, in that behind the barrel is a separate bolt, held in place by a two-piece locking bar. When the weapon is fired, the recoil forces the bolt and barrel backwards, until the barrel hits a stop. At this point, the locking bar hinges in the middle, releasing the bolt and allowing it to continue to the rear. The bolt motion pulls the empty case from the breech and re-cocks the hammer. The bolt is then driven forwards by a powerful spring, picking up the next round from the box magazine in the butt, and feeding it into the breech. The locking bar snaps straight again, and the pistol is ready to fire.

2 Mauser Model 1898

LENGTH: 11.75in (298mm)
WEIGHT: 40oz (1.13kg)
CALIBRE: 7.63mm (.30in)
CAPACITY: 10
MV: c.1400f/s (427m/s)

Mauser's first self-loading pistol was produced in 1896, and this improved model appeared in 1898. It uses a modified version of the Borchardt cartridge, and again depends on recoil energy to operate the mechanism. The weapon has to be cocked before firing the first shot, and this is done by pulling back the barrel and slide assembly by using the machined grips in front of the hammer. This feeds the a round into the breech while cocking the hammer. The firer than simply pulls the trigger to fire each shot until the ammunition supply is finished. Ten rounds are held in the integral box magazine in front of the trigger, which is loaded through the ejection port above. The hollow wooden holster also doubles as a detachable stock. Mausers were carried by both sides in the Boer War.

3 Mauser Model 1912

LENGTH: 11.75in (298mm)
WEIGHT: 44oz (1.25kg)
CALIBRE: 7.63mm (.30in)
CAPACITY: 10
MV: c.1400f/s (427m/s)

The early Mausers were not chosen for German military service, although other countries bought them in reasonable numbers. The Model 1912 is a slightly improved version of the Model 1898, although it is identical in many respects. It also uses a clip of ten rounds in an integral magazine and has a wooden stock/holster attachment. The main difference is an improved safety device, operated by a lever on the left of the frame which locks the hammer when cocked. Mausers of this type saw service around the world, and in the 1920s Spanish engineers devised a modification to allow fully automatic fire. Mauser responded by producing their own version in about 1930, which used detachable 10 or 20-round box magazines. The weapon was too short for accurate burst fire.

4 Mauser 9mm

LENGTH: 11.75in (298mm)
WEIGHT: 44oz (1.25kg)
CALIBRE: 9mm (.354in)
CAPACITY: 10
MV: c.1150f/s (351m/s)

By the time of the First World War, the German Army had standardised on Luger's P08 Parabellum automatic, firing specially-developed 9mm ammunition. Supply could not keep up with demand, so in 1916 Mauser modified the Model 1912 to fire the more powerful straight-sided cartridge. All such weapons are identified with a large figure '9' cut into the wooden grips and filled with red paint. This variant is also sometimes known as the Model 1916, and like all Mauser automatics, it has an adjustable leaf rearsight, which seems to be an unnecessary complication for a short-ranged pistol. This specimen does not have the wooden holster/shoulder stock fitted, which was a popular attachment for trench clearing operations. These pistols saw service well into the 1930s.

1 Bergmann Model 1896
LENGTH: 10in (254mm)
WEIGHT: 40oz (1.13kg)
CALIBRE: 7.63mm (.30in)
CAPACITY: 5
MV: c.1250f/s (380m/s)

Theodor Bergmann produced his first self-loading pistol in 1894, of which this is an improved 1896 model. It uses simple blowback, where the gas pressure in the breech pushes the bolt to the rear, leaving the barrel fixed in place. Blowback is only really viable with comparatively low-powered cartridges, and this design is on the limits of safety and effectiveness. There is no extraction system, instead the gas pressure just blows the empty case out of the breech, where it bounces off the next round and out of the ejection port. There is an integral box magazine which is opened by pulling down the catch in front of the trigger. Ammunition is loaded in a five-round clip. This is a well-made but unreliable weapon which was unsuited to the rigours of military service.

2 Bergmann Model 1897
LENGTH: 10.5in (267mm)
WEIGHT: 26.5oz (.75kg)
CALIBRE: 7.63mm (.30in)
CAPACITY: 5
MV: c.1100f/s (335m/s)

Developed from the Model 1896, this weapon uses a cam system to lock the bolt to the barrel until the gas pressure drops to a safe level. It also feeds from a detachable box magazine. An efficient and reliable pistol, its ammunition was considered to be too light for widespread service use.

3 Bergmann Simplex
LENGTH: 7.5in (190mm)
WEIGHT: 21oz (.59kg)
CALIBRE: 8mm (.315in)
CAPACITY: 6 or 8
MV: c.650f/s (198m/s)

Bergmann designed this pocket pistol which was licensed to a Belgian company in 1904. It uses the blowback principle and fires a special low-powered cartridge from a detachable box magazine. This is a light, handy, self-defence weapon but with poor stopping power.

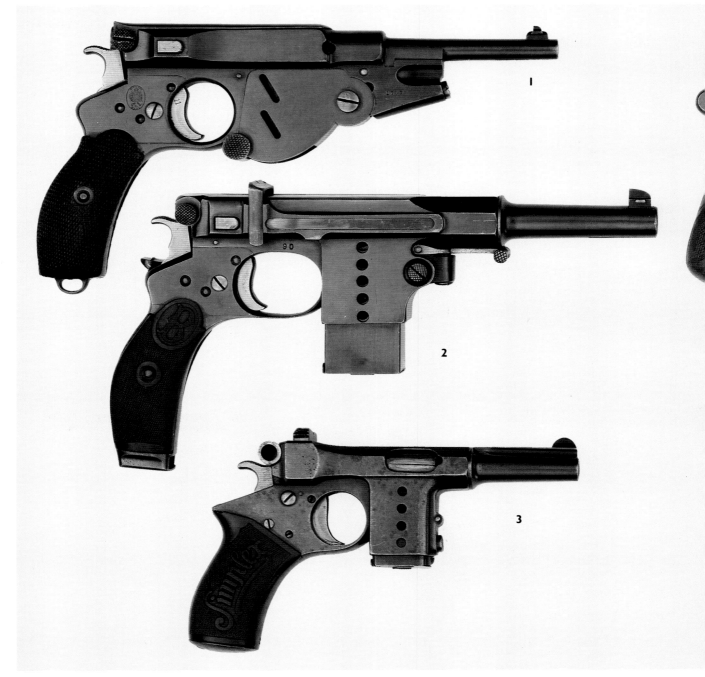

4 Bergmann-Bayard
LENGTH: 9.9in (251mm)
WEIGHT: 35.5oz (1.01kg)
CALIBRE: 9mm (.354in)
CAPACITY: 6
MV: c.1000f/s (305m/s)

This 1901 weapon was designed specifically for service use. It fires a powerful 9mm cartridge and uses the recoil principle, where the barrel and bolt are driven to the rear before the breech opens. It uses a detachable box magazine and saw service with the Spanish, Danish and Greek armies.

5 Mannlicher Model 1901
LENGTH: 9.4in (239mm)
WEIGHT: 33oz (.94kg)
CALIBRE: 7.63mm (.30in)
CAPACITY: 8
MV: c.1025f/s (312m/s)

The Steyr factory was built in Austria by Josef Werndl, whose son (also Josef) incorporated American mass production methods to manufacture a cheaper range of small arms. One of their early products was this automatic pistol, which was developed by Ritter von Mannlicher. This 1901 model is an improved version of the original 1894 pistol, and uses delayed blow-back principles of operation. The bolt is not locked to the fixed barrel, but instead relies on a mechanical retardation system to slow its operation until the gas pressure has dropped to a safe level. The magazine is in the butt, although it is an integral one which is reloaded through the top of the weapon from a charger. This is a well-made and reliable weapon firing a reasonably effective cartridge.

6 Mannlicher Model 1903
LENGTH: 10.5in (267mm)
WEIGHT: 35oz (.99kg)
CALIBRE: 7.65mm (.301in)
CAPACITY: 6
MV: c.1090f/s (332m/s)

This Mannlicher design has a positive locking recoil system for use with more powerful ammunition. Once cocked, a stop on the frame locks the bolt and barrel together until the gas pressure drops to a safe level. The safety lever above the trigger cocks and de-cocks the hammer.

1 Browning Model 1900

LENGTH: 6.75in (171mm)
WEIGHT: 22oz (.62kg)
CALIBRE: 7.65mm (.301in)
CAPACITY: 7
MV: c.940f/s (287m/s)

John Moses Browning first produced an automatic pistol in 1900, but after disputes with American manufacturers he sold the rights to the Belgian firm of Fabrique Nationale (FN), creating a link that would last for decades. This a tough and reliable pistol, which has the barrel fixed to the frame. The breech block is an integral part of the top slide, which also holds the recoil spring running above the barrel. This slide is pulled back to cock the weapon, then released to move forward and feed a round from the magazine. When the pistol is fired, the slide provides sufficient mass to delay rearwards movement until the gas pressures have dropped. An extractor on the slide also pulls the empty case from the breech and flips it out through the ejection port on the left side.

2 Browning Model 1900

LENGTH: 6.75in (171mm)
WEIGHT: 22oz (.62kg)
CALIBRE: 7.65mm (.301in)
CAPACITY: 7
MV: c.940f/s (287m/s)

Browning's automatics fired a specially developed cartridge, which some thought too light for military use. Even so, they were popular with many soldiers, and this early model was still being carried by a French officer in Algeria in the late 1950s. It has been fitted with non-standard grips.

3 Colt Model 1903

LENGTH: 6.75in (171mm)
WEIGHT: 24oz (.68kg)
CALIBRE: .32in (8.1mm)
CAPACITY: 8
MV: c.900f/s (274m/s)

Colt produced their own automatic pistol in 1903, but soon replaced it with this neat and handy design from John Browning. It uses simple blowback with the hammer concealed within the slide. There is a grip safety which has to be depressed before the weapon can be fired.

4 Webley-Mars

LENGTH: 12.25in (311mm)
WEIGHT: 48oz (1.36kg)
CALIBRE: .38in (9.6mm)
CAPACITY: 7
MV: c.1750f/s (533m/s)

At the turn of the century, Webley looked around for a suitable automatic pistol to manufacture. They were given this design by Hugh Gabbet-Fairfax, and put it into production under the tradename Mars. It is a heavy, cumbersome weapon which fires a specially-designed bottle-necked cartridge. The bolt is locked against the barrel, and has to rotate to unlock during the initial movement to the rear. The powerful cartridge gives this pistol a hefty recoil kick, while case ejection is somewhat erratic. It was rejected on these grounds for British military service, although there was also strong resistance to the automatic pistol in any shape or form. Gabbet-Fairfax attempted to market the weapon himself, but it did not sell. He went bankrupt in 1904.

5 Webley & Scott M1904

LENGTH: 10in (254mm)
WEIGHT: 48oz (1.36kg)
CALIBRE: .455in (11.5mm)
CAPACITY: 7
MV: c.750f/s (229m/s)

Webley persisted with the self-loader, however, and in 1904 produced this pistol, chambered for a round slightly bigger and rather more powerful than the British service cartridge. The M1904 is a large square pistol with the butt at an awkward angle for instinctive shooting. It uses recoil principles, with the barrel and breech are locked together by a vertical stop at the moment of firing. After a short distance, this locking piece drops away to allow the bolt to continue rearwards on its own. It is a heavy, somewhat complex design, and is easily jammed by dirt and grit, which could pose severe problems for a military user. The British services expressed little interest in this large pistol, and the Webley only gained limited commercial sales, although it set the pattern for later designs.

1 Webley No.1 Mk.1

LENGTH: 8.5in (216mm)
WEIGHT: 39oz (1.1kg)
CALIBRE: .455in (11.5mm)
CAPACITY: 7
MV: c.750f/s (229m/s)

Webley developed this improved automatic in 1906, which was accepted for service by the British Royal Navy in 1913. It is a large, square pistol, with a detachable box magazine in the butt, and fires a larger and more powerful version of the .455in (11.5mm) revolver cartridge. It is recoil-operated, with the barrel and slide locked together for the first part of their rearward travel. A cam system then forces the rear of the barrel downwards slightly, unlocking the slide and permitting it to move to the rear. There is a safety grip at the rear of the butt, which has to be depressed by the firer's hand before the weapon can be fired. There was also a later version with a detachable stock which was issued to the Royal Flying Corps, although it was soon replaced by a machine gun.

2 Webley Model 1909

LENGTH: 8in (203mm)
WEIGHT: 34oz (.96kg)
CALIBRE: 9mm (.354in)
CAPACITY: 7
MV: c.750f/s (229m/s)

This pistol was designed for police and para-military users who did not need the power of the .455in (11.5mm) service cartridge. Firing Browning's 9mm (.354in) round, it uses blowback without a delay system. It was bought in large numbers by the South African Police Force.

3 Webley & Scott .32in

LENGTH: 6.25in (159mm)
WEIGHT: 20oz (.57kg)
CALIBRE: .32in (8.1mm)
CAPACITY: 8
MV: c.900f/s (274m/s)

Webley saw a large market for a simple automatic firing reasonably light cartridges, and had this model in production by 1906. It is a simple, rugged and effective blowback design which proved to be extremely popular with police and service users. It remained in manufacture until 1940.

4 Harrington & Richardson
LENGTH: 6.5in (165mm)
WEIGHT: 20oz (.57kg)
CALIBRE: .32in (8.1mm)
CAPACITY: 6
MV: c.980f/s (299m/s)

Harrington and Richardson of Massachusetts produced this pistol based on Webley's lighter blowback designs. Unlike the British pistols it has a hidden hammer and a large cut-out above the slide. While an effective weapon, it never competed well against indigenous American designs.

5 Dansk Schouboe M1907
LENGTH: 8.8in (224mm)
WEIGHT: 42oz (1.19kg)
CALIBRE: 11.35mm (.447in)
CAPACITY: 6
MV: c.1600f/s (488m/s)

Lt. Jens Schouboe developed a simple blowback pistol in 1903, and in 1907 tried to scale up his design for use with a larger service calibre round. Unlocked blowback systems are not normally safe with full-powered service ammunition, so Schouboe developed a new lighter bullet made from wood with a thin metal jacket. This round reduces the recoil forces, and leaves the barrel faster, keeping gas pressure at a low level. His idea worked, in that this pistol is a reliable weapon which functions well in service conditions. Its problem is that the round itself is virtually useless. The light bullet has very little stopping power, while it loses accuracy very quickly. This weapon was an interesting technical solution that ignored real military requirements. It ceased production in 1917.

6 Schwarzlose Model 1908
LENGTH: 5.4in (137mm)
WEIGHT: 32oz (.91kg)
CALIBRE: 9mm (.354in)
CAPACITY: 6
MV: c.1000f/s (305m/s)

Andreas Schwarzlose produced this commercially unsuccessful pistol in 1908. The breech block is fixed to the frame, while the barrel is free to move forwards under gas pressure. When the recoil spring pulls it back, the barrel re-cocks the hammer and chambers the next round.

1 Luger Parabellum P08

LENGTH: 8.75in (222mm)
WEIGHT: 30oz (.85kg)
CALIBRE: 9mm (.354in)
CAPACITY: 8
MV: c.1150f/s (351m/s)

Georg Luger improved upon Borchardt's design to produce a series of weapons known as the Parabellum pistols (from the postal address of the factory). His early automatics fired a 7.65mm (.301in) round, but in 1908 Luger modified this cartridge to hold a 9mm (.354in) bullet, and developed a pistol to fire it. The P08 uses a similar recoil system to the Borchardt, in that the barrel and breech block recoil together for a short distance until a locking toggle bends upwards to release the breech block. The Luger was immediately successful, being adopted by the German Army and remaining in continuous manufacture until 1943. It saw widespread service in both world wars, and created a reputation somewhat greater than it perhaps deserves. This is a Mauser-built 1940 model.

2 Luger Artillery Model

LENGTH: 12.75in (324mm)
WEIGHT: 37oz (1.05kg)
CALIBRE: 9mm (.354in)
CAPACITY: 8/32
MV: c.1250f/s (380m/s)

In 1917, this carbine version of the Luger was issued as a defensive weapon for machine gun and artillery detachments. Known as the 'Artillery' model, it has a much longer barrel (190mm/7.5in) than the standard pistol, and is usually fitted with a detachable wooden stock. It can either use the standard box magazine in the butt, or a special 32-round clockwork driven 'snail drum' as seen on the photograph. The weapon is also fitted with an adjustable leaf sight. While there were initial problems with the magazine feed, this combination became popular for close-quarters combat such as night-raids and trench-fighting. It may have been the success of this and the Mauser that inspired German development of the submachine gun There was also a long-barrelled naval variant.

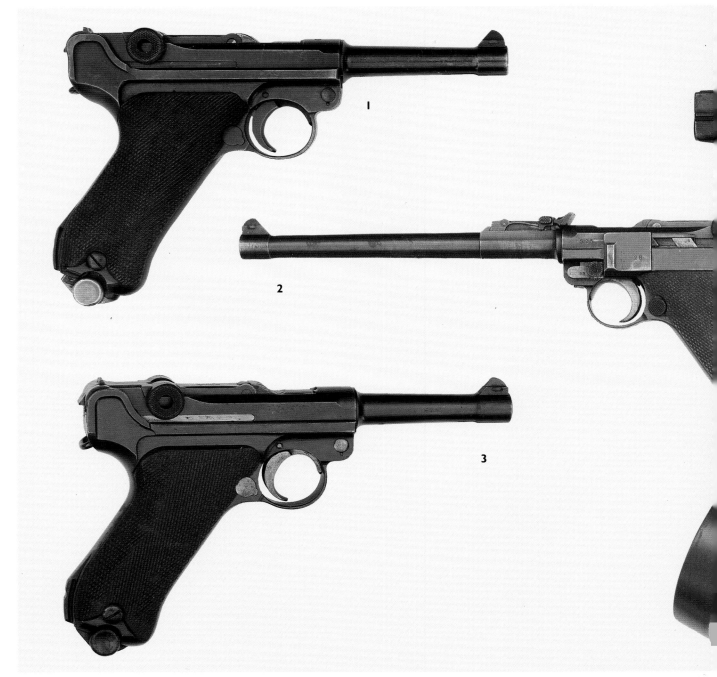

3 Luger P08/20

LENGTH: 8.75in (222mm)
WEIGHT: 30oz (.85kg)
CALIBRE: 7.65mm (.301in)
CAPACITY: 8
MV: c.1150f/s (351m/s)

This is another version of the Luger, produced after the First World War. It has a shorter barrel than the standard P08, and fires a less powerful 7.65mm (.301in) round, modifications which were designed to circumvent the restrictions imposed by the Allies in the Treaty of Versailles .

4 Rheinmetall Dreyse

LENGTH: 6.25in (159mm)
WEIGHT: 25oz (.71kg)
CALIBRE: 7.65mm (.301in)
CAPACITY: 7
MV: c.850f/s (259m/s)

This pistol was designed by Louis Schmeisser, and was first seen in 1907. The breech block is integral with the slide, and sits above the barrel, which lies in the trough in the frame. It is a simple blowback weapon firing medium-powered ammunition, with no locking or delay system necessary.

5 Savage Model 1907

LENGTH: 6.5in (165mm)
WEIGHT: 20oz (.57kg)
CALIBRE: .32in (8.1mm)
CAPACITY: 10
MV: c.800f/s (244m/s)

This American pistol first appeared in 1907, manufactured by a company that is still well-known for its sporting rifles. It uses blowback principles of operation, although with an unusual delay system. When the slide is forward, the barrel locks it in place with a lug engaging in a curved slot in the slide. When the weapon is fired, the slide is held forwards until the barrel rotates slightly to unlock the lug. The theory was that the mass of the bullet rotating in the rifling would be enough to prevent the barrel from moving until the bullet had actually left the barrel and the gas pressure had dropped to a safe level. Many engineers have disputed the details of the theory, but whatever the actual physical process, the Savage worked well enough, although the controversy hampered sales.

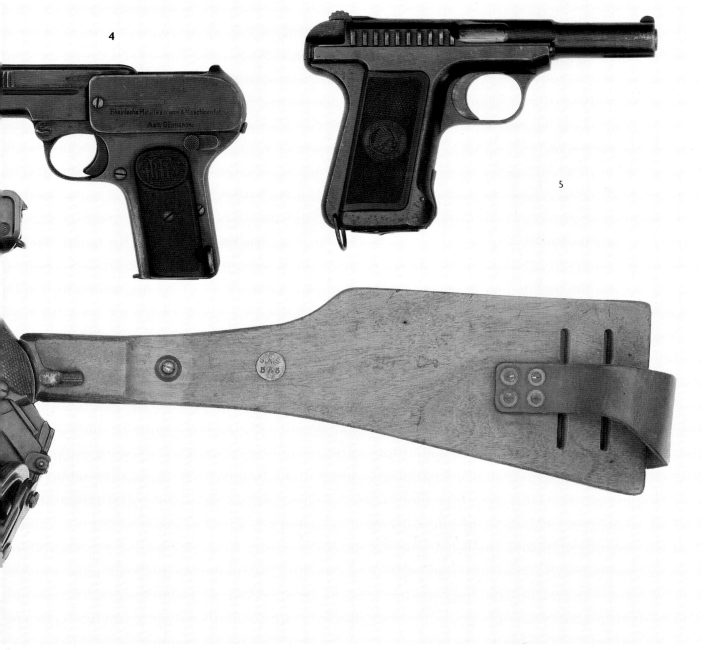

1 Roth-Steyr Model 1907

LENGTH: 9in (229mm)
WEIGHT: 36oz (1.05kg)
CALIBRE: 8mm (.315in)
CAPACITY: 10
MV: c.1090f/s (332m/s)

The 1907 entry into service of this pistol made the Austro-Hungarian Army one of the first military forces to adopt an automatic. The frame has a fixed, hollow receiver, inside which are the barrel and bolt. The weapon is cocked by pulling backwards on the large toggle at the rear of the bolt.

This is a large, heavy item with a hollow front end which surrounds the rear of the barrel. The two are locked together by studs on the barrel which fit into corresponding curved grooves on the inside of the bolt. When a round is fired, the barrel and bolt recoil together, while the curved grooves cause the barrel to rotate until the bolt is unlocked. The barrel then hits a stop, while the bolt continues to the rear to cock the hammer and feed the next round from the magazine.

2 Glisenti Model 1910

LENGTH: 8.25in (210mm)
WEIGHT: 29oz (.82kg)
CALIBRE: 9mm (.354in)
CAPACITY: 7
MV: c.1000f/s (305m/s)

This pistol was adopted by the Italian Army in 1910. It is a recoil design, where the barrel and bolt are locked together by a lug, and move together for a short distance. Once they are unlocked, the barrel stops its movement, while the bolt continues to the rear. When the barrel and bolt return to the forward position, a wedge on the frame rises to hold them in place. Unlike most automatics, the hammer is not cocked by the bolt movement. Instead, the first pull on the trigger raises the hammer, until a further pull causes it to drop onto the firing pin. The whole left side of the frame is detachable to allow access to the mechanism. The Glisenti is a rather fragile, complex and unreliable weapon, which requires a reduced power 9mm (.354in) cartridge. The long trigger pull reduces accuracy.

3 Steyr Model 1911

LENGTH: 8.5in (216mm)
WEIGHT: 35oz (.99kg)
CALIBRE: .357in (9.06mm)
CAPACITY: 8
MV: c.1100f/s (335m/s)

This recoil-operated pistol entered Austro-Hungarian service in 1911, and is a solid, reliable weapon. The barrel is locked to the slide by two lugs, and rotates during the initial movement to release the slide. The integral magazine is loaded with a clip, with the slide being held to the rear.

4 Frommer Model 1910

LENGTH: 7.25in (184mm)
WEIGHT: 21oz (.59kg)
CALIBRE: 7.65mm (.301in)
CAPACITY: 7
MV: c.1100f/s (335m/s)

This Hungarian pistol uses the principle of long recoil, where the barrel and bolt remain locked together for the whole of their rearwards travel. As they reach the rear limit, the bolt head rotates to unlock the barrel while a stop engages to hold it in place. The barrel is then driven forward, which helps the extractor remove the empty case and flip it away. When the barrel returns to the forward position, it trips a release catch which permits the bolt to come forwards, picking up the next round as it does so. This system requires two separate recoil springs, and is somewhat complex for a pistol firing such a light cartridge. The Frommer pistol saw service in a number of variants with Hungarian forces through the 1930s, and many were still in use during the Second World War.

5 Unceta Victoria

LENGTH: 5.75in (146mm)
WEIGHT: 20oz (.57kg)
CALIBRE: 7.65mm (.301in)
CAPACITY: 7
MV: c.750f/s (229m/s)

This copy of the Browning M1903 is from a Spanish company who specialised in pistols that were reasonably cheap but still effective. It uses the same blowback system as the Browning, with the recoil spring beneath the barrel and the hammer completely hidden within the frame.

1 Colt Model 1911

LENGTH: 8.5in (216mm)
WEIGHT: 39oz (1.1kg)
CALIBRE: .455in (11.5mm)
CAPACITY: 7
MV: c.860f/s (262m/s)

One of the best known and most popular military pistols of the modern era, the Colt was developed from a 1900 design by John Moses Browning. Chambered for a powerful .45in (11.4mm) cartridge, it was formally adopted by the US Army in 1911. The pistol uses a short recoil system, where the barrel is held in place by ribs on its top surface which lock into corresponding grooves on the inside of the slide. As the barrel and slide begin to move to the rear, a pivoting link pulls the rear of the barrel downwards, which unlocks the slide and allows it to continue separately. The Colt is a solid and tough pistol which proved reliable and effective in service. This specimen was actually made for the Canadian Army in the First World War, so fires the British service round.

2 Hafsada Pistol

LENGTH: 9in (229mm)
WEIGHT: 39oz (1.1kg)
CALIBRE: .45in (11.4mm)
CAPACITY: 7
MV: c.860f/s (262m/s)

Licensed production of the Colt M1911A1 was undertaken in a number of countries, and some of the better copies were made in Argentina. This specimen has no grip safety, while the butt plates and finger grips on the slide are a different pattern from those of the Colt original.

3 Colt Model 1911A1

LENGTH: 8.5in (216mm)
WEIGHT: 39oz (1.1kg)
CALIBRE: .45in (11.4mm)
CAPACITY: 7
MV: c.860f/s (262m/s)

While combat experience in the First World War proved the effectiveness of the basic Colt design, a number of minor improvements were still felt to be necessary. In 1926 the M1911A1 was formally adopted, and remained virtually unaltered as the standard US military pistol for nearly 60

years. It has a slightly shorter hammer than the earlier model, a re-shaped grip, and chamfered cut-outs on the frame, just behind the trigger. The grip safety is also slightly longer. Colts were made by a number of companies, including Remington and the Springfield Arsenal, and millions served with US and Allied forces during the Second World War. One of the all-time greats, the Colt was eventually replaced in US service in 1984 by the Beretta 92F (see page 115).

4 Llama Pistol

LENGTH: 9.5in (241mm)
WEIGHT: 40oz (1.13kg)
CALIBRE: .38in (9.6mm)
CAPACITY: 7
MV: c.850f/s (259m/s)

The Spanish firm of Gabilondo began to manufacture a range of automatic pistols in 1931 under the trade name Llama, basing their designs on the Colt M1911. Weapons have been produced in a number of calibres and in a wide range of models, some using simple blowback, others with Browning's locked breech. This is a locked breech weapon, designed to fire the powerful .38in (9.6mm) Colt Super cartridge. There is no grip safety, although there is a conventional safety catch on the left side, below the hammer. Like all the M1911 models, its only weakness is the limited number of rounds in the detachable box magazine, as most contemporary 9mm pistols can carry significantly more ammunition. This is a well-made and reliable Colt copy for military use.

5 Echeverria Star B

LENGTH: 8in (203mm)
WEIGHT: 34oz (.96kg)
CALIBRE: 9mm (.354in)
CAPACITY: 8
MV: c.1100f/s (335m/s)

The Star series of automatics were another range of Spanish pistols based on the Colt M1911. This one was adopted by the Spanish Army, chambered to fire the 9mm (.354in) Largo cartridge. It is a well-made and reliable weapon, although it lacks the grip safety of the Colt.

4

3

5

1 Bernedo Pocket Pistol

LENGTH: 4.5in (114mm)
WEIGHT: 15oz (.42kg)
CALIBRE: 6.35mm (.25in)
CAPACITY: 6
MV: c.800f/s (244m/s)

Pocket automatic pistols have often been used as concealed personal defence weapons for security and special duties personnel, while they are also sometimes carried as secondary weapons by uniformed soldiers. Normally chambered for small calibre, low-powered ammunition, they are able to use blowback principles to give a simple, reliable method of operation. This specimen is a Spanish design developed just after the First World War, and manufactured in Spain's gun-making region of Eibar. It is a blowback weapon, with the cylindrical barrel protruding a considerable distance ahead of the short slide. It is a neat, easily concealed firearm, although like all such weapons it is virtually useless at any distance further than extreme close range. The magazine has a short grip extension.

2 Frommer Baby

LENGTH: 4.75in (121mm)
WEIGHT: 14oz (.4kg)
CALIBRE: 6.35mm (.25in)
CAPACITY: 6
MV: c.800f/s (244m/s)

Rudolf Frommer also dabbled with miniature automatics, and this 1912 design is basically a scaled-down version of his service pistol of the same year. It uses long recoil, where the barrel and bolt travel to the rear together, hence the cylinderical tube above the barrel which houses the two recoil springs.

3 Walther Model 9

LENGTH: 4in (102mm)
WEIGHT: 9.5oz (.27kg)
CALIBRE: 6.35mm (.25in)
CAPACITY: 6
MV: c.800f/s (244m/s)

Carl Walther produced a range of automatic pistols from 1908, and this weapon dates from around 1930. It is a blowback weapon firing a small-calibre 6.35mm (.25in) round, and uses a fixed barrel and an open-topped slide to make a remarkably small, neat and easily concealed design.

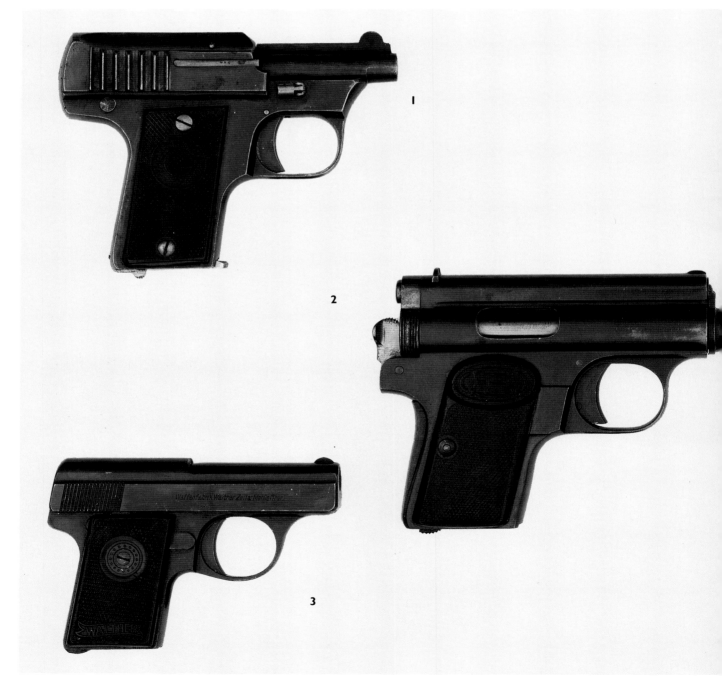

4 Lignose Einhand

LENGTH: 4.6in (117mm)
WEIGHT: 18oz (.51kg)
CALIBRE: 6.35mm (.25in)
CAPACITY: 9
MV: c.800f/s (244m/s)

This is actually a 1917 Bergmann design, but the rights were sold to Lignose, and it was under this name that it became best known. At the time it was produced, automatics did not display the same degree of safety features that they do now, and were normally carried un-cocked, with an empty chamber. This meant that the user had to pull back the slide before firing, which was a relatively time-consuming, two-handed process. The Einhand attempted to overcome this by connecting the front of the trigger guard to the slide. When the gun is gripped, all the firer needs to do is put his finger over the front of the guard and pull back, which moves the slide and cocks the weapon. He then simply moves his finger back to the trigger to fire the pistol which operates conventionally.

5 Colt Model 1908

LENGTH: 4.5in (114mm)
WEIGHT: 14oz (.4kg)
CALIBRE: .25in (6.35mm)
CAPACITY: 6
MV: c.800f/s (244m/s)

Another Browning design, this pocket blowback design was first produced in Belgium until Colt bought the patent and manufactured it in the United States. It is a simple personal defence weapon, and unusually for a pistol of this size, fitted with a grip safety at the rear of the butt.

6 Tomiska Little Tom

LENGTH: 4.7in (119mm)
WEIGHT: 15oz (.42kg)
CALIBRE: 6.35mm (.25in)
CAPACITY: 6
MV: c.800f/s (244m/s)

An Austrian design from around 1908, the Little Tom has a double-action lock, which means that it can safely be carried with a round in the chamber. It also has an exposed hammer to allow manual cocking. Pistols of this type were made in a number of European countries.

1 Gabilondo Ruby

LENGTH: 6in (152mm)
WEIGHT: 30oz (.85kg)
CALIBRE: 7.65mm (.301in)
CAPACITY: 9
MV: c.800f/s (244m/s)

In 1914, the Spanish firm of Gabilondo first began manufacture of this small blowback pistol. Cheap, simple, but effective, it appeared at a time when many countries were hastily rearming. The Ruby was taken up by the French Government, and remained in production until 1919.

2 Remington Model 51

LENGTH: 6.5in (165mm)
WEIGHT: 21oz (.6kg)
CALIBRE: .38in (9.6mm)
CAPACITY: 7
MV: c.900f/s (274m/s)

The first automatic pistols made by Remington were licensed copies of the M1911, manufactured in 1917 to supplement Colt's wartime production. The company had its own plans, however, and by 1919 had produced this weapon designed by J.D. Pedersen. It is a recoil-operated pistol, with the slide and barrel being locked together for the first part of the recoil movement. The front of the slide completely shrouds the barrel, and holds in place the recoil spring, which is wound around the barrel. The Model 51 has a well-shaped butt, with a grip safety at the rear, while there is a normal safety catch on the left of the frame, just under the hammer. This specimen is chambered for the .38in (9.6mm) Auto cartridge, although some also used the .32in (8.1mm) round.

3 Browning Model 1922

LENGTH: 7in (178mm)
WEIGHT: 25oz (.71kg)
CALIBRE: 9mm (.354in)
CAPACITY: 9
MV: c.875f/s (267m/s)

This is another Fabrique Nationale pistol to the designs of John Browning. It is a delayed blowback weapon, firing a reasonably powerful 9mm (.354in) Short cartridge. The slide has a cylindrical end cap which holds the recoil spring, which in turn surrounds the front of the barrel.

1

2

3

4 CZ Model 1924

LENGTH: 6.25in (159mm)
WEIGHT: 24oz (.68kg)
CALIBRE: 7.65mm (.301in)
CAPACITY: 8
MV: c.800f/s (244m/s)

The Ceska Zbrojovka factory was established in the new country of Czechoslovakia in 1919, and this was one of its first products. A delayed blow-back pistol, the barrel is rotated by a cam path, which unlocks the slide and allows it to continue moving to operate the reloading cycle.

5 CZ Model 1927

LENGTH: 6.25in (159mm)
WEIGHT: 25.5oz (.72kg)
CALIBRE: 7.65mm (.301in)
CAPACITY: 8
MV: c.900f/s (274m/s)

This is effectively an updated CZ Model 24 chambered for a smaller cartridge. The less powerful round means that the complexities of a locked barrel and slide are unnecessary, so the Model 27 uses a straightforward blowback system. The main visual difference is in the grooves in the slide.

6 Unceta Astra 400

LENGTH: 9.25in (235mm)
WEIGHT: 38oz (1.08kg)
CALIBRE: 9mm (.354in)
CAPACITY: 8
MV: c.1100f/s (335m/s)

Unceta had already manufactured a range of lightweight and pocket pistols, when in 1913 they produced a heavier service-calibre weapon which was later developed into the Astra. It fires a powerful 9mm (.354in) Largo cartridge, although the designers have managed to make do with a simple blowback system. The pistol has an extremely solid and weighty slide, which is cylindrical in section at the front. There is a separate end-cap at the muzzle, which holds in place the recoil spring which sits around the front end of the fixed barrel. To enable the safe use of blowback with such powerful ammunition, the heavy slide is combined with a very powerful recoil spring, both of which delay the rearward movement just enough to allow the pressure to fall to a safe level.

1 Nambu Taisho 14
LENGTH: 8.9in (226mm)
WEIGHT: 32oz (.91kg)
CALIBRE: 8mm (.315in)
CAPACITY: 8
MV: c.950f/s (290m/s)

The first automatic formally adopted by the Japanese Army, the Type 14 Nambu entered service in 1925. At the moment of firing, the barrel, bolt and receiver are locked together, and have to move a short distance before the bolt is released to continue travelling to the rear.

2 Le Francais Model 28
LENGTH: 7.9in (201mm)
WEIGHT: 35oz (.99kg)
CALIBRE: 9mm (.354in)
CAPACITY: 8
MV: c.1100f/s (335m/s)

A 1928 service-calibre weapon from St Etienne, it is an unlocked blowback pistol firing a low-powered cartridge. An unusual feature is the breech which hinges open rather like a shotgun, allowing single rounds to be loaded independently. Note the spare round beneath the magazine.

3 Walther PP
LENGTH: 6.4in (163mm)
WEIGHT: 25oz (.71kg)
CALIBRE: 7.65mm (.301in)
CAPACITY: 8
MV: c.1000f/s (305m/s)

Carl Walther produced this unlocked blowback weapon in 1929, specifically for police and security personnel. The PP (Polizei Pistole) quickly became adopted by several European police forces, and was also used extensively by the German military, especially the Luftwaffe. It was a revolutionary design, in that it was one of the first automatics that could be safely carried with a round in the chamber. When the weapon is cocked, applying the safety catch places a metal block between the hammer and the firing pin, while causing the hammer itself to fall back to the un-cocked position. There is also a metal signal pin that protrudes from the rear of the slide when a round is in the chamber. The lock is like that on a double action revolver, in that the user just needs to pull the trigger.

4 Walther PPK

LENGTH: 5.8in (147mm)
WEIGHT: 20oz (.57kg)
CALIBRE: 7.65mm (.301in)
CAPACITY: 7
MV: c.1000f/s (305m/s)

The PP was an immediate success, and in 1931 Walther produced a modified version for plain clothes use. The PPK (K = Kurz or 'Short') is smaller than its predecessor, and is a light, easily concealed weapon which can be carried with a round in the chamber. It has similar safety features to the PP, and likewise uses a double action lock to permit rapid shooting. The main difference between this weapon and the PP is that the butt grip is a one-piece plastic item that wraps around the rear of the frame. The 7.65mm (.301in) model was by far the most common, although there were versions produced firing 6.35mm (.25in) and 9mm (.354in) Short cartridges. The PPK became just as popular as its larger brother, finding a role with security troops, body-guards and others.

5 Tula-Tokarev 1930

LENGTH: 7.7in (196mm)
WEIGHT: 29oz (.82kg)
CALIBRE: 7.62mm (.30in)
CAPACITY: 8
MV: c.1350f/s (411m/s)

Feodor Tokarev took many of Browning's concepts as the basis for this Soviet design, which first entered production at the Tula arsenal in 1930. It is a typically Russian pistol, simple, tough, reliable, and easy to manufacture. It fires a Russian 7.62mm (.30in) cartridge and locks the barrel and slide at the moment of firing. The TT-30 has a number of new features introduced by Tokarev, including feed guides in the frame rather than the fragile lips found on Colt magazines. The single-action lock can also be removed in one piece for maintenance and cleaning. There is no safety catch, although the hammer can be dropped to half-cock. The design was slightly modified to become the TT-33, and as such was produced by the million for all arms of the Soviet military.

1 MAB Model D
LENGTH: 5.8in (147mm)
WEIGHT: 26oz (.74kg)
CALIBRE: 7.65mm (.301in)
CAPACITY: 9
MV: c.800f/s (244m/s)

A simple blowback design with no breech locking system, this French pistol is a modified version of the MAB (Manufacture d'Armes de Bayonne) Model C, first seen in 1933. It has the recoil spring wrapped around the barrel and held in place by a detachable end cap.

2 Type 94
LENGTH: 7.1in (180mm)
WEIGHT: 28oz (.79kg)
CALIBRE: 8mm (.315in)
CAPACITY: 6
MV: c.950f/s (290m/s)

Introduced in by Nambu in 1934, this pistol was purchased by the Japanese Government to supplement the existing Type 14 weapons. It is a delayed blowback weapon, with the barrel being locked to the slide at the moment of firing by a vertically-moving sliding block. It is a remarkably poorly-conceived design, often more dangerous to the firer than the target. Part of the trigger sear protrudes from the left of the frame when the weapon is cocked, making accidental discharge almost inevitable if the weapon is jolted or roughly handled. It is also possible to fire the weapon before the breech is properly closed, risking ruptured cartridge cases and injury to the firer. Nevertheless, tens of thousands were issued to unfortunate officers during the Second World War.

3 Beretta Model 1934
LENGTH: 6in (152mm)
WEIGHT: 23oz (.65kg)
CALIBRE: 9mm (.354in)
CAPACITY: 9
MV: c.750f/s (229m/s)

Produced in 1934, this compact automatic is a development of the 1915 Beretta service pistol. It fires the 9mm (.354in) Glisenti round, which is low-powered enough to allow the use of simple unlocked blowback. It is a well-made reliable weapon which saw widespread service.

4 Beretta Model 1935

LENGTH: 6in (152mm)
WEIGHT: 23oz (.65kg)
CALIBRE: 7.65mm (.301in)
CAPACITY: 7
MV: c.800f/s (244m/s)

The Model 1934 was so successful, that Beretta quickly developed a number of variants. This is the Model 1935, similar in most respects to the earlier weapon apart from being chambered for the smaller 7.65mm (.301in) cartridge. Like its predecessor it has a lightweight alloy frame, with the Beretta trademark of a large cut-out in the top of the slide. The hammer is external, while there is a safety catch on the left side of the frame. When the last round is fired, the magazine follower holds the slide open to give a positive visual indication. This can be inconvenient in service use, as the firer needs to pull back the slide to release the empty magazine, let it move forward as he inserts a fresh one, than pull it back again to load the top round into the breech. This was a neat and effective service arm.

5 Radom VIS-35

LENGTH: 8.3in (211mm)
WEIGHT: 37oz (1.05kg)
CALIBRE: 9mm (.354in)
CAPACITY: 8
MV: c.1150f/s (351m/s)

Radom began the manufacture of small arms in Poland soon after the First World War, and by 1935 had developed and manufactured this automatic. It fires the powerful 9mm (.354in) Parabellum cartridge first used in the Luger P08, and which was to gradually become a European military standard round. It fires from a locked breech, making use of Browning's concept of locking lugs on the barrel mating with corresponding grooves in the slide. The rear of the barrel is pulled down by a cam system to unlock the slide after the gas pressure has fallen to a safe level. There is a grip safety at the rear of the butt, but no safety catch as such. Instead there is a lever at the back of the slide which can be used to drop the hammer while moving a blocking piece between the hammer and the firing pin.

4

5

1 Lahti L35
LENGTH: 9.4in (239mm)
WEIGHT: 44oz (1.25kg)
CALIBRE: 9mm (.354in)
CAPACITY: 8
MV: c.1100f/s (335m/s)

At first glance resembling a Luger P08, this 1935 Finnish 9mm (.354) Parabellum pistol is closer to the Mauser designs in method of operation. Unusually for a pistol, it has a curved lever which accelerates the bolt to the rear, to ensure operation in severe conditions of dirt, grit or icing.

2 Browning GP35
LENGTH: 6in (152mm)
WEIGHT: 30oz (.85kg)
CALIBRE: 7.65mm (.301in)
CAPACITY: 9
MV: c.800f/s (244m/s)

The last pistol designed by Browning before he died in 1926, this weapon only entered large scale production with Fabrique Nationale of Belgium in 1935. Chambered for 9mm (.354in) Parabellum, it builds upon earlier Browning designs. There is no grip safety, but the hammer can be locked by a safety catch at the rear of the slide. It is a reliable, effective pistol, also known as the 'High-Power', which quickly entered service in Europe and China. When the Germans overran the factory in 1940, they put the GP35 into production for their own troops. Belgian engineers also managed to smuggle the plans to Canada, where it was manufactured for Canadian and Allied forces. After the war, it was adopted as the standard service pistol by over 30 countries.

3 Fegyvergyar Model 1937
LENGTH: 7.2in (163mm)
WEIGHT: 25oz (.71kg)
CALIBRE: 9mm (.354in)
CAPACITY: 7
MV: c.900f/s (274m/s)

Designed for the Hungarian Army by Rudolf Frommer, this is a simple but robust automatic firing a short 9mm (.354in) cartridge. It uses unlocked blowback, and has the recoil spring below the barrel. There is a grip safety, while this specimen has a magazine spur to improve grip.

4 Sauer Model 38H

LENGTH: 6.75in (171mm)
WEIGHT: 25oz (.71kg)
CALIBRE: 7.65mm (.301in)
CAPACITY: 8
MV: c.900f/s (274m/s)

This high-quality blowback military pistol was first produced in 1938 by the German firm of J.P. Sauer and Sohn, and most went to the Army during the Second World War. The Sauer introduced a number of features which were significantly more advanced than other pistols of the time.

To chamber a round, the slide is pulled back in the normal way. The weapon can then be fired, or alternatively made safe by depressing the catch just behind the trigger. When the trigger is pulled, this catch is released slowly to allow the internal hammer to drop to a un-cocked position. To fire, the user has two options. He can either just squeeze the trigger, which operates the hammer in double-action mode, or he can depress the de-cocking catch to raise the hammer for a more accurate shot.

5 Walther P38

LENGTH: 8.4in (213mm)
WEIGHT: 34oz (.96kg)
CALIBRE: 9mm (.354in)
CAPACITY: 8
MV: c.1150f/s (351m/s)

Developed by Carl Walther to replace the Luger P08 in German Army service, this 9mm (.354in) Parabellum pistol appeared in 1938. It shares some features of the PP and PPK series, although it uses recoil principles and has an external hammer. The barrel and slide are locked together by a wedge-shaped block, which is cammed down to release the slide during the first part of the movement. The P38 shares many of the PP safety features, including a signal pin which protrudes at the rear of the slide when a round is chambered. When the safety catch on the slide is operated, it locks the firing pin and causes the hammer to drop into an unlocked position. To fire, all the user needs to do is operate the catch to raise the hammer. The P38 was adopted post-war as the P1.

1 CZ Model 1939
LENGTH: 8.1in (206mm)
WEIGHT: 33oz (.94kg)
CALIBRE: 9mm (.354in)
CAPACITY: 8
MV: c.950f/s (290m/s)

Ceska Zbrojovka produced the first versions of this pistol in 1938, and this is a slightly modified 1939 model. It fires a low-powered 9mm (.354in) cartridge so can make use of simple blowback. It is a heavy weapon, with the grip at a somewhat awkward angle. The hammer is concealed

within the frame, while the lock is self-cocking only. The firer cannot raise the hammer by hand, nor is there any form of safety lever. Instead, the first trigger pull lifts the hammer, and continuing the movement fires the weapon. This requires a heavy trigger pull, and in combination with the shape of the grip, makes accurate shooting difficult. It has one redeeming feature, in that to make cleaning and maintenance easier, the slide and barrel are easily unlocked and tipped upwards.

2 MAS Model 1950
LENGTH: 7.6in (193mm)
WEIGHT: 34oz (.96kg)
CALIBRE: 9mm (.354in)
CAPACITY: 9
MV: c.1100f/s (335m/s)

After the Second World War, the French Army came to the belated conclusion that their standard 7.65mm (.301in) service pistol ammunition was inadequate for combat use. When they decided to change to 9mm (.354in) Parabellum, they chose a pistol based on their wartime MAS

(Manufacture Nationale d'Armes de St. Etienne) 35. The new weapon, the MAS 50, is yet another pistol that uses John Browning's locking system, where lugs on the barrel mate with corresponding grooves on the slide, and where a pivoting link pulls the end of the barrel down to unlock the slide. The MAS has a safety catch on the left of the frame, while the magazine has a device to hold the slide open after the last round has been fired. The hammer and lock can be removed as a single unit.

3 CZ Model 1950

LENGTH: 8.2in (208mm)
WEIGHT: 34oz (.96kg)
CALIBRE: 7.62mm (.30in)
CAPACITY: 8
MV: c.1000f/s (305m/s)

This post-war Czech design is basically a copy of the Walther PP modified for easier manufacture. It retains Walther's double-action mechanism, although the safety catch has been simplified, and is now positioned on the frame rather than the slide. The cartridge is really too light for service use.

4 Starfire Model DK

LENGTH: 5.7in (145mm)
WEIGHT: 15oz (.42kg)
CALIBRE: 9mm (.354in)
CAPACITY: 7
MV: c.1000f/s (305m/s)

A modernised version of a 1930 design, this Echeverria pistol first appeared in 1958. Like most of the weapons from this Spanish manufacturer, it uses Browning's locking system to fire the Spanish 9mm (.354in) Largo cartridge. Military use of this effective but cheap pistol was limited.

5 Makarov PM

LENGTH: 6.35in (161mm)
WEIGHT: 25oz (.71kg)
CALIBRE: 9mm (.354in)
CAPACITY: 8
MV: c.1075f/s (328m/s)

A Russian copy of the Walther PP, this pistol first appeared in the late 1950s, and went on to become the standard service arm for the Soviet Union, most of the Warsaw Pact, and many other Soviet allies. It fires a Russian-designed 9mm (.354in) cartridge of intermediate power, which permits the use of a simple blowback mechanism. The Makarov has Walther's double-action lock, and the pistol can safely be carried with a round in the chamber by applying the safety catch. This slide-mounted lever causes the firing pin to be locked at the same time as the hammer is decocked. To fire, the user just needs to release the catch and pull the double-action trigger. There is also a device on the magazine follower that pushes up a stop which holds the slide to the rear when the last shot is fired.

1 Beretta Model 81
LENGTH: 6.75in (171mm)
WEIGHT: 23.5oz (.67kg)
CALIBRE: 7.65mm (.301in)
CAPACITY: 12
MV: c.985f/s (300m/s)

Beretta introduced a new range of pistols in the mid-1970s, all sharing similar principles of construction and operation. A compact weapon in the Beretta tradition, the Model 81 makes use of light aluminium alloys in the frame, while weight is further reduced by the large cut-out in the top of the slide. Based on the successful 1951 service pistol, it fires a 7.65mm (.301in) cartridge and uses blowback principles of operation. It has a manual safety catch on the frame which can be operated with either hand. The hammer can also be manually dropped to the uncocked position to permit safe carriage when loaded. The magazine is typical of a modern pistol in that the rounds are in two staggered columns to permit many more to be stored than in earlier designs.

2 Beretta Model 84
LENGTH: 6.75in (171mm)
WEIGHT: 22oz (.62kg)
CALIBRE: 9mm (.354in)
CAPACITY: 13
MV: c.920f/s (280m/s)

This was introduced at the same time as the Model 81, and uses many of the same components. The main difference is that it is chambered for the 9mm (.354in) Short cartridge, which is about as powerful a round as can be used in a blowback pistol. A competent, well-made weapon.

3 Bernadelli P018
LENGTH: 8.4in (213mm)
WEIGHT: 35oz (.99kg)
CALIBRE: 9mm (.354in)
CAPACITY: 14
MV: c.1150f/s (350m/s)

Beretta is not the only Italian manufacturer of modern pistols, and this 9mm (.354in) Parabellum weapon is a solid and well-made competitor. It makes use of the Browning locking system, while a double-column magazine enables 14 rounds to be carried. The lock is double-action.

4 Beretta Model 92S
LENGTH: 8.5in (216mm)
WEIGHT: 35oz (.99kg)
CALIBRE: 9mm (.354in)
CAPACITY: 15
MV: c.1280f/s (390m/s)

The Model 92 appeared at around the same time as the Models 81 and 84, although it is a larger pistol intended primarily for service users. It fires the 9mm (.354in) Parabellum cartridge, so requires some form of breech locking system. A wedge-shaped block similar to that used on the Walther P38 was chosen, to give a safe and reliable method of operation. It has a two-column magazine to enable 15 rounds to be carried, while the lock is double-action. The Model 92S is a slightly improved version, with the safety catch on the slide, which also de-cocks the hammer to permit the weapon to be carried safely with a round chambered. When the catch is released, all the firer needs to do is pull the trigger. There is also a Model 92SB with further improved safety features.

5 Beretta Model 92F
LENGTH: 8.54in (217mm)
WEIGHT: 33.5oz (.95kg)
CALIBRE: 9mm (.354in)
CAPACITY: 15
MV: c.1280f/s (390m/s)

In a controversial 1984 decision, the US Army chose a version of the Beretta Model 92S to finally replace the venerable Colt. The Beretta designation is Model 92F, although in US service it is known as the Pistol M9. It has an ambidextrous safety and de-cocking lever on the slide, while the magazine catch behind the trigger guard can be shifted to either side. Extra safety features include a half-cock position for the hammer and a positive locking system for the firing pin. The butt has been reshaped, while the base of the magazine is extended to further improve grip. The front edge of the trigger guard has a reverse curve to suit a two-handed grip, while US service pistols are coated in a plastic material known as 'Bruniton'. This specimen is fitted with non-standard target sights.

1 S & W Model 39
LENGTH: 7.44in (189mm)
WEIGHT: 26.5oz (.75kg)
CALIBRE: 9mm (.354in)
CAPACITY: 8
MV: c.1150f/s (350m/s)

This was one of the first American automatics chambered for 9mm (.354in) Parabellum ammunition. It has a double-action lock and uses Browning's recoil system. A competent, well made pistol, it is used by some police forces. An updated version failed in the M9 contest.

2 S & W Model 469
LENGTH: 6.9in (175mm)
WEIGHT: 26.5oz (.75kg)
CALIBRE: 9mm (.354in)
CAPACITY: 12
MV: c.1150f/s (350m/s)

This Smith and Wesson design has proven to be popular as a concealable personal defence weapon. It is yet another Browning-type, with a double-action lock and a safety/de-cocking lever on the slide. The shaped trigger guard and magazine extension help to improve grip.

3 SIG-Sauer P220
LENGTH: 8.1in (206mm)
WEIGHT: 29.5oz (.84kg)
CALIBRE: 9mm (.354in)
CAPACITY: 9
MV: c.1132f/s (345m/s)

Designed in Switzerland and made in Germany, SIG-Sauer pistols are renowned for their quality of manufacture and reliability. The P220 has been adopted by the Swiss Army, while many are in service with other police and military forces. It is a recoil weapon, where a step on the barrel locks into the wide ejection port above the slide. A cam system drops the rear of the barrel to unlock the slide. There is a hammer de-cocking lever just above the trigger, which allows the pistol to be safely carried in the loaded state. Other mechanisms lock the firing pin until the trigger is pulled. There is no other safety catch, all the firer needs to do is point and shoot. The P226 is an improved model with wider butt and a two-column magazine to increase capacity to 15 rounds.

4 SIG-Sauer P225
LENGTH: 7.1in (180mm)
WEIGHT: 26oz (.74kg)
CALIBRE: 9mm (.354in)
CAPACITY: 8
MV: c.1115f/s (340m/s)

The P225 continues SIG's reputation for superbly-made precision weapons, being a compact version of the P220. It uses the same mechanism and safety systems as its larger brother, and has a light alloy frame to reduce weight. It is popular with police, bodyguard and security personnel.

5 FEG P9R
LENGTH: 7.75in (197mm)
WEIGHT: 37oz (1.05kg)
CALIBRE: 9mm (.354in)
CAPACITY: 14
MV: c.1150f/s (350m/s)

For many years FN seemed reluctant to bring out a double-action version of the Browning GP35, so in the mid-1980s the Hungarian state factory FEG did it for them. This pistol has a double-action lock with a safety/de-cocking lever. It fires 9mm (.354in) Parabellum.

6 H & K P7M13
LENGTH: 6.9in (175mm)
WEIGHT: 28.3oz (.8kg)
CALIBRE: 9mm (.354in)
CAPACITY: 13
MV: c.1150f/s (350m/s)

The Heckler and Koch P7 series was designed for police, bodyguard and special forces use, where the requirement was for a pistol that could safely be carried with a round chambered, but could be brought into action with no delay. The designers chose to use a spring-loaded firing pin to fire the cartridge. This is cocked by squeezing the lever which forms the front of the grip. If this lever is released, the firing pin is un-cocked and locked in place. It also uses an unusual form of delayed blow-back, where as the bullet is fired gas is bled off into a cylinder beneath the barrel, which acts as a piston on the front of the slide, keeping it locked shut until the pressure drops. The P7M13 has a two-column 13-round magazine, while the P7M8 carries 8 rounds in a single column.

1 Beretta 93R

LENGTH: 9.5in (241mm)
WEIGHT: 39oz (1.11kg)
CALIBRE: 9mm (.354in)
CAPACITY: 15/20
MV: c.1150f/s (350m/s)

Since the advent of the first automatic pistols, designers have persisted in attempts to give these weapons a fully-automatic burst fire capability, usually without much success. The Beretta 93R is one of a line stretching from the Mauser (see page 89), and shares most of the problems of its predecessors. The short recoil distance of a pistol invariably means a ferociously high rate of fire, which combined with the lack of a stock and fore grip, makes burst fire almost impossible to control. Beretta tried to get round this by fitting a folding front grip and an enlarged trigger guard to allow the forward hand to get a tight grip. There is also a flimsy folding stock which can be clipped to the butt. Automatic fire is limited to a three-round burst for every pull of the trigger.

2 H & K VP70

LENGTH: 8.6in (218mm)
WEIGHT: 34.5oz (.98kg)
CALIBRE: 9mm (.354in)
CAPACITY: 18
MV: c.1100f/s (335m/s)

Heckler and Koch's VP70 was an interesting technical exercise which failed to sell in large quantities. It is a large double-action blowback automatic which by use of a heavy slide and recoil spring is able to fire 9mm (.354in) Parabellum ammunition. Advanced plastics are used in the frame to keep the weight to a reasonable level, although the weapon is rather bulky. There is no safety catch as such, instead the action is only cocked by the heavy first pull on the trigger, with a lighter second pull being necessary to fire it. The VP70 comes complete with a rigid plastic holster, which clips on to the butt and frame to act as a stock. This also comes with a selector lever, which connects with the mechanism to permit three-round bursts to be fired from the 18-shot magazine.

3 Desert Eagle

LENGTH: 10.25in (260mm)
WEIGHT: 60oz (1.7kg)
CALIBRE: .375in (9.06in)
CAPACITY: 9
MV: c.1400f/s (427m/s)

Shooters who want the extra range and stopping power of Magnum cartridges have been traditionally limited to solid frame revolvers, but this American design now made in Israel is an attempt to use such powerful ammunition in an automatic. The Desert Eagle is massive and heavy, difficult to carry in a holster and impossible to conceal. It uses gas operation, where the bolt is locked to the barrel at the moment of firing, and gas is bled off from the chamber to activate a piston which unlocks the bolt and drives it back through the ejection and reloading cycle. Gas operation was supposed to make the weapon lighter and to reduce the recoil force, but it is still an intimidating handful, unsuited to all but the highly-trained user. The Desert Eagle is also available in .44in (11.2mm) Magnum.

4 Gyrojet

LENGTH: 9.2in (234mm)
WEIGHT: 17oz (.48kg)
CALIBRE: .5in (12.7mm)
CAPACITY: 6
MV: c.900f/s (274m/s)

This 1960 weapon was one that attempted to introduce radical new technical principles to the world of small arms. It is a rocket launcher rather than a pistol, firing a solid projectile carrying a propellant charge which vents through four tiny nozzles to produce thrust. The projectile is slotted into the breech, which has a fixed firing pin at the rear. When the trigger is pulled, a hammer flies upwards and to the rear, striking the front of the projectile and forcing it back on to the firing pin. This detonates a primer cap, which ignites the propellant and thrusts the projectile forward. As it begins to move, it pushes past the hammer, forcing it down to the cocked position. While the Gyrojet creates virtually no recoil forces, the rocket projectiles are inaccurate and their range poor.

EARLY MUSKETS AND RIFLES

The smooth bore flintlock musket remained more or less unchanged for about two hundred years. Having developed from the earlier 'snaphaunce', the perfected flintlock mechanism appeared in about 1630, and as a military longarm it was to reign supreme until the percussion lock ousted it in the 1840s. The only improvement was to develop rifled muzzle-loading muskets in order to improve accuracy, but these were generally confined to specialist formations. In the first place they were too expensive for general issue, and in the second place the rate of fire was too slow for the tactics which the smooth bore musket had engendered. Since the smooth bore was of poor accuracy, it was fired in volleys, rank by rank, to lay down a withering short-range carpet of bullets. The rifle, on the other hand, was far more accurate and longer-ranging, but slower to load due to the need to engage the lead bullet with the rifling; so that it was better suited to skirmishers and loose formations.

What rescued the rifle was improvement of the ammunition. The lead ball of the musket was not well suited to a rifled arm; rifling allowed the use of an elongated bullet, which derived greater benefit from the imparted spin. But to get the bullet down the barrel meant hammering it through the rifling, which was bad enough with a ball, but almost impossible with a long bullet. The eventual answer was to give the bullet a hollow base and make it of a diameter that would slip down the bore without engaging in the rifling. Then the explosion of the powder would expand the base outwards to bite into the rifling, so spinning the bullet as it departed. Known by various names, perhaps the most famous of these was the 'Minié' bullet widely used during the American Civil War.

Moving to the percussion system meant little change in the operation of long arms; instead of fixing a flint and priming a pan all that was now necessary was to place a percussion cap on the nipple leading to the chamber. Even so, loading was still the same performance of tipping in powder, wad and ball then ramming them down the barrel. But the simplicity of the percussion system led men to contemplate self-contained cartridges, and from that breech-loading. The advantages of breech-loading had long been appreciated, but so long as the cartridge stayed in the powder-and-ball era, effective breech-loading was almost impossible, except perhaps in an expensive hand-made weapon. As related elsewhere, the pinfire, then the rimfire, then the centre fire cartridge gradually changed the appearance and operation of small arms. The earliest practical percussion breech-loader to see military use was the Prussian 'needle gun', so called from the very long firing pin. The breech was closed by a bolt, the head of which was carefully ground to a cone so as to fit tightly into the rear of the chamber, also ground to a cone shape. The cartridge was of stiff paper and carried a charge of gunpowder and

Below: *A Federal marksman with his Sharps rifle. This percussion breech-loader fired a linen-wrapped cartridge ignited by a separate cap.*

Right: *This 19th Century French cavalryman carries a flintlock carbine.*

Far right: *A soldier from the 60th Rifle Regiment with an Enfield Rifle.*

the conical bullet at the front end. The percussion cap was at the base of the bullet, where it was well protected against accident and in a good place to ignite the charge. But the position of the cap was the reason for the long firing pin - the needle - that had to pierce the cartridge and pass through its full length to strike the cap.

The American Civil War saw a number of breech-loading rifles using rimfire cartridges, as well as several which used 'patent ignition' systems, cartridges of peculiar form which, put forward in good faith by their inventors, failed to last the course.

The Civil War also saw the arrival of a handful of repeating rifles - weapons which could, as a Confederate soldier said, "Be loaded every Sunday and fired for the rest of the week." Again, the success of this weapon relied entirely upon the availability of a reliable one-piece cartridge, and since some of them relied upon peculiar patent ignition designs, they generally failed to impress.

As the rifle moved from the musket to percussion to cartridge, and from single shot to repeating, so the ammunition was changing. Black powder, the traditional propellant, gave rise to fouling and volumes of smoke, and produced a relatively low velocity, so that a heavy, large-calibre lead bullet was necessary. But in the 1880s Vielle, a French chemist, produced the first smokeless powder, which also generated far more power for a given bulk. Such power allied to a heavy bullet gave rise to uncontrollable recoil, and thus a move to smaller calibres began with the French Army adopting an 8mm (.315in) solid copper bullet for their Lebel magazine rifle.

Making bullets of solid copper was probably acceptable in the early stages of the small-calibre revolution, but it was far from the ideal solution. For one thing, it left a thin layer of copper on the rifling of the weapon which built up until it was sufficient to prevent the passage of the bullet. What was needed was a small calibre bullet as heavy as lead but of a material which would not abrade the rifling in the barrel or leave deposits or cause undue friction. The solution came from a Major Rubin of the Swiss Army who developed the 'compound' bullet which had a core of lead, encased in a thin steel jacket. When fired, the lead gave the bullet its desirable mass, but the thin steel was easily compressed into the lead by the grooves of the rifling but left no deposit and generated little friction in its passage. In due course this design was improved by coating the steel jacket with a thin layer of gilding metal or nickel, which, at the velocities involved, virtually acted as a lubricant and reduced friction and abrasion to negligible proportions. And with that the military rifle was provided with all it needed to advance to the twentieth century.

1 Brown Bess (India)
LENGTH: 54.25in (1378mm)
WEIGHT: 158oz (4.48kg)
CALIBRE: .75in (19mm)
CAPACITY: 1
MV: c.900f/s (247m/s)

Brown Bess was the nickname given to a series of British military flintlock muskets from about 1730 onwards. This specimen was made in about 1800, and is to a pattern first used by the East India Company. It is reasonably well made, although the stock is of poor quality wood.

2 Model 1839 Musket
LENGTH: 46in (1168mm)
WEIGHT: 148oz (4.2kg)
CALIBRE: .75in (19mm)
CAPACITY: 1
MV: c.900f/s (247m/s)

Early British percussion muskets were converted from flintlock weapons, and the blanked holes for the frizzen and pan can be seen on this specimen produced for the Royal Navy. The lock was designed by George Lovell, who was responsible for many British developments of the time.

3 Baker Rifle
LENGTH: 46in (1168mm)
WEIGHT: 146oz (4.14kg)
CALIBRE: .625in (15.8mm)
CAPACITY: 1
MV: c.1000f/s (305m/s)

Adopted in 1800, this flintlock muzzle-loader was the first rifled weapon accepted for British military service. It was used by specially-trained riflemen, who could hit a single man-sized target at over 200yds (185m), and harass a large formation from much further away.

4 Jacob's Rifle
LENGTH: 40in (1016mm)
WEIGHT: 152oz (4.31kg)
CALIBRE: .524in (13.3mm)
CAPACITY: 1
MV: c.1000f/s (305m/s)

This double-barrelled percussion rifle was designed by General John Jacob, and equipped two regiments of the Indian Army in 1858. It fires elongated projectiles with four flanges which fit into the grooves of the rifling. Loading the tight-fitting projectile was difficult.

5 Thouvenin Rifle
LENGTH: 49.25in (1251mm)
WEIGHT: 144oz (4.09kg)
CALIBRE: .7in (17.5mm)
CAPACITY: 1
MV: c.1000f/s (305m/s)

A problem with early rifles was the need for a tight-fitting projectile, which made ramming the bullet down the barrel very difficult. One of the most successful attempts to overcome this was an 1844 design by Colonel Thouvenin, a French Army officer. His percussion rifle uses a central pillar which protrudes into the breech, along the axis of the barrel. Powder is poured into the space around this pillar, then the undersized elongated projectile rammed down the barrel. When the bullet rests against the pillar, it is struck a number of blows by the ramrod, which forces a flange on the base into the rifling to create a gas-tight seal. An effective weapon, its only weakness was the vulnerability of the central pillar to corrosion and eventual damage from the exploding charge.

6 Minié Rifle
LENGTH: 46in (1168mm)
WEIGHT: 148oz (4.2kg)
CALIBRE: .758in (19.25mm)
CAPACITY: 1
MV: c.1000f/s (305m/s)

Captain Minié was another French officer who developed a more effective muzzle-loading rifle bullet. His elongated projectile had a hollow base with an iron plug in the centre. The force of the explosion drove this plug into the soft lead, which forced the edges of the bullet out into the rifling and created a tight seal. The advantage of this system was that a plain breech could be used, with no need for an internal pillar or step. The British adopted the Minié in 1851, basing their first designs on the earlier 1842 pattern smooth-bore musket. The Royal Navy also converted existing stocks of the earlier weapon by rifling the bore and adding a rearsight. This specimen is one of these 'Altered Pattern 1842' weapons and is almost indistinguishable from the standard Army Minié rifle.

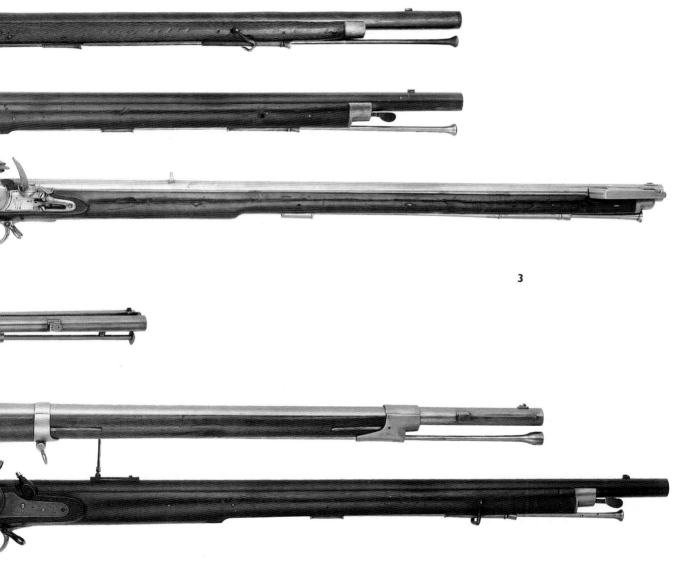

3

6

1 Enfield 1853 Pattern
LENGTH: 55in (1379mm)
WEIGHT: 138oz (3.9kg)
CALIBRE: .557in (14.6mm)
CAPACITY: 1
MV: c.1000f/s (305m/s)

The first British Minié rifles were large and heavy, and in 1854 this smaller-calibre weapon was produced by the government factory at Enfield. Lighter and easier to handle than its predecessors, it was remarkably effective, and soon became popular with British forces. Thousands also saw service with both sides in the American Civil War. It has a well-shaped stock, with a folding rearsight, and the barrel is held in place by three distinctive metal bands. The original bullet was a Minié type without the iron plug, although rounds were also made with wood, and even clay, plugs. It came wrapped in a paper cartridge, which also held the powder. To load, the paper cartridge is torn open, the powder poured into the barrel, then the bullet rammed in separately.

2 Belgian Short Rifle
LENGTH: 52in (1321mm)
WEIGHT: N/a
CALIBRE: .54in (13.7mm)
CAPACITY: 1
MV: c.1000f/s (305m/s)

This rifled percussion muzzle-loader was designed in Belgium, and was known in service as the Modele 1842. It uses a back-action lock, which results in a somewhat fragile stock. Thousands of obsolete weapons of this type were purchased by both sides in the American Civil War.

3 Enfield Short Rifle
LENGTH: 49in (1244mm)
WEIGHT: 130oz (3.7kg)
CALIBRE: .557in (14.6mm)
CAPACITY: 1
MV: c.1000f/s (305m/s)

A shorter version of the standard Enfield was first produced in 1856, and is readily identifiable by the use of two barrel bands instead of three. This is a later variant intended for naval use, with revised rifling, a brass end cap and trigger guard, and with a sling swivel ahead of the trigger.

6

4 Kerr Rifle
LENGTH: 58in (1473mm)
WEIGHT: 138oz (3.9kg)
CALIBRE: .557in (14.6mm)
CAPACITY: 1
MV: c.1000f/s (305m/s)

When the British formed volunteer militia regiments, government arms production could not keep pace with demand. Private contractors supplied a wide range of weapons such as this one, based on the Enfield 1853 pattern but with minor variations in the stock and sights.

5 Brunswick Rifle
LENGTH: 46in (1168mm)
WEIGHT: 147oz (4.17kg)
CALIBRE: .704in (17.9mm)
CAPACITY: 1
MV: c.1000f/s (305m/s)

This 1837 design was an attempt to replace the Baker rifle in British service. It fires a spherical bullet which has a single thick rib around it. This rib engages in two deep grooves in the barrel, which twist down its length to provide spin. The design of this system is credited to a Captain Berners, who was aide-de-camp to the Duke of Brunswick – hence the name. The British short rifle was a solid weapon with a back-action lock, brass furniture and a two-cavity patch box in the butt. It achieved spectacular results on the firing range, but soon ran into trouble in service. Mass-produced ammunition would often not fit the barrel properly, and loading could be a trial of strength and determination, especially when the barrel was fouled with powder residue.

6 Whitworth Rifle
LENGTH: 57in (1448mm)
WEIGHT: N/a
CALIBRE: .451in (11.4mm)
CAPACITY: 1
MV: c.1100f/s (335m/s)

Whitworth's rifles used a twisted octagonal barrel section to spin their specially-designed bullets. Superbly accurate but vulnerable to fouling, they were rejected for widespread military service. This civilian target rifle is fitted with an early telescopic sight and saw use in the American Civil War.

1 US Model 1841 Rifle
LENGTH: 49in (1245mm)
WEIGHT: 156oz (4.43kg)
CALIBRE: .54in (13.7mm)
CAPACITY: 1
MV: c.1000f/s (305m/s)

This was the first rifled percussion weapon adopted for US military service. It was an effective weapon, although the tight-fitting bullet was difficult to load, especially when the barrel was fouled. Many saw service in the Civil war, although most were rebored for Minié bullets.

2 US Model 1842 Musket
LENGTH: 58in (1473mm)
WEIGHT: 147oz (4.17kg)
CALIBRE: .69in (17.5mm)
CAPACITY: 1
MV: c.1000f/s (305m/s)

This was the last smooth-bore long arm issued to the United States Army, and served in the Mexican War of 1846–48. Many were later rebored and rifled for the Minié bullet, and thousands of these, along with the remaining unconverted smooth-bore weapons, were used in the Civil War.

3 US Model 1861 Rifle
LENGTH: 55in (1379mm)
WEIGHT: 138oz (3.9kg)
CALIBRE: .58in (14.7mm)
CAPACITY: 1
MV: c.1000f/s (305m/s)

First produced by the Springfield Armory, this rifled muzzle-loader was a development of the earlier Model 1855, which used a Maynard Tape Primer system. The new weapon reverted to a conventional percussion cap lock, and quickly proved itself to be reliable and effective. Light and easily handled, it could be relied upon to hit a man-sized target at over 300yds (277m). It became the most widely used longarm in the Union forces during the Civil War, and captured weapons were also sought after by Confederate soldiers. Later models were simplified to ease production, and a few minor manufacturing changes were made to produce the Model 1863. A superb rifle-musket, its nearest competitor was the Enfield, although the Model 1861 was more popular

4 Sharps New Model Rifle

LENGTH: 49in (1245mm)
WEIGHT: N/a
CALIBRE: .56in (14.2mm)
CAPACITY: 1
MV: c.1100f/s (335m/s)

Christian Sharps first patented his successful single-shot breech-loading system in 1848. A vertical breech block was opened by pulling down on a lever which doubled as the trigger guard. A paper (later linen) cartridge was inserted into the chamber, then the breech block pulled back up to seal the barrel. This movement also clipped off the rear of the cartridge, exposing the powder to the primer. A conventional external hammer then had to be cocked manually. Early versions used a Maynard Tape Primer, but this is one of the later 1859 models which used a patented percussion cap feeder. Sharps rifles were popular with cavalrymen and mounted infantrymen during the American Civil War, while two regiments of specialist marksmen became renowned as 'sharpshooters'.

5 Colt Model 1855 Rifle

LENGTH: 53in (1346mm)
WEIGHT: N/a
CALIBRE: .56in (14.22mm)
CAPACITY: 5
MV: c.1000f/s (305m/s)

Samuel Colt made his first revolver rifle in 1836, and sold a number in various calibres. The later 1855 Model was used in small quantities during the American Civil War, equipping a regiment of marksmen at Gettysburg. It has a five-chamber cylinder and an external side-mounted hammer, which has to be manually cocked to advance the cylinder. The barrel is 33in (838mm) long, which combined with the folding backsight makes for an accurate rifle. Even so, it was less than popular with the users, who disliked the fact that the exploding primer cap was so close to their face. Its greatest flaw, however, was the tendency of the flash from one chamber to ignite the powder in one or more of the others, with disastrous results for the firer's forward hand.

2

3

4

5

1 Morse Musket
LENGTH: 59in (1499mm)
WEIGHT: N/a
CALIBRE: .71in (18mm)
CAPACITY: 1
MV: c.1000f/s (305m/s)

George Morse of Greenville, South Carolina produced this smooth-bore percussion musket for Confederate forces. Also known as the 'inside lock' musket, it has a long 42in (1067mm) barrel, and is distinguishable by the simple, compact mechanism and minimal lock plate.

2 J.P. Murray Rifle
LENGTH: 48in (1219mm)
WEIGHT: N/a
CALIBRE: .58in (13.7mm)
CAPACITY: 1
MV: c.1000f/s (305m/s)

J.P. Murray was another Confederate manufacturer who tried to alleviate the shortage of firearms suffered by the southern states. This rifled muzzle-loader is based on the Model 1841 rifle (see page 126), although it fires a larger calibre bullet and is of slightly rougher construction.

3 Chapman Rifle
LENGTH: 49in (1245mm)
WEIGHT: c.156oz (4.43kg)
CALIBRE: .58in (13.7mm)
CAPACITY: 1
MV: c.1000f/s (305m/s)

Like most Confederate arms suppliers, C. Chapman used the Model 1841 rifle as the basis for this larger calibre rifle-musket. It uses two brass straps to hold the barrel to the stock, and has a slot underneath for the ramrod. The standard of workmanship on this weapon is quite crude.

4 Lamb Rifle
LENGTH: 49in (1245mm)
WEIGHT: c.156oz (4.43kg)
CALIBRE: .58in (13.7mm)
CAPACITY: 1
MV: c.1000f/s (305m/s)

Another Confederate weapon based on the Model 1841 rifle, the design has been simplified to make rapid production possible with relatively unskilled personnel. Even so, the standard of manufacture is poor, and this rifle would not have endured the rigours of heavy combat usage.

5 Cook & Bro. Rifle
LENGTH: 49in (1245mm)
WEIGHT: c.130oz (3.7kg)
CALIBRE: .58in (13.7mm)
CAPACITY: 1
MV: c.1000f/s (305m/s)

Ferdinand and Francis Cook were two Englishmen who made weapons in Georgia for the Confederacy. This rifle is closely based on the Enfield '2-band' short rifle (see page 124) and uses similar principles of construction. It is reasonably well made and proved as effective as the original.

6 Justice Rifle
LENGTH: 55in (1379mm)
WEIGHT: 138oz (3.9kg)
CALIBRE: .58in (14.7mm)
CAPACITY: 1
MV: c.1000f/s (305m/s)

The Union forces were also short of effective firearms at the start of the Civil War, and this rifle was one of the first attempts to boost production to meet wartime needs. P.S. Justice assembled most of these from spare parts from other designs, including locks from obsolete smoothbore muskets.

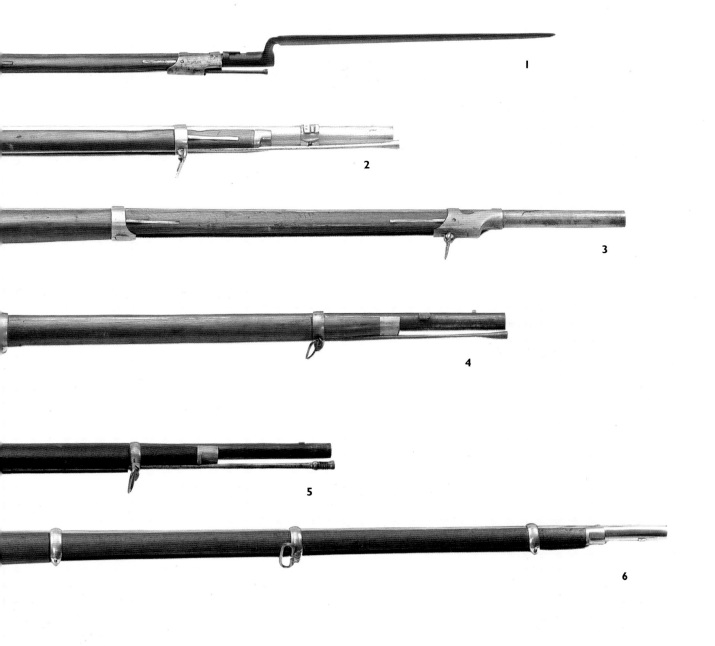

1

2

3

4

5

6

1 Dickson, Nelson & Co.
LENGTH: 40in (1016mm)
WEIGHT: N/a
CALIBRE: .58in (14.7mm)
CAPACITY: 1
MV: c.1000f/s (305m/s)

Dickson, Nelson and Company were one of the myriad concerns that manufactured weapons for the Confederate states during the Civil War. This well-made short cavalry carbine uses a lock based on that of the Model 1841 rifle, and is complete with a hinged ramrod.

2 Enfield Musketoon
LENGTH: 40in (1016mm)
WEIGHT: 120oz (3.43kg)
CALIBRE: .577in (14.6mm)
CAPACITY: 1
MV: c.1000f/s (305m/s)

This compact version of the Enfield rifle was first produced in 1853 as a carbine for artillery troops. It had a short 24in (610mm) barrel held by two bands, but in other respects was identical to the infantry rifles. The later 1860 model had the same improved rifling developed for the short rifle.

3 J.P. Murray Musketoon
LENGTH: 40in (1016mm)
WEIGHT: N/a
CALIBRE: .58in (14.7mm)
CAPACITY: 1
MV: c.1000f/s (305m/s)

J. P. Murray of Georgia made a few hundred of this carbine for Confederate artillerymen during the Civil War. It has a 24in (610mm) barrel and a lock based on the Model 1841 rifle. The barrel is held in place by two spring-locked bands, while there is also a brass end cap at the front of the stock.

4 J.P. Murray Carbine
LENGTH: 39in (991mm)
WEIGHT: N/a
CALIBRE: .58in (14.7mm)
CAPACITY: 1
MV: c.1000f/s (305m/s)

J.P. Murray also made a cavalry carbine, which is almost identical to the Musketoon but with a slightly shorter 23in (584mm) barrel. It has a hinged ramrod to make reloading on horseback easier. The lock is of based on the Model 1841 pattern, and the bands and endcap are of brass.

5 Terry Carbine
LENGTH: 38in (965mm)
WEIGHT: 99.5oz (2.8kg)
CALIBRE: .539in (13.7mm)
CAPACITY: 1
MV: c.1000f/s (305m/s)

This 1860 British carbine used a primitive form of bolt-action, where a breech cover was pulled outward and unlocked by the hinged bolt. It had a leather pad to seal the bolt head, although this would occasionally leak enough to blow the breech open, to the dismay of the firer.

6 Enfield Carbine
LENGTH: 37in (940mm)
WEIGHT: 108oz (3.06kg)
CALIBRE: .577in (14.6mm)
CAPACITY: 1
MV: c.1000f/s (305m/s)

In 1856, yet another variant of the Enfield rifle appeared, this time a cavalry carbine. It has an extremely short 21in (533mm) barrel held by two bands and with a hinged ramrod underneath. The chain attached to the trigger guard holds a protective cap over the percussion nipple.

1 Sharps Carbine

LENGTH: 39in (991mm)
WEIGHT: N/a
CALIBRE: .52in (13.2mm)
CAPACITY: 1
MV: c.900f/s (277m/s)

The first Sharps breech loading rifles occasionally had problems with gas leakage around the breech, and the 1859 models were an attempt to overcome this. They incorporated a redesigned seal which was only partially successful, and firers had to accept the occasional flash of gas and powder as the gun was fired. The 'New Model' Sharps also used a linen cartridge instead of paper, the fabric being coated with cellulose to improve combustion. The Maynard Tape Primer was replaced by a patent system of pellets held in a tubular magazine, although conventional percussion caps could still be used. This specimen is an 1859 cavalry carbine, and a skilled user could produce a rate of fire of more than ten aimed shots per minute. Note the raised backsight above the barrel.

2 Maynard Carbine

LENGTH: 37in (940mm)
WEIGHT: 96oz (2.74kg)
CALIBRE: .5in (12.7mm)
CAPACITY: 1
MV: c.900f/s (277m/s)

Edward Maynard was a Washington dentist known for his design of a paper tape primer system for percussion weapons. Maynard also devised this light breech-loading carbine, a number of which served with Union forces during the Civil War. The weapon was broken open (as seen in the photograph) by pulling down the trigger guard and tipping forward the barrel. A thick-rimmed brass cartridge was inserted into the breech then the weapon snapped shut. The cartridge had no primer but had a perforated base to allow external ignition. Early carbines used a paper tape primer, while later models reverted to a conventional percussion cap. While the Maynard was a reasonably effective breech loader, supply of its special cartridges could be a problem in service.

3 Richmond Carbine

LENGTH: 41in (1041mm)
WEIGHT: N/a
CALIBRE: .58in (14.7mm)
CAPACITY: 1
MV: c.1000f/s (305m/s)

The Richmond Armory made use of machinery and parts captured at Harpers Ferry in 1861, and throughout the war produced large numbers of weapons for the Confederate forces. This is the cavalry carbine with a 25in (635mm) barrel. Note the distinctive humped lock plate.

4 Starr Carbine

LENGTH: 38in (965mm)
WEIGHT: N/a
CALIBRE: .58in (14.7mm)
CAPACITY: 1
MV: c.900f/s (277m/s)

Ebenezer Starr's 1858 breech loading carbine uses a dropping breech block, opened by pulling down the trigger guard. Unlike the contemporary Sharps rifles, the Starr does not cut the combustible linen cartridge as it closes, which contributes towards its more effective gas seal.

5 Cook & Bro. Carbine

LENGTH: 37in (940mm)
WEIGHT: c.108oz (3.06kg)
CALIBRE: .58in (14.7mm)
CAPACITY: 1
MV: c.1000f/s (305m/s)

The Cook Brothers' rifle has already been described (on page 129), and this is their cavalry carbine design. Again closely based on the Enfield carbine, it has a similar 21in (533mm) barrel and hinged ramrod beneath. Unlike the Enfield, the stock is cut back from the muzzle.

6 Cook & Bro. Musketoon

LENGTH: 40in (1016mm)
WEIGHT: c.120oz (3.43kg)
CALIBRE: .58in (14.7mm)
CAPACITY: 1
MV: c.1000f/s (305m/s)

Francis and Ferdinand Cook also produced large numbers of this musketoon for the Confederate Army. Another Enfield-based weapon, it has a 24in (610mm) barrel and separate ram rod. In most other respects it is virtually identical to the Cook Brothers' rifle and carbine weapons.

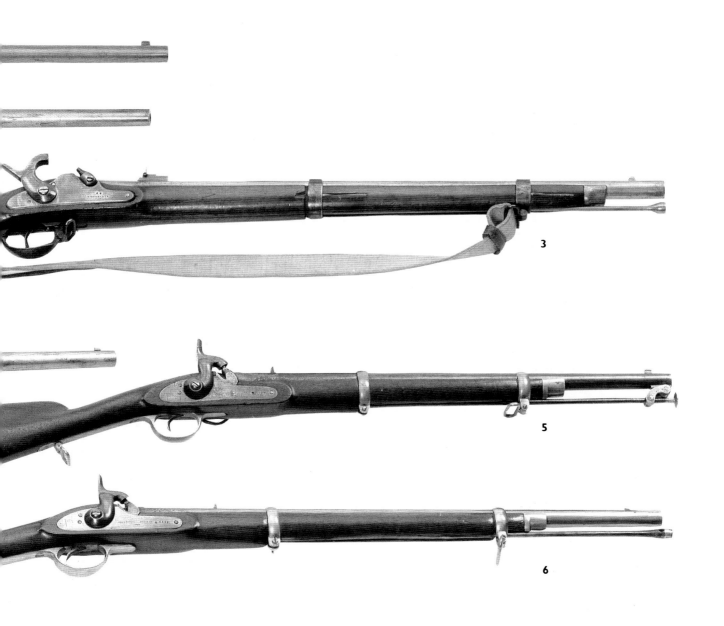

1 Robinson Carbine
LENGTH: 39in (991mm)
WEIGHT: N/a
CALIBRE: .52in (13.2mm)
CAPACITY: 1
MV: c.900f/s (277m/s)

The carbine version of the Sharps Model 1859 breech-loader was so effective that Confederate gun makers quickly produced copies. This specimen was made by S.C. Robinson and is reasonably well-made, although it lacks the patent pellet primer system of the original.

2 Chapman Musketoon
LENGTH: 41in (1041mm)
WEIGHT: c.120oz (3.43kg)
CALIBRE: .58in (14.7mm)
CAPACITY: 1
MV: c.1000f/s (305m/s)

C. Chapman followed up the production of his infantry rifle (see page 128) with this artillery musketoon. As with his previous weapon it is based on the Model 1841, although it has a much shorter 25in (635mm) barrel. Build quality was reasonable, even if the finish was somewhat rough.

3 Tallassee Carbine
LENGTH: 41in (1041mm)
WEIGHT: c.120oz (3.43kg)
CALIBRE: .58in (14.7mm)
CAPACITY: 1
MV: c.1000f/s (305m/s)

This is a close copy of the Enfield Musketoon (see page 130) but with a slightly longer 25in (635mm) barrel and a cavalry-style hinged ramrod. It was made by the Confederate Armory at Tallassee Alabama, although most were produced too late to see service in the Civil War.

4 Tarpley Carbine

LENGTH: 36in (914mm)
WEIGHT: N/a
CALIBRE: .58in (14.7mm)
CAPACITY: 1
MV: c.900f/s (277m/s)

Jere Tarpley designed this unusual looking breech-loading carbine, and a few hundred were made for the Confederacy during the Civil War. It uses a paper cartridge, while the lock is a normal percussion mechanism. Of simple, crude construction, it was too fragile to withstand service use.

5 Morse Carbine

LENGTH: 36in (914mm)
WEIGHT: N/a
CALIBRE: .5in (12.7mm)
CAPACITY: 1
MV: c.900f/s (277m/s)

George Morse invented this breech loading carbine which fired an early brass centre-fire cartridge. A few hundred were made for Confederate forces, but the cartridge was not really powerful enough for combat use. This specimen has the breech block tilted open to allow reloading.

6 Le Mat Carbine

LENGTH: 38in (965mm)
WEIGHT: N/a
CALIBRE: .42in (10.7mm)
CAPACITY: 9/1
MV: c.900f/s (277m/s)

Le Mat percussion revolvers have already been described on page 45, and this carbine uses similar principles. A nine-chamber revolver cylinder fires through the main barrel, while below is a single shot .63in (16mm) smooth-bore shotgun barrel usually loaded with a charge of buckshot.

1 Gallager Carbine
LENGTH: 39in (991mm)
WEIGHT: N/a
CALIBRE: .5in (12.7mm)
CAPACITY: 1
MV: c.1000f/s (305m/s)

Gallager's breech loading carbine used metal cartridges, although it still relied on an external cap for ignition. Pulling down the trigger guard moves the barrel forward and tips it down for access to the breech. It was an unpopular weapon, with a tendency to jam when in action.

2 Joslyn Carbine
LENGTH: 39in (991mm)
WEIGHT: N/a
CALIBRE: .56in (14.2mm)
CAPACITY: 1
MV: c.1000f/s (305m/s)

Benjamin Joslyn designed his breech-loading carbine in 1861, although this is actually the 1864 improved model. It fired Spencer or Joslyn brass rimfire cartridges, and was loaded by unlocking the large breech block and swinging it laterally to the left. Most were too late to see active service.

3 Smith Carbine
LENGTH: 40in (1016mm)
WEIGHT: N/a
CALIBRE: .5in (12.7mm)
CAPACITY: 1
MV: c.900f/s (277m/s)

Gilbert Smith's 1860 carbine was a simple but effective breech-loader that originally fired a rubber-cased cartridge, although later models used a metal-cased round. To load, a catch above the breech is released and the barrel tipped forward. A conventional percussion cap is still required.

4 Merrill Carbine
LENGTH: 38in (965mm)
WEIGHT: N/a
CALIBRE: .54in (13.7mm)
CAPACITY: 1
MV: c.900f/s (277m/s)

Merrill had tried a number of breech-loading designs before settling on this improved Jenks-type. The breech is opened by pulling up the long locking lever which lies along the top of the weapon. The Merrill used ordinary linen combustible cartridges, ignited by a percussion lock.

5 Gross Carbine
LENGTH: 39in (991mm)
WEIGHT: N/a
CALIBRE: .52in (13.2mm)
CAPACITY: 1
MV: c.900f/s (277m/s)

Henry Gross's 1859 carbine was also known as the Gwyn & Campbell (after the owners of the factory). It has a breech block which pivots open when the trigger guard lever is actuated, and fires unprimed combustible cartridges. A later model had a simpler and more reliable breech design.

6 Burnside Carbine
LENGTH: 39in (991mm)
WEIGHT: N/a
CALIBRE: .54in (13.7mm)
CAPACITY: 1
MV: c.900f/s (277m/s)

Ambrose Burnside designed a useful breech-loader before going on to become a Union Major General. This is the later 4th pattern, which has a double-pivot breech block attached to the trigger guard lever. The Burnside used special metal cartridges, although required external priming.

4

6

1 Dreyse Needle Carbine
LENGTH: 40in (1016mm)
WEIGHT: c.120oz (3.43kg)
CALIBRE: .607in (15.4mm)
CAPACITY: 1
MV: c.950f/s (290m/s)

The Prussian army issued this breech-loading rifle in 1848, long before the American Civil War. It is a solidly-built weapon, and has a manually operated rotating bolt which locks the breech. The bullet is a non-expanding one, held by a thick paper sabot which acts on the rifling to impart spin. It is held in a paper cartridge, which has its own primer at the base of the bullet. When the trigger is pulled, a long thin needle drives through the cartridge to hit the primer and fire the round. The needle gun was not particularly accurate and was also prone to gas leaks from the breech, although in Prussian hands it developed an almost mythical reputation. The infantry rifle was some 56in (1422mm) long and weighed 144oz (4.08kg); the shorter cavalry carbine is shown in the photograph.

2 Greene Rifle
LENGTH: 52.5in (1333mm)
WEIGHT: c.160 oz (4.54kg)
CALIBRE: .54in (13.7mm)
CAPACITY: 1
MV: c.1000f/s (305m/s)

James Greene developed this single-shot bolt action rifle in 1862, and a few hundred were used by Confederate forces in the Civil War. It has no rifling, instead the barrel has a slightly oval cross-section, which twists down its length to impart spin to the bullet. The self-primed combustible cartridge is also unusual, in that it has the projectile at the rear, facing forwards. To load, the user unlocks the bolt by pressing a release catch, then pulls it back to expose the breech. He then pushes a single bullet into the breech, following it with a full cartridge, with its own bullet at the rear. When the rifle is fired, the first bullet is propelled out of the barrel, while the rear one acts as a gas-seal. The firer then simply opens the bolt and inserts a new cartridge, which will fire the remaining bullet.

3 Green Carbine
LENGTH: 34in (837mm)
WEIGHT: 120oz (3.4kg)
CALIBRE: .55in (14mm)
CAPACITY: 1
MV: c.1000f/s (305m/s)

This carbine was another attempt at an effective breech-loader. A front trigger releases the barrel, which is unlocked by twisting. It is then pulled forward and swung to the right to allow insertion of the combustible cartridge. The chamber for the tape primer is shown open on this specimen.

4 Snider Mk II
LENGTH: 49in (1244mm)
WEIGHT: 130oz (3.7kg)
CALIBRE: .557in (14.6mm)
CAPACITY: 1
MV: c.1100f/s (335m/s)

For their first general issue breech-loaders, the British chose to convert their existing Enfield weapons. The Snider system has a breech which opens at the top, with the block swinging out to the right. It uses a paper cartridge with a brass base, which also holds the primer.

5 Chassepot Carbine
LENGTH: 40in (1016mm)
WEIGHT: c.120oz (3.43kg)
CALIBRE: .433in (11mm)
CAPACITY: 1
MV: c.1300f/s (396m/s)

Also known as the Modele 1866, this French single-shot bolt-action rifle fires an expanding bullet from a self-primed silk-wrapped cartridge. A thick rubber ring on the bolt helps seal the breech. This is the carbine; the rifle was 52in (1320mm) long and weighed 132oz (3.74kg). The consum-able cartridge caused great problems with fouling in the breech, and burning gasses tended to leak around the bolt and firing pin. Neverthless the Chassepot had a remarkably long effective range, and was significantly superior to the Dreyse needle gun in terms of firepower and reliability, although it couldn't tip the balance in the 1870 Franco-Prussian War. The Prussians themselves admired it so much that many of their soldiers were quick to arm themselves with captured French rifles.

2

5

1 Remington Rifle

LENGTH: c.40in (1016mm)
WEIGHT: 148oz (4.2kg)
CALIBRE: .45in (11.4mm)
CAPACITY: 1
MV: c.1350f/s (411m/s)

This design was never used officially by American soldiers, although it was popular with the armies of France, Denmark, Norway and others. It fires an expanding bullet from a self-primed brass case, and uses a 'rolling block' breech system. The breech block sits just in front of the hammer, and is pulled back and down to open. It is simply pushed forwards again once the cartridge is loaded, with no other lock applied. The hammer has a shaped projection which locks the bolt as it flies forward to hit the striker pin. Whiles this appears to be a weak point, the Remington was a remarkably sturdy weapon. This specimen is a Danish service cavalry carbine, with a metal rack for ten rounds fixed to the butt and a canvas ammunition pouch attached to the stock.

2 Springfield Rifle

LENGTH: 51in (1295mm)
WEIGHT: 132oz (3.74kg)
CALIBRE: .45in (11.4mm)
CAPACITY: 1
MV: c.1350f/s (411m/s)

The end of the Civil War saw American forces equipped with a multitude of weapons of various types. Money was short, so it was decided to convert existing .58in (14.7mm) Model 1863 rifles into general issue infantry breech-loaders. The Springfield-Allin system was chosen, where a hinged breech block (also known as a trap-door) was fixed in front of the existing side hammer. To load, the firer simply unlocks a short lever alongside the hammer, then tips the breech block up to expose the breech and loading trough. A metal self-primed cartridge is then inserted and the block closed. The hammer still has to be cocked manually before the trigger is pulled. The system was rugged, simple and effective, and was later applied to new weapons built in .45in (11.4mm) calibre.

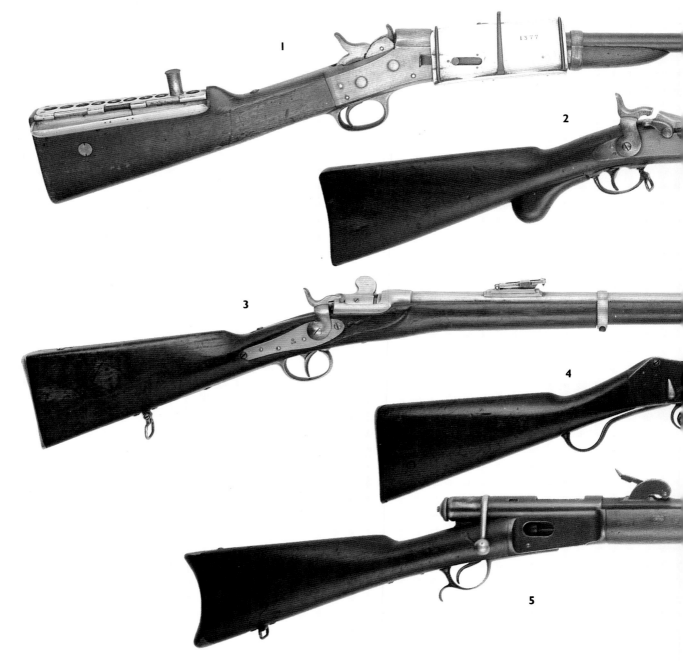

3 Werndl Rifle

LENGTH: 50.5in (1238mm)
WEIGHT: 144oz (4.1kg)
CALIBRE: .42in (10.7mm)
CAPACITY: 1
MV: c.1350f/s (411m/s)

After their 1866 defeat at the hands of the Prussians, the Austrian Army decided upon this single shot breech-loader. The breech block rotates around the axis of the weapon to reveal a slot which allows insertion of a brass cartridge. Rotating it back locks the cartridge in place, ready to fire.

4 Martini-Henry Rifle

LENGTH: 48in (1219mm)
WEIGHT: 138oz (3.9kg)
CALIBRE: .45in (11.4mm)
CAPACITY: 1
MV: c.1350f/s (411m/s)

This weapon combined the falling block system first seen on the American Peabody rifle and adapted by Martini, with a rifling system devised by Alexander Henry. It became the official British service rifle in 1871, and saw action in many parts of the wide-flung Empire. Pulling down the lever behind the trigger drops the block, and a round is fed into the breech by hand. Pulling up on the lever snaps the breech back and cocks the mechanism. The Martini-Henry was rugged, simple and cheap, and in skilled hands could put up a devastating rate of fire. The only weak spot was the early cartridges, which were made from brass tape wound into a cylinder. These would sometimes split and jam the rifle at critical moments, especially in hot, dusty or sandy conditions.

5 Vetterli Rifle

LENGTH: 51in (1295mm)
WEIGHT: 136oz (3.86kg)
CALIBRE: .41in (10.4mm)
CAPACITY: 1/11
MV: c.1350f/s (411m/s)

The Italian Army chose this Swiss bolt-action rifle in 1870. The bolt is pulled back to expose the breech, then pushed forward and rotated to lock it in place. The Swiss later developed the design themselves, converting it to a tubular magazine-fed weapon, which is shown here.

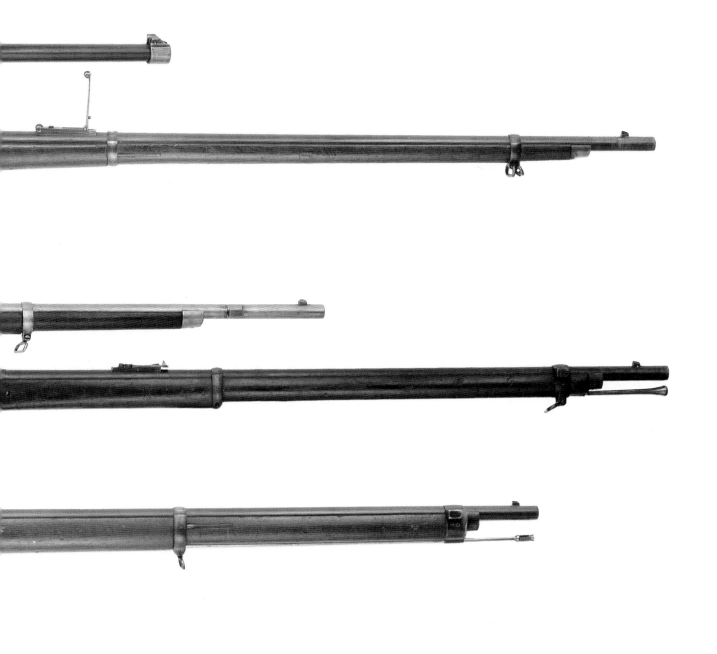

REPEATING RIFLES

The repeating rifle – a rifle with a magazine which, by some simple operation, could be reloaded and fired so long as ammunition was in the magazine – very soon divided into two camps, namely the lever action and the bolt action. Of these the lever action (e.g. the Winchester) was soon dropped, since it was virtually impossible to use in the prone position. Thus the bolt action became the preferred military system.

The first magazines were tubular, mounted beneath the barrel, (e.g. the German Mauser and French Lebel) but these were found wanting. They worked well enough with blunt-nosed lead bullets, but when the pointed and jacketed bullet appeared it was found that the bullet point, resting against the cartridge cap of the round in front of it, was liable to act as a firing pin under the recoil shock, resulting in the explosion of the entire magazine. So box magazines became the chosen system, though some elected for removable magazines (the British Lee) while others preferred a magazine of lesser capacity concealed within the rifle's stock (the Mauser)

There were, of course, some who stood out from the crowd, such as the Norwegian Krag-Jorgensen rifle which had a magazine which loaded from the side and fed, in a tortuous path, running underneath and around the bolt. Most chose to load their magazines from chargers - shaped clips of metal which carried five rounds and were inserted into the top of the breech, whence the rounds could be squeezed down by the thumb to load the magazine. The charger was then thrown away.

Others chose the clip-loading system pioneered by Mannlicher. In this, the clip actually formed part of the loading system. The full clip (usually of five rounds) was dropped into the magazine; a spring-loaded arm then pushed the rounds up in the clip as they were stripped off by the action of the bolt. When the last round was loaded, the empty clip fell through the bottom of the magazine; unless, of course, the hole had become stopped up by mud.

There was even disagreement about the bolt action itself; should the bolt turn or not? The Austrian Mannlicher and the Swiss Schmidt-Rubin rifles chose to use 'straight-pull' bolts rather than the turnbolt adopted by virtually everyone else. With these, as the term implies, the soldier merely grasped the bolt handle and pulled it straight back. In fact, what he pulled was a sleeve carrying a cam which interacted with the bolt itself, which was inside the

Below: *The bolt-action Lee-Enfield in various forms served the British Army for over 50 years. This man fighting in the Western desert carries an SMLE MK III.*

Right: *The Japanese used the Type 30 rifle in the 1904-5 war with Russia.*

Below right: *Mauser's front-locking bolt system was strong and reliable.*

sleeve. It was a turnbolt, but the turning was done by the mechanism and not by the man's hand. Theorists claimed that a straight pull bolt was faster than a turnbolt, but experience was to show that it all depended upon the design. Very few bolts of any kind are faster than the Lee turnbolt, due to the design of its locking lugs.

By the early 1900s, therefore, every army was equipped with a basic infantry rifle which was a bolt-action, magazine fed weapon, firing a powerful cartridge of about 8mm (.31in) calibre to a range of about 2000yds (1850m) And, by and large, there they remained until the 1950s.

The prospect of an automatic rifle had been appreciated even before the turn of the century and, indeed, one such weapon was actually issued to Danish Marines in the late 1890s; it was not entirely successful, was soon withdrawn, but the design was adapted and eventually re-appeared as the Madsen machine gun. Various other inventors put forward automatic rifles, and most armies issued lists of desirable features, but very few designs were ever turned into weapons, and none of them was ever considered robust enough for military service. In the 1920s the US Army busied itself with two designs which were developed in Springfield Arsenal. One was the Pedersen, using a toggle lock similar to that of the well-known Parabellum pistol; the other was a gas-operated design by John Garand. Both were in

.276in (7mm) calibre, but eventually the Pedersen design was turned down since it demanded lubricated cartridges. Garand's design was selected for adoption, but at the last moment General MacArthur, then Chief of Staff, insisted that it be in the existing .30in (7.62mm) calibre, since vast stocks of ammunition existed and much capital was invested in ammunition-making plant. This meant a re-design, but in 1936 the .30 M1 Garand rifle was approved, and the US Army became the first to adopt an automatic rifle as the standard infantry weapon. True, production was slow, due to financial restraints, but the days of the bolt-action rifle were numbered.

The heavy calibre bolt action rifle lives on, however, in the specialised sniping role. With few exceptions, automatic rifles are not sufficiently accurate for long range accuracy of the standard demanded by snipers. The British Army uses the same Lee-Enfield action that it did at the turn of the century, though it is in 7.62mm NATO calibre; the Americans use bolt-action WInchester rifles, the Germans bolt-action Mausers. Only the Russians, with their semi-automatic Dragunov, totally abandoned the manual bolt for a sniper weapon.

Below: *Men of the 7th Illinois Infantry pose with their Henry rifles. The* *Henry was one of the first successful repeaters, feeding from a tubular magazine.*

1 Spencer Rifle

LENGTH: 47in (1194mm)
WEIGHT: 160oz (4.54kg)
CALIBRE: .56in (14.2mm)
CAPACITY: 7
MV: c.1200f/s (366m/s)

This repeating rifle was first patented in early 1860 by Christopher Spencer, and its effectiveness in Union hands was shown in the battles of 1863, and especially at Gettysburg. Seven copper rim-fire cartridges are held in a long tube inside the butt, aligned so that they face the front. When the trigger guard is pulled down, the breech block drops, pulling the empty case with it until the ejector flips it away. When the lever is pulled back up, the breech block catches the rim of the next cartridge in the tube, inserting it into the breech as it locks. The hammer still has to be cocked by hand, but a skilled firer can shoot more than 12 rounds per minute. The Spencer was a tremendous success in action, and its firepower swung the balance in a number of key battles of the Civil War.

2 Spencer Carbine

LENGTH: 39in (991mm)
WEIGHT: 136oz (3.9kg)
CALIBRE: .56in (14.2mm)
CAPACITY: 7
MV: c1200f/s (366m/s)

The Spencer was also ideal for cavalry soldiers, and this carbine version entered service from 1863 onwards. The mechanism was identical to that of the rifle, the only changes were the shorter barrel and cut-back stock. The specimen shown here has the breech open, while the tubular magazine is partially withdrawn from the butt. The rate of fire of the rifle and carbine could be further improved by use of the Blakeslee reloader. The firer carried a wooden box on his belt which held six reloading tubes, each holding seven rounds. When the butt and magazine were opened, the rounds were just pushed from their tube into the magazine, the whole process taking just a few seconds. Resisted by traditionalists, the repeating Spencers pointed to the rifle of the future.

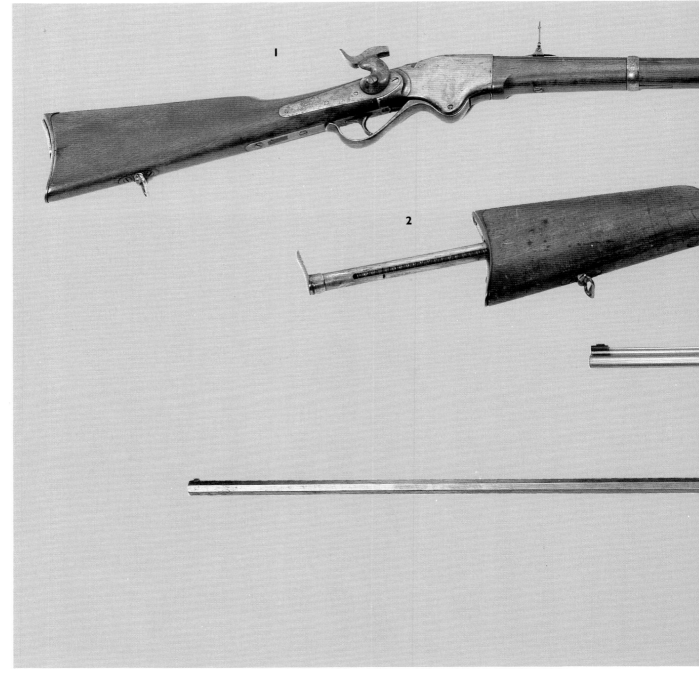

3 S & W Revolver Rifle

LENGTH: 35in (889mm)
WEIGHT: 80oz (2.27kg)
CALIBRE: .32in (8.1mm)
CAPACITY: 6
MV: c.820f/s (250m/s)

First appearing in 1879, this is one of those carbine-style weapons which could be thought of as a short rifle or a large pistol. The action and frame are based on that of the Smith & Wesson No.3 revolver (see page 66) with a few minor differences in the mechanism. It has an 18in (457mm) barrel screwed onto a short stub barrel protruding from the frame, while 16in (406mm) and 20in (508mm) models were also available. There is a post foresight, while there is a two-position back sight. An optional pillar-mounted backsight is also fitted to the detachable wooden butt. Very few of these weapons were made, and their effectiveness is questionable – being too large and cumbersome for a pistol but not sufficiently powerful or accurate for use as a rifle.

4 Webley Revolver Rifle

LENGTH: 45.5in (1156mm)
WEIGHT: 72oz (2.04kg)
CALIBRE: .5in (12.7mm)
CAPACITY: 5
MV: c.800f/s (244m/s)

This percussion weapon is based on the Webley longspur revolver, and was first made in 1853. It has a 27in (610mm) barrel, a detachable stock and one fixed and one hinged backsight. The firer was advised not to grip the barrel, as the flash from one chamber could sometimes ignite others.

Instead he had to grip under the cylinder, keeping his fingers well clear. Note that the metal in front of the cylinder is also grooved to prevent such a multiple discharge from damaging the weapon. Revolving rifles enjoyed a short period of limited popularity in the early years of the 19th Century, where their multiple shot capability was seen as a bonus. After the American Civil War and the advent of repeating rifles firing metal cartridges, they virtually disappeared from the military scene.

3

4

1 Jennings Rifle

LENGTH: 43in (1092mm)
WEIGHT: 124oz (3.5kg)
CALIBRE: .54in (13.7mm)
CAPACITY: 20
MV: c.600f/s (183m/s)

Before the advent of the brass cartridge, an engineer called Walter Hunt devised a self-contained conical projectile which carried its propellant in a hollow base. The idea was that a separate primer cap or pill would ignite this charge, firing the bullet while leaving no case behind. Hunt's 'voli-tion ball' was taken up by Lewis Jennings, who designed this 1849 repeating rifle around it. Twenty projectiles are held in the tube beneath the barrel, and are fed into the chamber by pulling the ring trigger down and to the front. The hammer is cocked, then the trigger pulled to the rear, an action which pushes the projectile into the breech then drops the hammer onto a percussion 'pill'. A good concept in theory, the volition ball had little power, while the unstable propellant was dangerous.

2 Volcanic Rifle

LENGTH: 45in (1143mm)
WEIGHT: N/a
CALIBRE: .41in (10.4mm)
CAPACITY: 30
MV: c.600f/s (183m/s)

The patents for the volition ball (also known as the 'volcanic ball') were acquired by Smith and Wesson then sold to the Volcanic Repeating Firearms Company. During the 1850s a range of tubular magazine pistols and rifles were produced, including the rifle seen here. The long magazine holds 30 self-contained volcanic rounds, which are fed into the chamber by operating the lever trigger guard. While the combination of tubular magazine and lever action made for a rapid rate of fire, these weapons were still relatively unsuccessful. The projectile was too low-powered for military use, while shooters became wary of the unstable propellant. Nevertheless, the volcanic arms were an interesting concept that held many pointers to the future of repeating rifles.

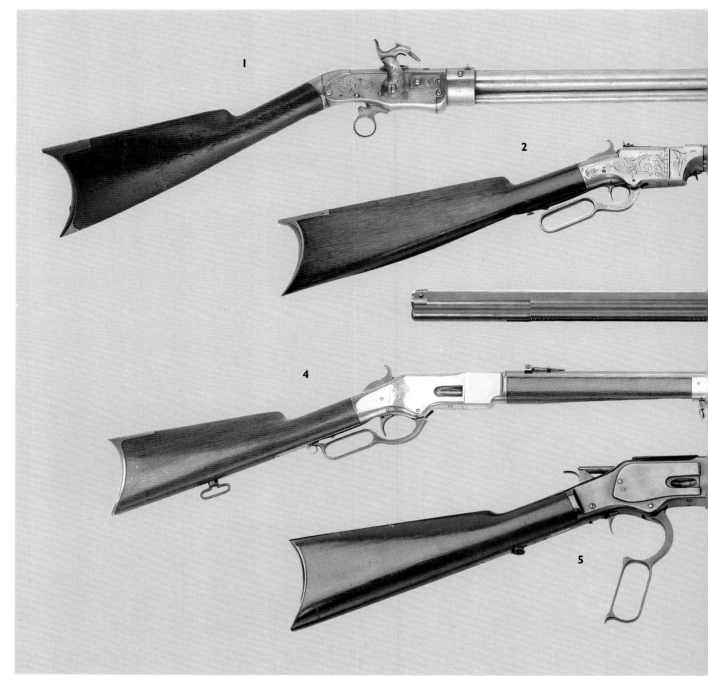

3 Henry Rifle

LENGTH: 48in (1219mm)
WEIGHT: 160oz (4.54kg)
CALIBRE: .44in (11.2mm)
CAPACITY: 16
MV: c.900f/s (275m/s)

When businessman Oliver Winchester acquired the assets of the Volcanic company, he employed Benjamin Henry to improve the design of the rifle. Henry devised a new .44in (11.2mm) brass rimfire cartridge, and redimensioned the rifle to suit. The Henry holds 16 rounds in a tubular magazine under the barrel, which are loaded by operating the lever trigger guard. It first became available just at the start of the Civil war, and soon became the most prized infantry weapon of that conflict. Its rate of fire is prodigious, although new rounds have to be fed into the magazine from the muzzle end. Its only weak spots are a rather fragile magazine which has its spring exposed to dirt and dust, and the fact that the ammunition is of revolver type and has limited effective range.

4 Winchester Model 1866

LENGTH: 39in (991mm)
WEIGHT: 124oz (3.5kg)
CALIBRE: .44in (11.2mm)
CAPACITY: 13
MV: c.1100f/s (336m/s)

The Henry was eventually fitted with a magazine loading gate on the right of the receiver, which allowed the use of a sealed magazine. It was now known as the Winchester Model 1866, or 'yellow boy' (from the brass receiver). This is the short carbine variant of this successful weapon.

5 Winchester Model 1873

LENGTH: 48in (1219mm)
WEIGHT: 160oz (4.54kg)
CALIBRE: .44in (11.2mm)
CAPACITY: 16
MV: c.1300f/s (397m/s)

The Model 1866 was a fine rifle which suffered from lack of hitting power. Winchester tried to overcome this in the Model 1873, which was chambered for a longer cartridge. Even so, it never really caught on as a military weapon, although it was successful in the American West.

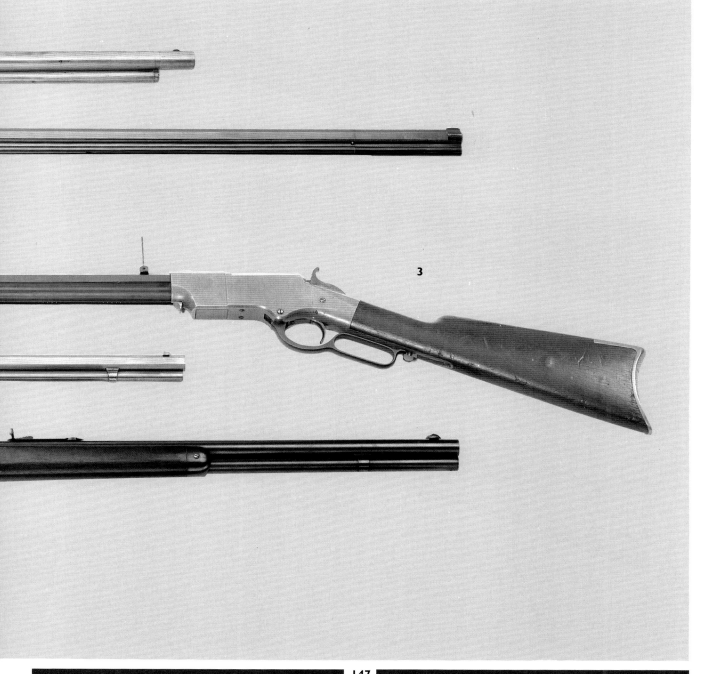

3

1 Lebel Modele 1886

LENGTH: 51in (1295mm)
WEIGHT: 149oz (4.22kg)
CALIBRE: 8mm (.315in)
CAPACITY: 8
MV: c.2350f/s (716m/s)

Introduced into French service in 1886, this magazine-fed bolt-action rifle is based on the Austrian Kropatschek. It retains a tubular magazine which sits under the barrel and is loaded via an opening beneath the chamber. A cut-off is fitted to allow single rounds to be loaded into the chamber, only being removed when a burst of rapid fire is necessary. The Lebel was the first service weapon to use small bore cartridges fired by smokeless propellant instead of the old black powder. This had two effects. Lack of smoke meant that the target would not be obscured after the first shot, while the firer could stay concealed. The second feature was that the new propellant was much more powerful than the old, which made really long-range shooting viable for the first time.

2 Commission Rifle

LENGTH: 49in (1245mm)
WEIGHT: 136oz (3.86kg)
CALIBRE: 7.92mm (.31in)
CAPACITY: 5
MV: c.2035f/s (620m/s)

The advent of the Lebel and its smokeless powder gave the Germans something to think about, so in 1888 their Small Arms Commission approved this weapon, which used design ideas from Mannlicher and Mauser. Referred to as the Gewehr 88, it holds five cartridges in a single column in the permanently attached box magazine. This sits underneath the breech and forms an integral component with the trigger guard. The rounds come pre-packed in a light metal clip or charger, which is simply pressed into the empty magazine. When the last is fired, a catch drops the charger out of the magazine. Surprisingly perhaps, for a weapon designed by a committee, this turned out to be an effective rifle which also saw service in carbine form and in a later improved 1891 version.

3 Schmidt-Rubin Rifle

LENGTH: 43in (1092mm)
WEIGHT: 128oz (3.63kg)
CALIBRE: 7.5mm (.295in)
CAPACITY: 12
MV: c.1920f/s (585m/s)

This Swiss design fires a small-calibre copper-jacketed bullet propelled by smokeless powder. The magazine, which protrudes beneath the stock, holds two chargers of six rounds each. The bolt is a straight pull type, where a separate operating rod acts on a cam slot to turn and lock the bolt.

4 Carcano M1891

LENGTH: 36.2in (920mm)
WEIGHT: 106oz (3kg)
CALIBRE: 6.5mm (.256in)
CAPACITY: 6
MV: c.2300f/s (701m/s)

This was an Italian service rifle, modified from Mannlicher and Mauser concepts by a Lt. Col. S Carcano of the Italian Government Arsenal. It fires an exceptionally small bullet from a Mannlicher-type magazine, which can be loaded using a six-round charger or clip. It also has rifling which increases in twist towards the muzzle - a design feature which is supposed to increase performance but which only makes the weapon more expensive to manufacture. The Mannlicher-Carcano was produced as a full-length infantry rifle and in an number of carbine variants, and it is one of these that is illustrated. Note the permanently attached folding bayonet, a sign that the Italian cavalry were already thinking along the lines of fighting as horse-mobile dismounted infantry.

5 Berthier Carbine

LENGTH: 37.2in (945mm)
WEIGHT: 109oz (3.1kg)
CALIBRE: 8mm (.315in)
CAPACITY: 3
MV: c.2380f/s (725m/s)

While French infantry stayed with the Lebel, in 1890 the cavalry and artillery were issued with this short carbine, fed from a permanently fitted box magazine. This is shrouded by the wooden stock, and is loaded using a three-round charger. A rifle version was also made for colonial troops.

1 Lee Model 1895

LENGTH: 47in (1194mm)
WEIGHT: 128oz (3.63kg)
CALIBRE: 6mm (.236in)
CAPACITY: 5
MV: c.2400f/s (732m/s)

Designed to fire a small-bore high-velocity cartridge, this rifle was designed by James Lee, a Scot who became an American citizen. The breech block is angled downwards slightly, and locks in place behind the breech. It is lifted and unlocked by simply pulling the bolt handle to the rear, which also ejects the empty cartridge case. Five cartridges are held in the box magazine in front of the trigger. This rifle was adopted by the United States Navy in 1895, although it was quickly superseded by the Springfield Model 1903. While the straight pull bolt was faster than a rotating one in theory, in practice it was found to be cumbersome and tiring to operate, especially with the rifle in the aiming position. Sporting models of this rifle were also made.

2 Gewehr 98

LENGTH: 49in (1250mm)
WEIGHT: 144oz (4.1kg)
CALIBRE: 7.92mm (.31in)
CAPACITY: 5/20
MV: c.2850f/s (870m/s)

This weapon first entered German service in 1898 and was intended to replace the Model 1888 Commission rifle (see page 148). It fires the same cartridge, but this time makes use of the rugged bolt locking system devised by Paul Mauser. When the bolt handle is rotated, two lugs at the front of the bolt fit into corresponding recesses just behind the chamber, making a strong and positive lock. A five round box magazine is flush within the stock, although some later rifles were fitted with a 20-shot detachable box (as in the photograph). This was a fine, reliable rifle which saw German service in both World Wars, while many were purchased by other countries. It only faults were limited ammunition storage and a straight bolt handle, which made rapid fire difficult, especially when prone.

3 Krag-Jorgensen
LENGTH: 41.5in (1054mm)
WEIGHT: 124oz (3.51kg)
CALIBRE: .30in (7.62mm)
CAPACITY: 5
MV: c.2000f/s (610m/s)

When the United States Army finally decided to replace their single-shot Springfields (see page 140), they chose a weapon designed by two Danes, a Captain Ole Krag and an engineer called Eric Jorgensen. It had an effective turnbolt locking system, which was fed from a five-round box magazine. This lay horizontally under the breech, and the rounds had to pass around the barrel into the loading trough at the top. The magazine was loaded by unlocking a flap on the right side of the receiver and feeding the rounds in one by one. As no charger was used, this could be a slow process, although it meant that the magazine could be easily kept topped up. The specimen shown here is the shorter half-stocked carbine version, one of the last such weapons ordered by American Forces.

4 Kar 98k
LENGTH: 43.7in (1110mm)
WEIGHT: 138oz (3.9kg)
CALIBRE: 7.92mm (.31in)
CAPACITY: 5
MV: c.2400f/s (732m/s)

The Germans updated their Gewehr 98 by cutting back the barrel and stock, while turning down the bolt handle. The ensuing Kar 98k became their standard rifle through the Second World War, giving excellent and reliable service. This is a sniper version, fitted with a Czech telescopic sight.

5 Ross Rifle
LENGTH: 50.5in (1283mm)
WEIGHT: 158oz (4.48kg)
CALIBRE: .303in (7.7mm)
CAPACITY: 5
MV: c.2600f/s (794m/s)

This Canadian rifle has a straight pull bolt which uses a cam to rotate the locking lugs. Accurate enough, it was found to be hopelessly unreliable in Canadian service during the First World War. Mud and dirt would jam it solid, while the bolt was sometimes blown back into the firer's face.

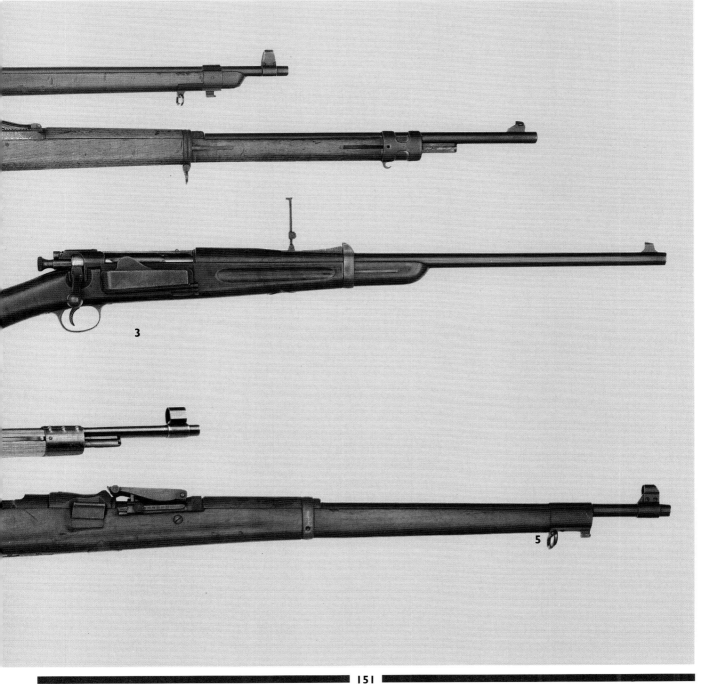

1 Springfield M1903

LENGTH: 43.2in (1097mm)
WEIGHT: 139oz (3.94kg)
CALIBRE: .30in (7.62mm)
CAPACITY: 5
MV: c.2800f/s (813m/s)

Soon after the Krag-Jorgensen rifle entered US service, the Army came to the same conclusion as the British, that the days of the long infantry rifle and short cavalry carbine were over. What was needed was a 'short' rifle, which would be used by all arms, and would have adequate power at likely combat ranges. They eventually settled on the M1903, a turnbolt rifle developed by the Springfield Armory and which used Mauser's bolt locking system. A five-round box magazine was fitted into the stock, and a cut-off allows single rounds to be loaded into the breech, keeping the magazine as a reserve. This rifle saw extensive service during the First World War, while many were still in use during the Second World War. Sniper variants remained in service until the 1950s.

2 Meiji 38 Arisaka

LENGTH: 34.2in (868mm)
WEIGHT: 158oz (3.3kg)
CALIBRE: 6.5mm (.256in)
CAPACITY: 5
MV: c.2400f/s (732m/s)

Japan's 1894 war with China showed up defects in equipment and weapons, so a commission led by Colonel Arisaka was tasked with developing an improved infantry rifle. They came up with a series of weapons based on the Mauser, chambered for a smaller round. Known as the Meiji Type 30 (from the 30th year of the Meiji dynasty) they were introduced in 1897. A shorter carbine variant was adopted in 1905, and was known as the Type 38. All the Arisaka rifles were reasonably sound designs, although they suffered from a small calibre round. The Type 30s were cumbersome for the average Japanese soldier to handle, while the Type 38 suffered from excessive muzzle flash and recoil. A later variant had a permanent folding bayonet attached to the muzzle, lying alongside the stock.

3 SMLE Mk III

LENGTH: 44.5in (1130mm)
WEIGHT: 131oz (3.71kg)
CALIBRE: .303in (7.7mm)
CAPACITY: 10
MV: c.2440f/s (738m/s)

After the South African War, the British decided that they needed a universal 'short' rifle which would be used by all arms. The Short Magazine Lee Enfield Mk II appeared in 1907, and the Mk III a few years later. It uses a turnbolt system which locks towards the rear of the bolt rather than at the front, like the Mauser. This was criticised at the time for being a weak design, but the fast, smooth action enables a trained shooter to fire 15 aimed shots per minute. Ten rounds are held in the box magazine, loaded in clips of five, while there is a magazine cut-off device fitted. This rifle proved itself to be one of the best and most reliable combat weapons of all time, serving superbly through the First World War. Later Mk IIIs were simplified to ease mass production.

4 1913 Pattern Rifle

LENGTH: 46.3in (1176mm)
WEIGHT: 139oz (3.94kg)
CALIBRE: .276in (7mm)
CAPACITY: 5
MV: c.2785f/s (843m/s)

This British weapon was designed using the Mauser bolt system and an experimental cartridge. Awkward to use, clumsy and unreliable, it was hastily shelved, but a later 1917 version chambered for .30in (7.62mm) was adopted as a stop-gap by the US Army who used it for sniping.

5 SMLE Mk V

LENGTH: 44.5in (1130mm)
WEIGHT: 131oz (3.71kg)
CALIBRE: .303in (7.7mm)
CAPACITY: 10
MV: c.2440f/s (738m/s)

In the 1920s the British modified the SMLE MK III to produce the 'interim' Mk V. Apart from simplified sights, it was almost identical to its predecessor. The Mk V was intended to be replaced by the Rifle No.4, but millions were still in use by Allied soldiers during the Second World War.

1 Lee Enfield No.4
LENGTH: 44.5in (1130mm)
WEIGHT: 146oz (4.12kg)
CALIBRE: .303in (7.7mm)
CAPACITY: 10
MV: c.2440f/s (738m/s)

Developed in 1928, this replacement for the SMLE did not enter production until 1941. A simplified version of the earlier weapon, it had new sights and a revised front end. Millions were made during the Second World War, and the No. 4 Rifle remained in British service until 1957.

2 Mosin-Nagant M1944
LENGTH: 40in (1016mm)
WEIGHT: 142oz (4kg)
CALIBRE: 7.62mm (.3in)
CAPACITY: 5
MV: c.2700f/s (823m/s)

When the Russians looked for their first small-calibre rifle, they combined features from designs by the Belgian Nagant brothers with others from a weapon by Captain S. I. Mosin. The first Mosin-Nagant models appeared in 1891, and were effective turn-bolt designs with a fixed five-shot box magazine loaded from a charger. They were made in Russia and many other European countries, while some were even manufactured in the United States. Later models had shorter barrels and simplified receivers. This is one of the last made, produced in 1944 at the height of the Second World War. It is a short carbine with a permanently fitted cruciform bayonet folded alongside the barrel. The bolt-action Mosin-Nagants served the Russians well for over five decades.

3 Carcano M1938
LENGTH: 40.2in (1022mm)
WEIGHT: 122oz (3.45kg)
CALIBRE: 6.5mm (.256in)
CAPACITY: 6
MV: c.2300f/s (701m/s)

When the Italians updated their M1891 rifles (see page 149), they produced the M1938 carbine. Early weapons used a new 7.35mm (.288in) cartridge, but most stayed with the 6.5mm (.256in) round. A weapon of this type was supposedly used to assassinate President Kennedy in 1963.

4 MAS 36

LENGTH: 40.15in (1020mm)
WEIGHT: 133oz (3.76kg)
CALIBRE: 7.5mm (.295in)
CAPACITY: 5
MV: c.2700f/s (823m/s)

After the First World War, the French realised that their 8mm (.315in) Lebel cartridge had its limitations, especially when used in automatic weapons. In 1924 they began development of a new cartridge optimised for machine guns. Once they had produced the new 7.5mm (.295in) round and the gun to go with it, they turned to the design of a rifle. The MAS 36 uses a modified Mauser system, where the bolt actually locks into the receiver behind the magazine. This is a slightly weaker design than Mauser's, although it allows a shorter bolt stroke. It also means that the bolt handle has to be angled forward, which makes rapid manipulation difficult. The five round box magazine is loaded using a charger, while a cruciform bayonet is normally carried in a tube beneath the barrel.

5 Type 99 Short Rifle

LENGTH: 44in (1117mm)
WEIGHT: 138oz (3.9kg)
CALIBRE: 7.7mm (.303in)
CAPACITY: 5
MV: c.2350f/s (715m/s)

By the late 1930s, the Japanese had found that their standard 6.5mm (.256in) rifle cartridge lacked stopping power, and began development of a new weapon firing a more powerful 7.7mm (.303in) round. The new Type 99 rifle was made in two lengths; one was a traditional long rifle while the other was a shorter 'all arms' type. (shown here). The Type 99 uses similar Mauser principles as the earlier Meiji 38 (see page 152), with a front-locking bolt and a five round box magazine. An unusual feature is the permanently fitted wire monopod under the barrel, which is supposed to support the weapon when firing from the prone position. The rearsight is also fitted with extensions to enable the (optimistic) engagement of low-flying aircraft. This rifle did not see widespread service

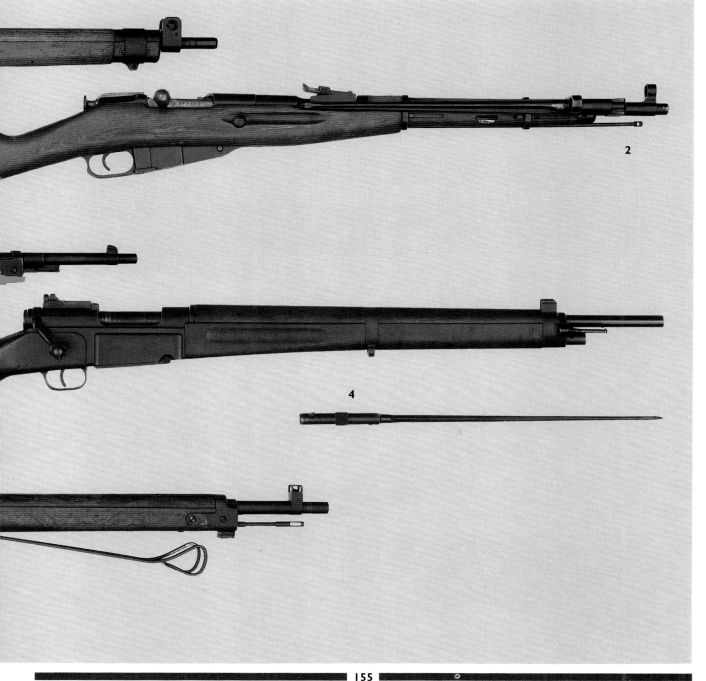

1 Type 2 Para Rifle
LENGTH: 44in (1117mm)
WEIGHT: 138oz (3.9kg)
CALIBRE: 7.7mm (.303in)
CAPACITY: 5
MV: c.2350f/s (715m/s)

The Japanese Type 99 (see page 155) was modified for paratroop use by splitting the weapon just in front of the breech. This is the later Type 2 Rifle, which is separated by sliding a horizontal wedge out of a cut-out in the top of the barrel. In most other respects it is identical to the Type 99.

2 Lee Enfield No.5
LENGTH: 39.5in (1003mm)
WEIGHT: 120oz (3.4kg)
CALIBRE: .303in (7.7mm)
CAPACITY: 10
MV: c.2000f/s (610m/s)

Wartime experience convinced the British Army that they needed a short carbine for use in the thickly-forested and jungle terrain of the Far East. They took the No.4 Rifle as the basis of the new weapon, cutting back the barrel by 5in (127mm) and the stock by more. The weight was also reduced by 26oz (.72kg). A lighter weapon meant that a greater recoil force was felt by the firer, while the short barrel created a much bigger muzzle flash. A conical flash hider was fitted to overcome this, while recoil pads were fitted to the butt. Even with these modifications, the No.5 rifle remains an unpleasant weapon to shoot, although it successfully met the need for a jungle carbine. It was briefly considered as the basis for the post-war standard rifle, but was withdrawn in 1947.

3 L42 Sniper
LENGTH: 42.15in (1071mm)
WEIGHT: 156oz (4.42kg)
CALIBRE: 7.62mm (.3in)
CAPACITY: 10
MV: c.2750f/s (838m/s)

For their post-war sniper weapon, the British Army chose an accurised version of the No.4 Rifle which had the front of the stock cut back and a cheek pad on the butt. The L42 is chambered for the NATO 7.62mm (.3in) round and is a remarkably tough and rugged sniper weapon.

4 L96A1 Sniper

LENGTH: 44.25in (1124mm)
WEIGHT: 229oz (6.5kg)
CALIBRE: 7.62mm (.3in)
CAPACITY: 10
MV: c.2830f/s (840m/s)

Most armies switched to automatic and assault rifles from the mid 1950s onwards, although manual action has survived on sniper weapons. Firing from a fixed bolt makes for a much more accurate shot, especially when combined with a telescopic sight. The Accuracy International PM is typical of a modern sniper rifle, and was chosen by the British Army in 1986, who refer to it as the L96A1. It has a solid aluminium frame coated in plastic, within which the stainless steel barrel floats freely. The bolt has a short throw, and can be operated without the firer moving his head. It has adjustable iron sights, but is normally used with a telescopic sight, which gives a high hit probability out to at least 875yds (800m). The weapon shown is the Accuracy International AW, an updated version of the PM.

5 SSG Sniper

LENGTH: 44.88in (1140mm)
WEIGHT: 138oz (3.9kg)
CALIBRE: 7.62mm (.3in)
CAPACITY: 5/10
MV: c.2820f/s (860m/s)

The Austrian Army selected this sniper weapon in 1969, and many other forces soon followed suit. Made by Steyr-Mannlicher of Austria, it is a superb example of the classic bolt-action precision rifle. The stock is of high-impact plastics, and holds a rotary 5-shot magazine. An alternate 10-round detachable box can also be fitted. The SSG has a cold-hammered steel barrel, and uses an extremely rigid bolt which is locked by six lugs. Iron sights are fitted, although most shooters will use a telescopic sight, which gives a good hit probability at up to 875yds (800m). This has proven to be a highly successful weapon, and a number of variants have been developed, including a model with a built-in suppressor. The version shown is actually intended for police marksmen and special forces.

SELF-LOADING AND ASSAULT RIFLES

From the earliest days of the self-loading rifle the question of fully-automatic fire has been a vexed one; most theorists demanded it, claiming that each automatic rifle would then bestow the power of a machine gun on every soldier. Most practical men argued against it, claiming that a lightweight weapon with automatic fire was inaccurate at best and uncontrollable at worst.

This was true enough in view of the heavy and powerful cartridges of the pre-1939 years; but as early as 1916 one experimenter had seen the way forward. This was V.G.Fyedorov, a Russian designer who developed his 'Avtomat' around the 6.5mm Japanese service cartridge. This was a less powerful round than the current Russian 7.62mm cartridge, and he produced a reasonably controllable weapon due to the lesser recoil force

There the matter rested until the mid-1930s, when a group of German infantry officers sat down to discuss a possible future rifle. Drawing upon the experience of the First World War, they reached the conclusion that the current type of rifle and cartridge were too powerful. When they had been designed, at the turn of the century, the South African War had been uppermost in everyone's mind, and long range rifle shooting was the ultimate goal. But 1914-18 showed that the front line infantryman rarely fired his rifle at ranges greater than 300-400yds (277-370m), and that with modern uniforms and tactics, it was a rare soldier who could even see his enemy at 500yds (460m). So why have a weapon capable of killing at 2000yds (1840m)?

Eventually, a short-cased 7mm (.276in) cartridge was designed, a round adequate for all purposes out to about 600yds (552m). Being short it allowed the design of a short breech action and a short rifle; being low powered it had less recoil, so the rifle could be lighter and might even fire automatic; and smaller and lighter ammunition meant that each man could carry more. But when the officers reported their conclusions to their masters, they were reminded that the war reserves held thousands of millions of 7.92mm (.31in) rifle cartridges, which nobody could afford to throw away.

Nevertheless, the design went ahead, in 7.92mm (.31in) calibre, so as to utilise existing ammunition-making machinery, but with a short case. A suitable automatic rifle was designed around it, sent for troop trials on the Eastern Front, improved, and finally adopted. It was given the official title of 'Assault Rifle' (Sturmgewehr 44) by Adolf Hitler himself.

Even before the 1939-45 war ended the British Army was studying the adoption of an automatic rifle and by the late 1940s had developed the EM1 and EM2 (Enfield Model 1 and 2). These were the

first military 'bullpup' rifles, a term of unknown origin which indicates that the barrel is set back in the stock so that the action is alongside the firer's face and the magazine is behind the trigger. This allows a barrel of almost the same length of a conventionally stocked rifle to be accommodated in a much shorter overall length, giving the desired compact and handy size. The cartridge selected was a 7mm (.280in) short design, and the weapon was also unique in incorporating a low-power optical sight as part of the basic structure.

Unfortunately, at that time the North Atlantic Treaty Organisation (NATO) was in the process of being put together, and a prime first requirement was standardisation of the common rifle calibre. After much bickering, a 7.62mm (.3in) cartridge, a version of the earlier American service round slightly shortened in order to pay lip-service to the reduced power concept, was proclaimed the NATO standard. Most of the participants then equipped their armies with semi-automatic weapons firing this powerful cartridge as a compromise between the firepower of the true assault rifle and the range of a classic bolt-action weapon.

At the same time as the EM2 was being designed, though unknown in the west, the Soviets had adopted the Kalashnikov AK47 (Avtomat Kalashnikova obraz 1947) which was built around a short-cased 7.62mm (.3in) cartridge developed in 1943/44. This was compact, had the capability of automatic fire, was reasonably accurate to 500yds (460m), and was simple and reliable. It went into Soviet service in 1953 and thereafter was licence-built (sometimes with modifications) in other Warsaw Pact countries, and also in Communist countries such as China and North Korea.

During the later 1950s/early 1960s the US Army conducted several trials to discover ways of improving the firepower of the infantry soldier. One suggestion put forward was to reduce the calibre so as to reduce the weapon recoil, which should improve the accuracy of the shooting. It would also allow automatic fire from a rifle with a better chance of hitting the target, due to the lower recoil force. As a result of these conclusions, Eugene Stoner of the Fairchild ArmaLite company designed a compact rifle in .223inch calibre called the AR15.

Eventually (it is a long and involved story which need not concern us here) the AR15 was adopted by the US Army as the M16 and the calibre became 5.56mm. In the late 1960s this became the standard US Army infantry rifle, thus effectively destroying NATO standardisation of rifle calibres.

By this time the compact cartridge had attracted the eye of manufacturers, and such companies as Fabrique Nationale, Heckler & Koch, Beretta and Steyr-Mannlicher were developing 5.56mm (.223in) assault rifles with considerable success. Some of these designs were adopted by various armies, though NATO still adhered to the 7.62mm (.3in) standard. Finally, in the late 1970s, a NATO trial took place over three years to decide upon the future NATO standard calibre. To nobody's surprise the 5.56mm (.223in) calibre was adopted, though with a new and heavier bullet than that used by the original US design.

By the early 1990s, therefore, the full-sized military rifle firing a full-sized cartridge capable of accurate fire to over 1000 metres, was almost extinct as a general-issue weapon. Unfortunately, the object in view in the 1950s – to improve the hit probability and thus the effectiveness of infantry rifle fire – has not been achieved. The adoption of the assault rifle was paralleled by the adoption of many other new weapons which made heavy demands upon training time, so that the amount of time given to training soldiers in the use of the rifle has been drastically reduced. If the armies using today's rifle used yesterday's musketry training curriculum, we might see an improvement. If not, not.

Far left: *An Ecuadorian paratrooper on exercise with his Steyr AUG.*

Top left: *The British L85 assault rifle has gained a mixed reputation for reliability.*

Bottom left: *Grenades can be fired from most modern rifles (such as this South African R4).*

Right: *The M1 Garand self-loading rifle saw large scale US service in the Second World War.*

1 Cei-Rigotti Rifle

LENGTH: 39.4in (1000mm)
WEIGHT: 153oz (4.3kg)
CALIBRE: .6.5mm (.256in)
CAPACITY: 25
MV: c.2400f/s (730m/s)

Captain Cei-Rigotti of the Italian Army developed this gas operated automatic rifle in around 1900. High pressure gas from the chamber is tapped into a cylinder to drive back a short-stroke piston. This is connected to a long rod (seen alongside the barrel) which unlocks the bolt and takes it to the rear to open the breech and eject the empty case. The powerful recoil spring then pushes the bolt forwards, where it lifts the next round from the fixed box magazine and pushes it into the breech, ready to fire once more. By operating a selector lever the firer could choose either single shots or bursts. A number of armies evaluated this weapon, although none accepted it for service. It was felt to be too complex and unreliable for sustained combat operations.

2 Farquhar-Hill Rifle

LENGTH: 41in (1042mm)
WEIGHT: 232oz (6.58kg)
CALIBRE: .303in (7.7mm)
CAPACITY: 10
MV: c.2400f/s (732m/s)

First seen in 1908, this British automatic weapon was rejected for service owing to its weight, complexity and unreliability. It uses long recoil, where the barrel and bolt move to the rear together. The 1924 redesign (seen here) has a conical magazine with a fragile clockwork spring.

3 Pederson T2E1

LENGTH: 41in (1042mm)
WEIGHT: 144oz (4.1kg)
CALIBRE: .276in (7mm)
CAPACITY: 10
MV: c.2500f/s (762m/s)

After designing an automatic fire attachment for the M1903 Springfield, John Pedersen went on to produce this toggle-lock blowback operated self-loading rifle in the 1930s. To operate reliably, it required waxed cartridge cases, which was regarded as too restrictive for a service weapon.

4 MI Garand

LENGTH: 43.5in (1103mm)
WEIGHT: 152oz (4.37kg)
CALIBRE: .30in (7.62mm)
CAPACITY: 8
MV: c.2800f/s (853m/s)

This was the first self-loading rifle to be accepted as a general service weapon when it was adopted by the US Army in 1932. Robust, reliable and effective, it uses gas pressure to drive a short-stroke piston in the cylinder beneath the barrel. This actuates a long rod connected to the bolt which

unlocks it before pushing it to the rear. Ammunition is held in an internal box magazine, loaded using a special eight-round clip which is ejected as the last round is fired. Weak points were its weight and limited ammunition storage, but overall the Garand was a fine rifle which served its users well. It became the standard US rifle of the Second World War, and over 5.5 million had been made by the time production ceased in 1950. After the war it was also developed in Italy as the BM 59 assault rifle

5 Gewehr 41(W)

LENGTH: 44.5in (1130mm)
WEIGHT: 176oz (4.98kg)
CALIBRE: 7.92mm (.31in)
CAPACITY: 10
MV: c.2550f/s (776m/s)

The German Army had experimented with self-loading rifles as early as 1901, and developments continued until two designs, made by Mauser and Walther respectively, were trialled in 1940. The Gewehr 41 (Mauser) was soon dropped, and efforts concentrated on the Gewehr 41 (Walther), shown

here. This weapon uses a muzzle cap to deflect some of the gasses back onto an annular piston, which drives a bolt actuating rod. The bolt is locked by two hinged flaps protruding into the receiver, a method first seen on the Russian DP light machine gun. The Gewehr 41(W) is heavy, poorly-balanced and prone to fouling, but was an effective enough weapon for a few tens of thousands to see combat service, mainly on the Eastern Front. It was eventually replaced by the MP 43.

1 Gewehr 43
LENGTH: 44in (1130mm)
WEIGHT: 153oz (4.33kg)
CALIBRE: 7.92mm (.31in)
CAPACITY: 10
MV: c.2450f/s (746m/s)

The Gewehr 43 was developed from the Gewehr 41(W), and is lighter, more reliable and easier to handle. The muzzle cap has been replaced by a more conventional gas and piston system, while the box magazine is detachable. The Gewehr 43 was often used as a sniper weapon.

2 M1 Carbine
LENGTH: 35.7in (905mm)
WEIGHT: 87.2oz (2.48kg)
CALIBRE: .30in (7.62mm)
CAPACITY: 15/30
MV: c.1950f/s (585m/s)

This lightweight self-loading 'carbine' entered US service in 1941 as a personal defence weapon for officers, drivers, gunners, radiomen and others for whom a standard rifle would be an unnecessary encumbrance. It fires a short pistol-style cartridge which it is effective at short ranges, and is fed from a 15- or 30-round detachable box. The bolt rotates to lock to the breech, and is unlocked and driven back by an actuating rod connected to a short-stroke gas piston. The M1 Carbine quickly became popular with US and Allied forces, and was prized for its handiness, light weight and general ease of use. The M2 was a selective fire variant, and the M3 was equipped with an early infra-red night sight. The M1 series became the most widely used US weapon of the war.

3 M1A1 Carbine
LENGTH: 36.7in (931mm)
WEIGHT: 87.2oz (2.48kg)
CALIBRE: .30in (7.62mm)
CAPACITY: 15/30
MV: c.1950f/s (585m/s)

This variant of the M1 carbine was intended for use by para-troops, and had the butt replaced by a simple tubular metal folding stock. This was attached to a wooden pistol grip, and in an emergency the weapon could be fired with the stock folded. An oil bottle was held in the stock bracing plate.

4 Sturmgewehr 44
LENGTH: 37in (940mm)
WEIGHT: 180oz (5.1kg)
CALIBRE: 7.92mm (.31in)
CAPACITY: 30
MV: c.2125f/s (647m/s)

One of the most significant weapons of modern times and the first true assault rifle, The StG 44 paved the way for virtually all the infantry rifles of the late 20th century. German studies in the 1930s showed that the normal rifle bullet was too powerful, so two automatic weapons were designed around a short-cased 7.92mm (.31in) round. After combat experience, one of these was further developed to become the MP43. Designed by Louis Schmeisser, this was a gas operated selective fire short rifle, which was intended to replace the rifle, submachine gun and light machine gun. It quickly proved to be a resounding success. The designation was changed in 1944 to MP44, and later that year it was further renamed the Sturmgewehr ("Assault Rifle") StG 44, supposedly by Hitler himself.

5 Fallschirmgewehr 42
LENGTH: 37in (940mm)
WEIGHT: 159oz (4.5kg)
CALIBRE: 7.92mm (.31in)
CAPACITY: 20
MV: c.2500f/s (762m/s)

Developed for use by German paratroops during the Second World War, this technically advanced weapon is often regarded as a forerunner of the modern assault rifle. It is gas operated, and can fire single shots or continuous bursts, with the bolt being held open to cool the breech when burst fire is selected. It is fitted with a folding bipod and an integral bayonet, and ammunition is fed from a detachable 20-shot box fitted to the left side of the receiver. The problem was that the FG 42 was expensive to make, while the use of a full-powered rifle cartridge and the position of the magazine made control difficult in burst fire. With the decline of the German paratroop force during the war, further development of this intriguing and sophisticated weapon was not promoted.

1 SKS

LENGTH: 40.2in (1022mm)
WEIGHT: 136oz (3.86kg)
CALIBRE: 7.62mm (.3in)
CAPACITY: 10
MV: c.2410f/s (735m/s)

The Russians had experimented with a number of self-loading and selective fire weapons from the turn of the century, but this is one of the most successful and significant. Introduced during the Second World War, it fires a specially developed intermediate 7.62mm (.3in) cartridge with a short 39mm (1.54in) case. Gas operated, the SKS is a simple and robust, if somewhat heavy, self-loading rifle. Rounds are fed from the fixed 10-shot box, and can be loaded singly or in clips. A folding bayonet is fitted under the barrel. The SKS saw service during the war, and millions were used by Soviet allies and clients afterwards. Simple to use and requiring little maintenance, it also became popular with communist-backed guerrilla organisations in Africa and the Middle East.

2 AK 47

LENGTH: 34.65in (880mm)
WEIGHT: 151oz (4.3kg)
CALIBRE: 7.62mm (.3in)
CAPACITY: 30
MV: c.2350f/s (717m/s)

Once the Russians saw the MP 43/44 in action, they were so impressed by the concept that they quickly developed their own assault rifle. Mikhail Kalashnikov led the team which created this well-balanced and rugged weapon, designed around the Russian 7.62mm intermediate cartridge. The AK 47 is tough, simple to use and maintain, and rugged enough to operate in the most severe environments. It is gas operated, but is tolerant of fouling, mud and grit to a remarkable degree. It is in service with dozens of armies around the world, and many of its design concepts have been copied in other weapons. Like its SKS predecessor, it has also found favour with guerrilla forces and terrorist organisations, who value its toughness, simplicity, reliability and ease of handling.

3 AK 47 (folding)

LENGTH: 34.65in (880mm)
WEIGHT: 151oz (4.3kg)
CALIBRE: 7.62mm (.3in)
CAPACITY: 30
MV: c.2350f/s (717m/s)

Early AK 47s had crudely-made wooden butts, but the Russian designers soon incorporated a folding metal stock. This weapon was initially intended for paratroopers, but is also used by vehicle crews, rear-echelon troops, and as a concealable weapon by guerrillas and terrorists. Like the standard AK it is of typically Russian manufacture. There are no frills and it has a crudely finished appearance, but precision engineering is apparent where it is needed. The inside of the barrel is even chrome plated for longevity. The AK is a good balance of portability and firepower, and while hardly the last word in accuracy, it is prized by combat soldiers who value its reliability and ruggedness. The rifle has been made under license in many countries, and copied in several others.

4 AKM

LENGTH: 34.65in (880mm)
WEIGHT: 151oz (4.3kg)
CALIBRE: 7.62mm (.3in)
CAPACITY: 30
MV: c.2350f/s (717m/s)

This is an improved version of the AK-47, with many components made from stampings and pressings rather than machined from solid. It is recognised by the three ribs on top of the receiver. An amazing 35 million AKs of all types are thought to have been made around the world.

5 Type 56

LENGTH: 34.65in (880mm)
WEIGHT: 151oz (4.3kg)
CALIBRE: 7.62mm (.3in)
CAPACITY: 30
MV: c.2350f/s (717m/s)

The most widespread AK 47 copy is this Chinese rifle, many of which saw service with the North Vietnamese during the Vietnam War. It has been made both with fixed and folding butts, and is recognisable by the strangely old fashioned permanently-fixed cruciform bayonet under the barrel.

1 VZ 52

LENGTH: 40in (1016mm)
WEIGHT: 144oz (4.08kg)
CALIBRE: 7.62mm (.3in)
CAPACITY: 10
MV: c.2440f/s (740m/s)

This Czech gas operated self-loader first appeared towards the end of the Second World War, firing a 7.62mm (.3in) intermediate round of local design. It was a mediocre weapon which was quickly replaced by the AK 47 when the Czech Army was incorporated into the Warsaw Pact.

2 Rifle No. 9 (EM2)

LENGTH: 34.65in (880mm)
WEIGHT: 151oz (4.3kg)
CALIBRE: .280in (7mm)
CAPACITY: 30
MV: c.2350f/s (717m/s)

After the end of the Second World war, the British Army realised that they needed a new rifle to replace their bolt-action Lee-Enfields. The Royal Small Arms factory at Enfield produced this gas operated selective fire assault rifle prototype in the late 1940s. It fired a specially-developed short-cased .280in (7mm) cartridge, and was unusual in that the magazine and mechanism sat behind the grip and trigger. This 'bullpup' configuration permitted a reasonably long barrel to be used in a compact weapon. The EM2 also had an optical sight built into the carrying handle, and its appearance was a startling innovation for the times. It never saw military service, as Britain instead followed the NATO decision to standardise on a full-powered 7.62mm (.3in) rifle cartridge, and chose the FAL.

3 SAFN Model 49

LENGTH: 44in (1117mm)
WEIGHT: 152oz (4.31kg)
CALIBRE: 7.92mm (.31in)
CAPACITY: 10
MV: c.2400f/s (730m/s)

A Belgian gas-operated self loader produced just after the Second World War, this was actually a pre-war design. It proved remarkably popular and was used by a number of countries in various calibres, although it was an expensive weapon to make. This specimen fires the Mauser round.

4 M14

LENGTH: 44in (1117mm)
WEIGHT: 137oz (3.88kg)
CALIBRE: 7.62mm (.3in)
CAPACITY: 20
MV: 2800f/s (853m/s)

Once the American Government had persuaded NATO to standardise on a round modified from their wartime .30 (7.62mm) cartridge, they turned to the M1 Garand as the basis for a new selective-fire rifle. The ensuing M14 feeds from a detachable 20-round box magazine, and does away with the Garand's awkward loading clip. Firing a full-powered rifle cartridge makes the weapon hard to control in automatic fire, and most service weapons had the selector permanently fixed for single shots only. Some were fitted with a bipod for use as a light machine gun, but were really too light, and with a fixed barrel were prone to overheating. The M14 was a well-balanced and accurate rifle, although it was superseded in US Army service rather quickly by the lighter M16.

5 M14 (Modified)

LENGTH: 44in (1117mm)
WEIGHT: 216oz (6.12kg)
CALIBRE: 7.62mm (.3in)
CAPACITY: 20
MV: 2800f/s (853m/s)

The M14 proved to be surprisingly accurate for a semi-automatic rifle, and a number of sniper and target variants have been produced. While a gas operated system is intrinsically less accurate than a fixed turnbolt, semi-automatic fire and a 20-shot magazine allows the sniper more tactical options, and gives him a better chance of shooting his way out of trouble The specimen shown here is a highly modified marksman's weapon, with just about every major component modified or replaced. The barrel is made from stainless steel, while the stock has been replaced with a heavier and more stable laminated item. The normal sights have been retained, but the primary aiming device is a Schmidt and Bender telescope. This is a phenomenally accurate precision weapon.

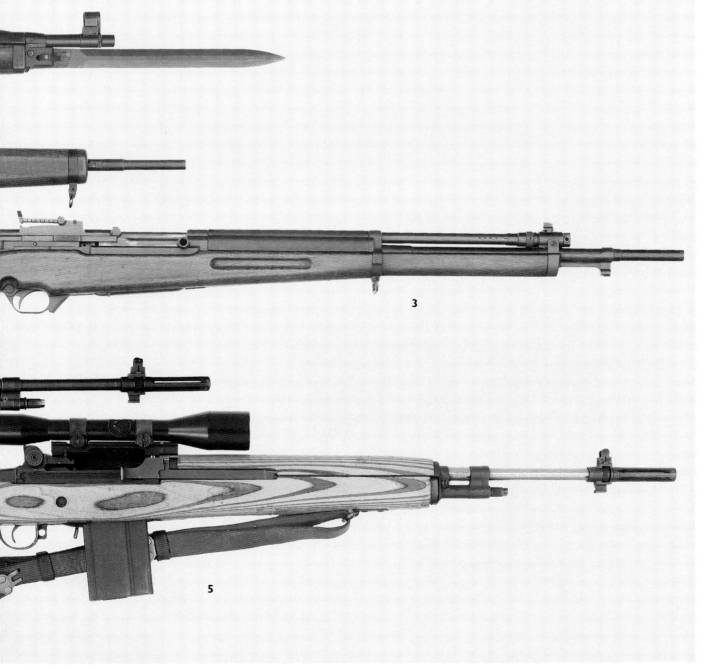

3

5

1 FN FAL (7.62mm)

LENGTH: 41.5in (1054mm)
WEIGHT: 152oz (4.31kg)
CALIBRE: 7.62mm (.3in)
CAPACITY: 20
MV: 2800f/s (853m/s)

The Fusil Automatique Légère was first produced by Fabrique Nationale of Belgium in 1950, and was based on the successful Model 49 (see page 166). Initially intended to fire the wartime German intermediate round, it was soon modified to take the standard NATO 7.62mm (.3in) cartridge. Once converted, it became an amazing success, being taken up by more than 70 countries. It is a robust, simple and well-made weapon, operated by gas impinging on the long piston in the cylinder running above the barrel. The rear of the bolt tips downwards to lock it to the breech at the moment of firing. Most FALs can fire bursts as well as single shots, although the full-powered round makes the weapon difficult to control. There is also a heavy-barrelled light machine gun version.

2 FN FAL (Experimental)

LENGTH: 41.5in (1054mm)
WEIGHT: 152oz (4.31kg)
CALIBRE: .280in (7mm)
CAPACITY: 20
MV: 2800f/s (853m/s)

When the British were experimenting with the EM 2 (see page 166), the Belgians produced this FAL chambered for the new British .280in (7mm) ammunition in case it was chosen by NATO. In the event a 7.62mm (.3in) cartridge was chosen, and this rifle remained a prototype.

3 L1A1 SLR

LENGTH: 41.5in (1054mm)
WEIGHT: 152oz (4.31kg)
CALIBRE: 7.62mm (.3in)
CAPACITY: 20
MV: 2800f/s (853m/s)

After the EM 2 foundered, Britain joined the many others who decided upon the FN FAL as their infantry rifle. Made under license in Britain and Australia, the L1A1 Self-Loading Rifle has plastic furniture and no burst fire option, but in other respects is identical to the Belgian original.

4 Gewehr 3
LENGTH: 40.35in (1025mm)
WEIGHT: 155oz (4.4kg)
CALIBRE: 7.62mm (.3in)
CAPACITY: 20
MV: 2625f/s (800m/s)

The FAL's main competitor through the 1960s and 70s was the German G3, a selective-fire automatic rifle, which while it looks similar, actually uses a completely different method of operation. Instead of a gas system, the G3 uses straightforward blowback, with the bolt delayed by two tiny rollers which are forced outwards into recesses in the receiver. First used on the wartime MG 42 (see page 223) this system demands precision engineering, but makes for a reliable method of operation which is less susceptible to fouling and variations in ammunition. The G3 has been made under license in a number of countries, including Pakistan. The rifle shown here has a 40mm (1.57in) grenade launcher clipped under the barrel to give the infantryman useful HE firepower.

5 SG510
LENGTH: 40in (1016mm)
WEIGHT: 150oz (4.25kg)
CALIBRE: 7.62mm (.3in)
CAPACITY: 20
MV: 2592f/s (790m/s)

The Swiss have always tended to go their own way in military matters, and the development of small arms has been no exception. This SIG rifle is a modification to the 7mm (.28in) Stgw 57, the first Swiss post-war automatic rifle. The SG510 is effectively the same weapon converted to NATO 7.62mm (.3in), and it is a heavy, accurate, straight stocked weapon with a built-in bipod (fixed above the barrel on this example). This is a superbly-engineered rifle which has a similar roller-delayed blowback mechanism to that of the G3, and by using the bipod is able to fire controlled bursts. Ideally suited to the Swiss concept of defensive operations from protected positions, the SG510 has proven to be too expensive for most other countries, and foreign sales have been poor.

1 M16A1

LENGTH: 39in (991mm)
WEIGHT: 152oz (2.88kg)
CALIBRE: 5.56mm (.223in)
CAPACITY: 20/30
MV: 3250f/s (991m/s)

Eugene Stoner's 1950s experiments with new materials and small calibres eventually resulted in the ArmaLite AR 15, which entered US military service as the Colt M16. This model was quickly superseded in Army service by the M16A1, almost identical apart from the addition of a bolt-closing device. Made from light alloys and black plastic, the M16A1 fires a tiny bullet which depends upon its muzzle energy to have decent stopping power. It is light, handy and easy to aim, and quickly proved popular in the jungles of Vietnam. It is gas operated, although there is no piston; the gas directly impinges on the bolt carrier. In early service use there were problems with unreliability and lack of accuracy, but improved cleaning drills and weapons training solved most of these.

2 M16A2

LENGTH: 39.63in (1006mm)
WEIGHT: 126oz (3.58kg)
CALIBRE: 5.56mm (.223in)
CAPACITY: 20/30
MV: 3250f/s (991m/s)

After initial teething problems, the M16A1 became a widespread success, entering service with dozens of nations and ushering in a new concept in assault rifle ammunition. When NATO decided to standardise on 5.56mm (.223in) in the 1970s, the more effective SS109 round was chosen over the original M193 Remington cartridge fired by the M16A1. The 'black rifle' was thus re-engineered into the improved M16A2, recognisable by the ribbed front end. The rifling was modified to suit the new round, and a three-round burst limiter fitted instead of an automatic fire selector. This is a superb, well-proven weapon, such that when the Army searched for a replacement in the 1990s, they found no design which gave a sufficiently greater hit probability to warrant development.

3 Colt Commando

LENGTH: 28in (711mm)
WEIGHT: 105oz (2.88kg)
CALIBRE: 5.56mm (.223in)
CAPACITY: 20/30
MV: 3250f/s (991m/s)

There are two shortened 'carbine' variants of the M16, namely the M4 and the Colt Commando (shown here). The Commando has a 10in (25.4mm) barrel (half the length of the rifle) and is fitted with a telescopic butt and large flash hider. It is used by US and other Special Forces.

4 ArmaLite AR 18

LENGTH: 38in (965mm)
WEIGHT: 107oz (3.04kg)
CALIBRE: 5.56mm (.223in)
CAPACITY: 20/30
MV: 3248f/s (990m/s)

When Stoner and the AR 15 went to Colt, ArmaLite worked on an improved design of 5.56mm (.223in) rifle, eventually coming up with the AR 18. Rather than complex alloy forgings, the receiver is pressed steel, and the weapon is designed to be made using less sophisticated industrial facili-

ties than those needed for the M16. It also uses a different mechanism, with a conventional piston operating the bolt, which runs back on two guide rods which also hold the recoil springs. The AR 18 is reliable, accurate and effective, although it has turned out to be a commercial failure. The US military were committed to the M16, and even though a few were made in other countries, no major army took up the AR 18. The mechanism forms the basis of that in the British L85A1.

5 H & K 33

LENGTH: 37in (940mm)
WEIGHT: 123oz (3.5kg)
CALIBRE: 5.56mm (.223in)
CAPACITY: 20/30/40
MV: 3145f/s (960m/s)

To produce a 5.56mm (.223in) rifle, Heckler & Koch of Germany simply scaled down the existing G3 7.62mm (.30in) service rifle (see page 169). The result formed the basis for a successful family of weapons, all using the same delayed blowback mechanism from the MG 42.

1 Valmet M62
LENGTH: 36in (914mm)
WEIGHT: 128oz (3.6kg)
CALIBRE: 7.62mm (.3in)
CAPACITY: 30
MV: c.2350f/s (717m/s)

The Finnish Army first adopt-ed an assault rifle in the late 1950s, taking the AK 47 as the basis for their new weapon, which was known as the M60. A later improved model was the M62 or Valmet, also cham-bered for the Russian 7.62mm (.3in) intermediate round, and it is this weapon that is shown

here. The mechanism and gen-eral structure is almost identi-cal to that of the AKM, although there are a number of external differences. The butt is a crude metal tube with a metal plate welded on to the end. The rearsight has been moved back over the plastic pistol grip, while the forward grip is perforated steel with a plastic coating. The foresight is over the gas tube. The trigger guard can easily be removed to allow operation while wearing the thick gloves necessary for the harsh Finnish winter.

2 Galil AR (5.56mm)
LENGTH: 38.54in (979mm)
WEIGHT: 153oz (4.35kg)
CALIBRE: 5.56mm (.223in)
CAPACITY: 30/50
MV: c.3117f/s (950m/s)

The Israelis developed this rifle to replace their FN FALs after the 1967 war, and like many others chose the AK 47 (see page 168) as the starting point for their design. The basic rifle is chambered for the M193 5.56mm (.223in) cartridge, although the mechanism is largely Kalashnikov. In Israeli

service it has a folding metal butt, plastic grip and metal fore grip, but variants are available with a fixed wooden or plas-tic butt and a wooden fore grip. An optional 50-shot magazine and folding bipod can be used to bestow a lim-ited fire support capability, although the Galil is really too light for this role. A short 'car-bine' version is also available. In the Galil, the Israelis have an excellent series of weapons which combine quality manu-facture with the AK 47's leg-endary reliability.

3 Galil ARM (7.62mm)

LENGTH: 42in (1050mm)
WEIGHT: 157oz (4.45kg)
CALIBRE: 7.62mm (.3in)
CAPACITY: 25
MV: c.2800f/s (853m/s)

The Galil is also made in NATO 7.62mm (.3in) calibre for export, in both rifle and carbine forms. This specimen has the folding metal butt and wooden fore grip, with a folding bipod under the barrel. There is also a specially modified 7.62mm (.3in) Galil sniper rifle.

4 FA MAS

LENGTH: 29.8in (757mm)
WEIGHT: 127oz (3.61kg)
CALIBRE: 5.56mm (.223in)
CAPACITY: 25
MV: c.3150f/s (960m/s)

Once NATO had decided upon the SS109 as their standard 5.56mm (.223in) cartridge, the French were the first to deploy a rifle designed for it. The FA MAS entered service in the early 1980s, and is a compact and effective 'bullpup' design which can fire single shots, automatic fire or three-round bursts. It uses the blowback method of operation, with a lever system to delay opening of the bolt. The sights are fitted into the long carrying handle, while a permanent bipod is usually attached to the front grip. The FA MAS is one of the few bullpups that can easily set up for a left- or right-handed firer, just by moving a few components. This is a reliable and effective weapon which provides French soldiers with effective firepower in a remarkably neat package.

5 FN FNC

LENGTH: 39.25in (997mm)
WEIGHT: 134oz (3.8kg)
CALIBRE: 5.56mm (.223in)
CAPACITY: 30
MV: c.3165f/s (965m/s)

It took FN some time to develop a successful 5.56mm (.223in) assault rifle, and this attractive weapon only appeared in the 1980s. It uses an M16-style rotary bolt and has a three-round burst facility. The FNC is used by Belgium, Indonesia and Sweden (as the AK5).

I AK 74

LENGTH: 36.6in (930mm)
WEIGHT: 127oz (3.6kg)
CALIBRE: 5.45mm (.215in)
CAPACITY: 30
MV: c.2952f/s (900m/s)

The Russians already had a world-beating assault rifle in the shape of the AKM, so when they decided to change to a smaller calibre the obvious move was to use this as the basis for the new design. The AK 74 was first seen publicly in 1977, and is simply the older weapon updated to take a new 5.54mm (.215in) cartridge. The new rifle is recognisable by the plastic-coated steel magazine, and the elongated muzzle brake which reduces recoil force to an negligible level. The AK 74 retains the reliability of its predecessor while being lighter and while firing a small calibre round which is remarkably effective. The AKS is a version with a folding steel butt, while the AKSU is a significantly shorter submachine gun variant, although it fires the standard rifle ammunition.

2 4.85mm IW

LENGTH: 30.3in (770mm)
WEIGHT: 136oz (3.86kg)
CALIBRE: 4.85mm (.191in)
CAPACITY: 20
MV: c.2952f/s (900m/s)

In the mid 1970s, British designers were again looking at lightweight 'bullpup' rifles firing a small calibre cartridge. They eventually settled on a weapon, which while looking similar to the earlier EM2 (see page 166), actually owes more to ArmaLite's AR 18 (see page 171). It is chambered for a spe-cially developed 4.85mm (.191in) cartridge, and can fire single shots or bursts. Fitted with a 2x optical sight as standard equipment, it is exceptionally accurate, while the bullpup configuration makes for a handy and compact weapon. As did the EM 2, the new British rifle ran foul of NATO, who chose the 5.56mm (.223in) SS109 round as their new standard. This time the designers were prepared, and the IW was quickly and easily modified to suit the new cartridge.

3 L85A1

LENGTH: 30.9in (785mm)
WEIGHT: 177oz (4.98kg)
CALIBRE: 5.56mm (.223in)
CAPACITY: 30
MV: c.3084f/s (940m/s)

Also known as the SA 80, this is the earlier IW modified for 5.56mm (.223in) as used by the British Army. It has a larger magazine and reshaped body, but is generally the same weapon. While accurate enough, early models gained a reputation for unreliability and fragility.

4 Steyr AUG

LENGTH: 31.1in (790mm)
WEIGHT: 127oz (3.6kg)
CALIBRE: 5.56mm (.223in)
CAPACITY: 30/42
MV: c.3180f/s (970m/s)

Startlingly futuristic in appearance, the AUG (Armee Universal Gewehr) is actually a family of 'bullpup' weapons built around modular components. The basic rifle was first seen in 1977 and has a one piece plastic body into which the aluminium receiver and steel barrel are fixed. The 1.4x optical sight is an integral part of the barrel assembly, while the trigger guard is moulded with the grip and body. Fire selection is simple - first pressure on the rigger fires single shots while a stronger pull selects bursts. In a neat touch, the plastic 30-shot magazine is transparent, allowing an easy visual check on the contents. The AUG has a reputation for being amazingly tough and reliable, and has been adopted by a number of armies. It is probably the main western competitior to the M16.

5 Steyr AUG (9mm)

LENGTH: 24.6in (626mm)
WEIGHT: 108 oz (3.05kg)
CALIBRE: 9mm (.354in)
CAPACITY: 30
MV: c 1312f./s (400 m/s)

This handy pistol-calibre carbine shows how the standard AUG frame is easily modified for a completely new role. In single shot form, this weapon is used by police, anti-terrorist and security teams who need extreme accuracy but who find the power of a full-blown rifle excessive.

1 CETME L
LENGTH: 36.4in (925mm)
WEIGHT: 120oz (3.4kg)
CALIBRE: 5.56mm (.223in)
CAPACITY: 30
MV: c.2878f/s (875m/s)

The original 1950's Spanish CETME made use of a roller-delayed blowback system similar to that on the German MG 42, and the 1980s Model L is basically the same rifle updated for the SS109 NATO round. There is also a shortened LC 'carbine' version with a telescopic stock.

2 Armscor R5
LENGTH: 34.6in (878mm)
WEIGHT: 129oz (3.65kg)
CALIBRE: 5.56mm (.223in)
CAPACITY: 30/50
MV: c.3215f/s (980m/s)

This is a South African version of the Galil (see page 172) with a few minor modifications. The first to see service was the R4, which is basically the long-barrelled Galil with folding stock and bipod. The main change is a slightly longer stock which is made from high-impact plastic rather than steel, and is easier to handle in extremely hot conditions. The normal magazine is a 30-shot fibreglass item, although there is also a 50-round option for use in a fire support role. The weapon shown is the later R5, which is a lighter variant of the standard rifle with a slightly shorter barrel and the bipod removed. These weapons are the standard infantry rifles of the South African Defence Force, and have proven themselves in some of the most harsh and hostile operating environments in the world.

3 AR70/223
LENGTH: 37.6in (955mm)
WEIGHT: 124oz (3.5kg)
CALIBRE: 5.56mm (.223in)
CAPACITY: 30
MV: c.3117f/s (950m/s)

This light weight assault rifle was first developed by Beretta in the late 1960s, and was designed around the US M193 cartridge. Made from steel pressings with plastic furniture, it was issued to Italian Special Forces and taken up by Jordan, Malaysia and others. It fires single shots or bursts,

4 SCS70/90

LENGTH: 32.3in (820mm)
WEIGHT: 130.5oz (3.7kg)
CALIBRE: 5.56mm (.223in)
CAPACITY: 30
MV: c.3117f/s (950m/s)

With more and more soldiers travelling in armoured personnel carriers and other vehicles, the need for a short rifle remains, long after the demise of the cavalry for whom carbines were originally designed. These handy weapons are also used by paratroopers and as self-defence weapons for Special Forces. They are usually less accurate than their rifle counterparts and often suffer from excessive muzzle flash, but are just as effective at short range. This is the 'carbine' variant of the AR70/90. It has a shorter barrel than standard, while the fixed butt is replaced by a folding metal tubular item with a plastic top cover. The magazine catch can be reached from either side, and the gun can be operated in an emergency even when the butt is folded. It has been adopted by Italian Special Forces.

5 AR70/90

LENGTH: 39.29in (998mm)
WEIGHT: 141oz (3.99kg)
CALIBRE: 5.56mm (.223in)
CAPACITY: 30
MV: c.3117f/s (950m/s)

Service use showed the need for improvements in the AR70/223, which were incorporated in a late 1980s redesign known as the AR70/90. The new weapon has a more robust construction, although it is still largely made from steel pressings and plastic. The design of the receiver has been extensively modified to improve reliability and longevity. The AR70/90 is gas operated with a rotary bolt, and can fire single shots, fully automatic or controlled three-round bursts. It feeds from an M16-type magazine, and fires the more powerful NATO SS109 round. The sights are in the long carrying handle, while the fixed butt is plastic. This well made rifle has been adopted as the Italian service weapon for the 1990s, along with a light support variant.

1 Browning A5
LENGTH: 44.5in (1130mm)
WEIGHT: 138oz (3.9kg)
CALIBRE: 12 Gauge
CAPACITY: 5
MV: c.1313f/s (400m/s)

The smooth-bore combat shotgun can be thought of as a descendant of the blunderbuss (see page 20), being used for short range work where quick reaction and a wide spray of shot is required. One of the most widely used of all such weapons is John Browning's A5, the first ever semi-auto-matic shotgun, which entered production in 1903. It uses a long recoil action, where the barrel and bolt both slide back together under the force of the recoil. The barrel then moves back into place before the bolt comes forward and picks up the next shell from the tubular magazine. It is a reliable and effective piece, which was devastating in the trenches of the First World War, and equally deadly as a jungle weapon in the Second World War and with British forces in Malaya in the 1950s.

2 Ithaca 37
LENGTH: 44in (1118mm)
WEIGHT: 108oz (3.06kg)
CALIBRE: 12 Gauge
CAPACITY: 5/8
MV: c.1313f/s (400m/s)

The Ithaca Model 37 featherlight was introduced as a sporting shotgun in 1937, but went on to become equally popular with military and police users. It is of remarkably robust construction, using a machined solid steel receiver with the ejection port sitting underneath.

3 Remington 870
LENGTH: 45.5in (1156mm)
WEIGHT: 120oz (3.4kg)
CALIBRE: 12 Gauge
CAPACITY: 5/8
MV: c.1313f/s (400m/s)

This 1950's pump-action design has dominated the military and Special Forces shotgun world for many years, being a firm favourite for close-quarters urban combat and for hostage rescue teams. Some models have a folding stock, while this one has an extended 8-shot magazine.

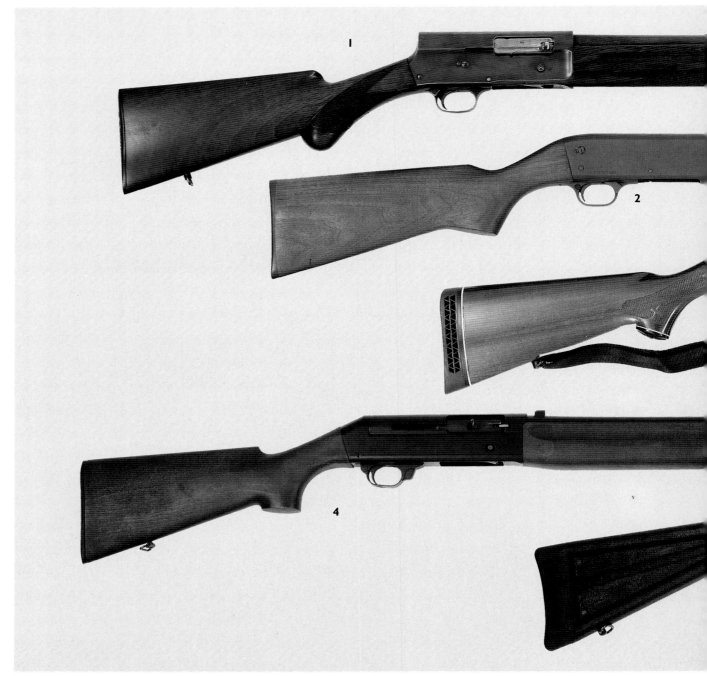

4 Benelli M 121

LENGTH: 39.75in (1010mm)
WEIGHT: 115oz (3.27kg)
CALIBRE: 12 Gauge
CAPACITY: 7
MV: c.1313f/s (400m/s)

Apart from the Browning A5, the semi-automatic shotgun has remained relatively rare in military circles. The need for total reliability in close-quarters combat and the requirement to shoot a wide range of ammunition has mitigated against the extra complexity of automatic loading, but new designs are now challenging the supremacy of the pump-action gun. Typical of these is the Benelli M 121, a neat Italian-made sports and combat weapon with an unusual mechanism. It uses a form of recoil operation, although the barrel remains fixed and the bolt is unlocked by an inertial lever. It a superbly-made weapon which is light and handy to use (although with a rather sharp recoil), and which is capable of pushing out an amazing five aimed shots per second in trained hands.

5 SPAS 12

LENGTH: 41in (1041mm)
WEIGHT: 154oz (4.35kg)
CALIBRE: 12 Gauge
CAPACITY: 8
MV: c.1313f/s (400m/s)

Designed from the outset as a military weapon, Franchi's SPAS (Special Purpose Automatic Shotgun) is a gas-operated semi automatic which is compatible with a wide range of military ammunition. It is relatively heavy and solidly-built, and is normally supplied with a folding stock which can hook under the forearm to allow one-handed operation. This specimen has an optional fixed plastic butt. When the weapon is fouled, or when non-standard ammunition is being used, the gas system can easily be disabled and the shotgun used as conventional pump-action weapon. This is a well-thought out military weapon which is rapidly gaining in popularity. A later development, the SPAS 15, looks rather like an over-sized M16, complete with detachable box magazine.

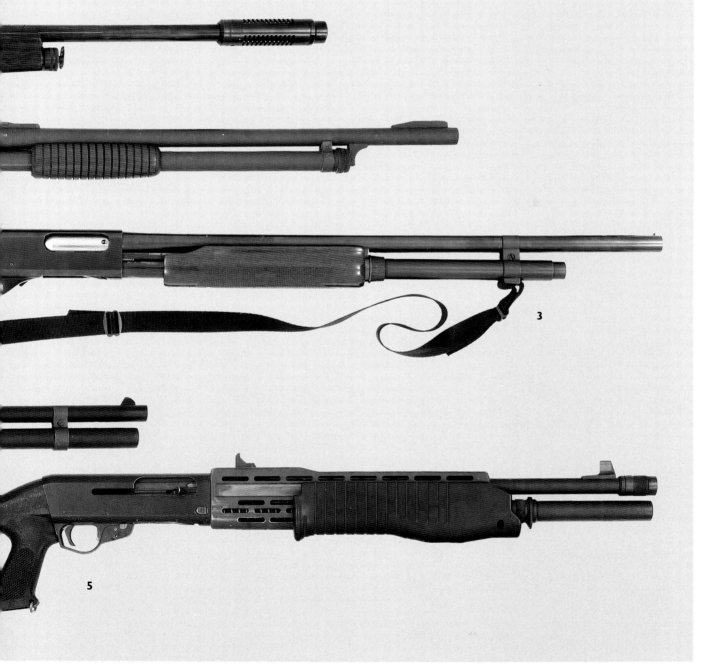

SUBMACHINE GUNS

The deadlock on the Western Front in 1916/17 is well known; it is less well known that there were similar deadlocks on the Eastern Front. In September 1917 General von Hutier attacked Russian-held Riga with a new concept of 'storm troops', small parties of men who probed the front, found weak spots, infiltrated and then held the gate for the main attack. These men needed portable firepower, and the weapon chosen for them was a light machine gun designed by Theodor Bergmann, known as the 'Bergmann Musquete'. Bergmann had developed this in 1916 and a few specimens were sent to the Western Front, but with little result. But the portable machine gun, firing pistol bullets, fitted von Hutier's conception very well, and the Bergmann 'maschinen pistole 18' became the first true submachine gun.

The submachine gun is thus defined as a hand-held automatic weapon firing pistol bullets; there are a few exceptions which prove the rule, but in general this is an accurate description. The Bergmann weapon was little known outside military circles, and might well have died out after 1918; but another inventor had been on the same track and he was to bring the submachine gun to the world's notice; indeed, he invented the title.

John T. Thompson was an American officer who had been concerned with small arms for most of his service. He retired in 1915 and began developing an automatic rifle. Searching for a suitable breech locking system he hit on a design known as the Blish system, after its inventor, which relied upon allowing sliding faces of a locking device to slip or lock according to the pressure applied. He was recalled to duty when the US entered the war and left a designer called Oscar Payne to work on the rifle. Payne soon found the system would not function with a rifle cartridge but worked well with the .45in (11.4mm) automatic pistol round. Thompson told him to design a suitable weapon for trench warfare, calling it the 'Trench Broom'. By the time the design was completed the war was over, so Thompson re-named it the 'Sub Machine Gun' and offered it as a police weapon. Unfortunately the gangsters got hold of it as quickly as the police, and the rest is history.

The Finns, seeking a weapon for use in thick forests, developed an excellent model, the Suomi of 1931. The Germans developed a number of designs, and the Russians also carried out experiments. Relatively few submachine guns were seen in any of the pre-1939 small wars, but by late 1937 the German Army had fastened upon a use for these weapons. They were ideal for mechanised infantry, who needed a compact weapon they could easily carry in and out of personnel carriers. And from

Left: *A Weimar police officer with a Bergmann MP28, an updated version of the first submachine gun.*

Below: *During the Second World War, the Russians used millions of submachine guns.*

that came the archetypal German weapon, the Machinen Pistole 38, more commonly, and wrongly, known as the 'Schmeisser'.

The MP38 broke a lot of new ground; it introduced the submachine gun into a modern army; it was the first military weapon to have no wood in it; and it had a folding butt, making it even more compact to carry. And it looked the part – modern, efficient, sinister. It was enough to scare the Russians into developing an equivalent design of their own, the PPS-38, with its characteristic drum magazine and slotted barrel jacket; this was to transmute into the PPSh, which became as much the trademark of the Red Army as the MP38 became that of the Wehrmacht.

The 1939-45 war fostered a number of submachine guns, some of which gained widespread renown and many of which sank without trace. The British contribution to the legend was the famous (or infamous) Sten gun, a cheap and cheerful weapon produced by the million and distributed to resistance groups all over Europe with a generous hand. The American parallel was the M3 'grease gun' but this never seemed to achieve the popularity of the Sten. Most of these weapons used the blowback system, where the weight of a large bolt was sufficient to delay opening until the gas pressure had dropped to a safe level.

In postwar years the design of new submachine guns became a minor industry, but it was one which did not produce very much satisfaction – there were too many cheap wartime guns available for anyone

to make a fortune by replacing them. Moreover the postwar years, notably the 1960s, saw the rise of the assault rifle, and one of the propositions which accompanied this weapon was that it could replace both the rifle and the submachine gun. Indeed, it did just that in Soviet service, and what the rest of the world considers to be the ultimate assault rifle – the Kalashnikov AK – is actually officially referred to in Russia as a submachine gun.

While the rise of the assault rifle caused a decline in the importance of the submachine gun in military forces; their came a rise in demand from police and para-military security and anti-terrorist groups. For them, the submachine gun was the ideal weapon. It was fast-firing, compact, easily handled and perfectly adequate for the short range shooting demanded in anti-terrorist and police operations. But the police wanted something rather more elegant and sophisticated than the rough and ready weapons which the military were casting off, and thus the designers finally had their opportunity.

The result of that can be seen in the Heckler & Koch MP5, the Spanish Star and the Israeli Uzi, to name but three. These have been widely adopted throughout the world. But a further demand came from the security forces, for smaller and even more compact weapons, which led to the Mini and Micro-Uzi models, the MP5K and several others. There has also been a development of these compact weapons into semi-automatic models, until it is becoming hard to tell where the submachine gun stops and the pistol begins.

Below: *The AKSU is a submachine gun variant of the AK 74, and fires the same ammunition.*

Right: *An Italian paratrooper with a Beretta 12, a simple and effective blowback design.*

1 Bergmann MP18.1

LENGTH: 32in (813mm)
WEIGHT: 147oz (4.18kg)
CALIBRE: 9mm (.354in)
CAPACITY: 32
MV: c.1250f/s (365m/s)

Developed from a 1916 prototype designed by Hugo Schmeisser, this weapon entered German service in 1918 as the first true submachine gun. The method of operation is blowback, where the bolt is a large heavy piece which is driven back by the recoil force from the 9mm (.354in) Parabellum pistol cartridge. A powerful recoil spring fills the tubular receiver and returns the bolt to the firing position, picking up a new round from the magazine as it moves. Ammunition is fed from a 32-round 'snail drum' magazine, similar to that seen on the Luger Artillery Model (see page 96) and which also proved to be unreliable in service. The original concept was for a section of six guns to be allocated to every infantry company, each gun having a No.2 to carry the ammunition.

2 Bergmann MP28.II

LENGTH: 32in (813mm)
WEIGHT: 141oz (4kg)
CALIBRE: 9mm (.354in)
CAPACITY: 20/30/50
MV: c.1250f/s (365m/s)

After the war, Schmeisser modified the MP18 in the light of experience, eventually coming up with the MP28.II. Instead of the 'snail drum' magazine of the earlier weapon, the new gun uses a side-feeding box, available in a number of sizes. A selector switch has also been incorporated to allow single shots to be fired as well as bursts, while an optimistic tangent backsight is fitted. This was a highly successful design which first saw service with the German police and was made under license in Belgium and Spain. It served with the Belgian Army and with a number of South American armies and police forces. It was also made in 7.65mm (.301in) and .45in (11.4mm), while many of its design features were copied by later weapons from a number of other countries.

3 ZK383

LENGTH: 35.4in (899mm)
WEIGHT: 150oz (4.25kg)
CALIBRE: 9mm (.354in)
CAPACITY: 30
MV: c.1250f/s (365m/s)

A Czech design which first appeared in 1933, this is another weapon made to high standards of construction and finish. It has a changeable barrel, while the rate of fire can be modified by the addition of a weight to the bolt. A folding bipod is fitted to the perforated cooling sleeve as standard.

4 Steyr-Solothurn S100

LENGTH: 33.5in (833mm)
WEIGHT: 138oz (3.9kg)
CALIBRE: 9mm (.354in)
CAPACITY: 32
MV: c.1375/s (417m/s)

In order to evade Versailles restrictions, this German design was manufactured in Austria. A reliable and effective blowback submachine gun, it used machined components and was expensive for its intended role. The S100 was used by some South American countries and Austria.

5 Suomi Model 1931

LENGTH: 34.25in (870mm)
WEIGHT: 165oz (4.69kg)
CALIBRE: 9mm (.354in)
CAPACITY: 20/50/40/71
MV: c.1312f/s (400m/s)

Aimo Lahti had designed a number of submachine guns before this model was taken up by the Finnish Army in 1931, a few years before they also adopted Lahti's automatic pistol (see page 110). It is a large, heavy weapon, well made from machined components and quality materials. It uses conventional blowback, and with its 12.5in (317mm) barrel is more accurate than most submachine guns. A wide range of magazines was used with the Suomi, including a 20-round box, a two-column 50-round box, a 40-round drum and a 71-round drum (later copied by the Russians). In the 1950s, many were converted to take a modern 36-round box. The weapon was also made in Sweden, Denmark and Switzerland, and saw service in Poland and Scandinavia.

1 MP40

LENGTH: 32.8in (833mm)
WEIGHT: 142oz (4.02kg)
CALIBRE: 9mm (.354in)
CAPACITY: 32
MV: c.1250f/s (365m/s)

Widely and incorrectly known as the 'Schmeisser' (Hugo Schmeisser had nothing to do with its design), this was the first 'modern' all-metal sub-machine gun fitted with a folding stock. A simple blowback weapon, it was designed by an employee at the Erma Werke and was adopted by the German Army in 1938, initially for use by tank crews and mechanised infantry. Known as the MP38, this short, handy and effective gun quickly became popular with the troops. However, the pressures of wartime production created a need to replace the machined receiver with one made from welded steel pressings, and the ensuing redesign became known as the MP40. Equally as effective as its predecessor, this went on to serve in large quantities wherever the German soldier fought.

2 Beretta Modello 38A

LENGTH: 37.25in (946mm)
WEIGHT: 148oz (4.97kg)
CALIBRE: 9mm (.354in)
CAPACITY: 10/20/40
MV: c.1378f/s (420m/s)

A typical 1930s design from Beretta, this was developed from a self-loading carbine to become a fully-fledged sub-machine gun. The original Modello 38 was made to a high standard, with a wooden stock and machined receiver. It used blowback operation with a separate firing pin, and early versions had a folding bayonet and slotted cooling holes in the barrel jacket. This later variant has round cooling holes, no bayonet, and a slotted compensator at the forend to help prevent muzzle climb when firing bursts. There are two triggers, the forward being used for single shots while the rear one is for automatic fire. This specimen also shows wartime standards of mass production, with a pressed and welded receiver. The Modello 38 was used by both Italian and German troops.

3 Beretta Modello 38/42
LENGTH: 31.5in (800mm)
WEIGHT: 115oz (3.26kg)
CALIBRE: 9mm (.354in)
CAPACITY: 20/40
MV: c.1250f/s (381m/s)

The Modello 38/42 was the Modello 38 simplified for mass production. The barrel jacket has been removed, the stock reshaped, and the bolt modified into a simple one-piece item. There was also a later Modello 38/44 with further simplifications, and both were effective combat weapons.

4 Thompson M1928
LENGTH: 33.75in (857mm)
WEIGHT: 172oz (4.88kg)
CALIBRE: .45in (11.4mm)
CAPACITY: 20/50
MV: c.920f/s (281m/s)

Another classic submachine gun, this weapon was developed during the First World War by then Colonel J.T. Thompson of the US Army. It is a heavy and well-made weapon, firing the Colt .45in (11.4mm) pistol round. It uses a form of blowback, but in the M1928 model there is a delay device, consisting of a metal bridge which needs to be forced upwards in two oblique slots before the bolt can open. The cocking handle protrudes above the receiver, and is slotted so as not to obscure the sights. The first magazine was a 50-shot spring-driven drum, although a 20-shot box could also be used. There were variations in the foregrip, while not all models had the cooling fins seen here. Military sales were poor, until the British and French placed large orders in 1939.

5 Thompson M1A1
LENGTH: 32in (813mm)
WEIGHT: 167oz (4.74kg)
CALIBRE: .45in (11.4mm)
CAPACITY: 20/30
MV: c.920f/s (281m/s)

In M1A1 form, the Thompson was simplified for wartime mass production for the US Army. The Blish delay system was removed, the receiver and bolt redesigned, and the cooling fins and foregrip deleted. This was a popular and effective weapon which was used by many countries.

1 Reising Model 50

LENGTH: 35.75in (908mm)
WEIGHT: 108oz (3.06kg)
CALIBRE: .45in (11.4mm)
CAPACITY: 15/20
MV: c.920f/s (281m/s)

Eugene Reising produced this submachine gun in 1938, and it was accepted for service by the US Marine Corps in 1941. The Reising operated rather like a self-loading rifle, with a separate firing pin operating through the closed bolt, which was locked in place at the moment of firing. Cocking was achieved by pulling back a finger catch recessed into a slot under the front of the gun. The weapon performed well enough on the range, but combat experience soon proved it to be a disaster. Unnecessary complexity was combined with a vulnerability to dirt and fouling, which first became apparent in the Guadalcanal campaign. Stoppages and jams were legion, and most Marines tried to dispense with their Reisings in favour of any other rifle or submachine gun they could get their hands on.

2 Lanchester Mk I

LENGTH: 33.5in (851mm)
WEIGHT: 154oz (4.38kg)
CALIBRE: 9mm (.354in)
CAPACITY: 50
MV: c.1200f/s (365m/s)

The summer of 1940 saw Britain in a desperate situation, facing shortages of weapons of all kinds. In an effort to get a submachine gun into production quickly, British engineers turned to a design they knew worked - the Bergmann MP28 (see page 182). Known as the Lanchester, this is a straight-forward copy with only a few modifications, and is a rugged and reliable blowback weapon. It fires from a side-mounted 50-shot box magazine, and early models had a selector switch to enable single shots or automatic fire. This specimen is the later model with simpler sights and no selector. In the event, the Lanchester was quickly superseded in Army service by the Sten, and most went to the Royal Navy who continued to use it until the 1960s, until its replacement by the L2 Sterling (see page 193).

3 S & W Light Rifle

LENGTH: 32.5in (825mm)
WEIGHT: 128oz (3.63kg)
CALIBRE: .45in (11.4mm)
CAPACITY: 20
MV: c.1300f/s (396m/s)

This 1930s weapon was originally designed as a semi-automatic carbine, but a few were later modified to fire bursts. Well made to peacetime standards, its 9mm (.354in) calibre ensured rejection by the US military. The development batch of 2000 was bought by the British in 1940.

4 United Defense M42

LENGTH: 32.3in (820mm)
WEIGHT: 146oz (4.14kg)
CALIBRE: .45in (11.4mm)
CAPACITY: 20
MV: c.1312f/s (400m/s)

This blowback submachine gun was designed in 1938 to fire the Colt .45in (11.4mm) round, although production models were chambered for 9mm (.354in). Made to a high standard, it was rejected for US service in favour of the M1A1 Thompson and the M3, which were easier to mass-produce.

5 M3A1

LENGTH: 29.8in (757mm)
WEIGHT: 130oz (3.7kg)
CALIBRE: .45in (11.4mm)
CAPACITY: 30
MV: c.920f/s (281m/s)

The M3 'Grease Gun' was designed in 1942 to be easy to make in the vast quantities needed for wartime. Manufactured largely from welded stampings, it is a simple and reliable 'no-frills' blowback design. A 30-shot box magazine feeds from below, its housing doubling as the fore-grip. There is also a steel pistol grip and an extendable wire stock. The mechanism fires bursts only, although the cyclic rate is slow enough to enable a trained user to fire single shots. This specimen is the later M3A1, which has no cocking handle. Instead the hinged ejection port cover is opened to reveal the bolt, into which is cut a recess to enable it to be pulled back by the firer's forefinger. A crude and simple design maybe, but the M3A1 worked well enough to do the job for which it was intended.

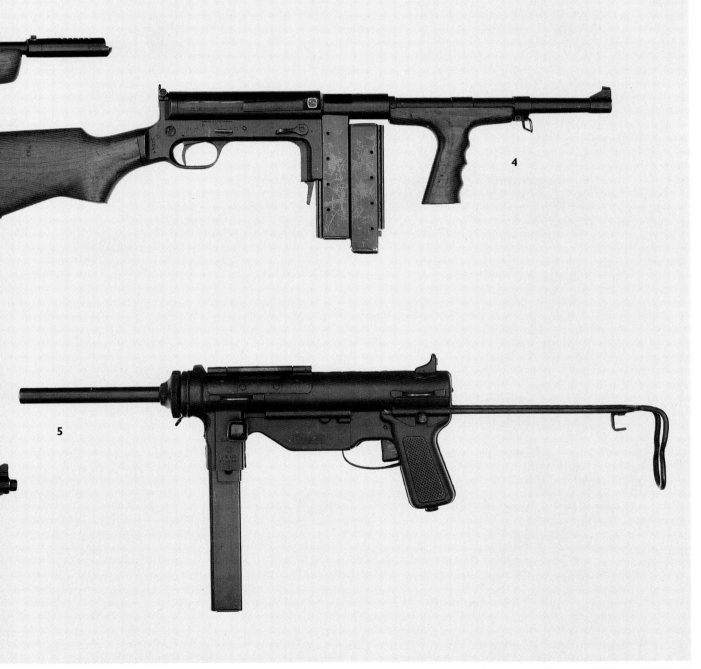

1 Sten Mk. I

LENGTH: 32.25in (896mm)
WEIGHT: 115oz (3.27kg)
CALIBRE: 9mm (.354in)
CAPACITY: 32
MV: c.1200f/s (365m/s)

After the disasters of 1940, the British were in need of huge numbers of cheap, easily manufactured infantry weapons. In early 1941 a Major Shepherd and Mr Turpin came up with a simple blowback submachine gun, and by June of that year the Sten (named after Shepherd Turpin and Enfield)

was entering Army service. The Mk. 1 Sten has a tubular receiver which holds the one-piece bolt and recoil spring, while the barrel has a perforated cover and ends with a cone-shaped flash hider and compensator. There is a folding wooden foregrip and a fixed steel skeleton stock. The 32-shot single column box magazine feeds from the right side, and its poor construction proved to be the only real weak point of the design. Crude and simple, the Sten worked remarkably well.

2 Sten Mk. 2

LENGTH: 30in (762mm)
WEIGHT: 106oz (3kg)
CALIBRE: 9mm (.354in)
CAPACITY: 32
MV: c.1200f/s (365m/s)

After further simplifications, Enfield came up with the Sten Mk. 2, the cheapest, nastiest and ugliest weapon ever used by the British Army. The butt is a crude tube with a simple endplate and a thumb-hole at the front, while the truncated barrel jacket forms the foregrip. The magazine feeds from

the side as before, but in a neat touch the feed collar can be rotated upwards to protect the ejection port from dirt and sand. This version of the Sten still suffered from feed problems, and was rather fragile in use, although care and training helped overcome the worst problems. The Mk. 2 was made in vast numbers, often in workshops with no experience of firearms, and was ideal for supply to resistance groups in occupied Europe. Never really popular with the troops, this weapon did what was needed.

3 Sten Mk. 2 (2nd Type)
LENGTH: 30in (762mm)
WEIGHT: 106oz (3kg)
CALIBRE: 9mm (.354in)
CAPACITY: 32
MV: c.1200f/s (365m/s)

This Canadian-built Mk. 2 is typical of those made by some of Britain's allies during the war. Better finished than the previous weapon, it also has a stronger skeleton butt while there are fittings for a bayonet. Over four million Stens of all types were made during the Second World War.

4 De Lisle Carbine
LENGTH: 35in (889mm)
WEIGHT: 112oz (3.18kg)
CALIBRE: .45in (11.4mm)
CAPACITY: 10
MV: c.1200f/s (365m/s)

The British De Lisle was an unusual silenced carbine intended for special operations. It marries the bolt from the Lee Enfield rifle to a 9in (228mm) long silenced barrel, chambered for the Colt .45in (11.4mm) round. This was a remarkably effective and extremely silent weapon.

5 Sten Mk. 6(S)
LENGTH: 35.75in (908mm)
WEIGHT: 157oz (4.45kg)
CALIBRE: 9mm (.354in)
CAPACITY: 32
MV: c.1000f/s (305m/s)

The Mk. 3 Sten was little better than the Mk. 2, but the Mk. 5 was made to a higher standard, with a wooden pistol grip and fixed wooden butt. After experiments with a silenced Mk. 2, a version of the Mk. 5 was produced which incorporates an integral silencer assembly. The barrel has numerous small holes along its length which bleed off gas into the surrounding silencer tube and its array of baffles. The bullet is now subsonic, and the only noise that can be heard is the sound of the bolt as it slams forward. The silencer heats up quickly so single shots are advisable, with bursts being reserved for emergencies. Known as the Mk.6 (S), this weapon was used by paratroopers and commandos, who would use it on night raiding operations to kill key personnel such as sentries.

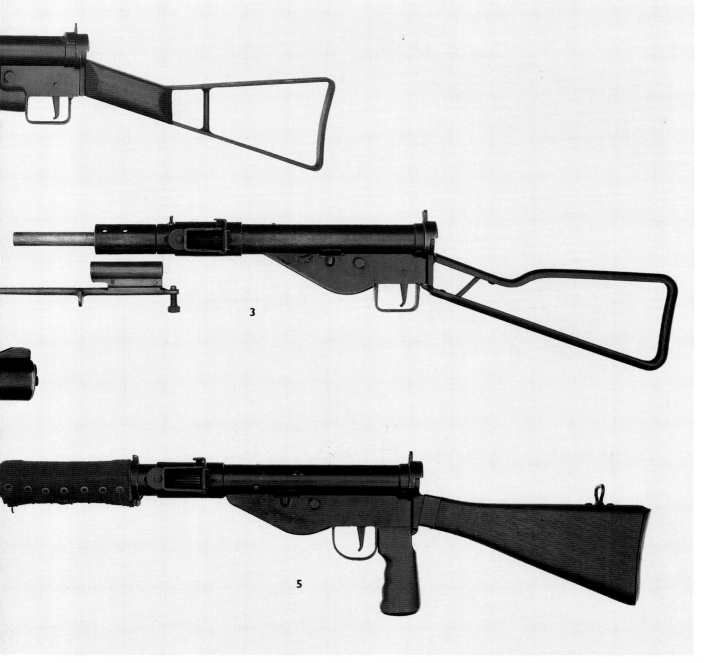

1 PPD 34/38

LENGTH: 30.6in (779mm)
WEIGHT: 128oz (3.74kg)
CALIBRE: 7.62mm (.3in)
CAPACITY: 25/71
MV: c.1600f/s (489m/s)

Using similar principles to the Bergmann MP 28 (see page 182), this neat and well made Russian weapon was designed by Vasiliy Degtyaryev. It is a simple blowback weapon chambered for the Russian 7.62mm (.3in) pistol round, which whilst having a higher muzzle velocity than the 9mm (.354in) Parabellum was no more effective. The PPD could be fed from a 25-shot box magazine, although it was more commonly seen with a spring driven 71-shot drum, based on that used on the Suomi (see page 183). Reliable and effective enough, the PPD 34/38 was replaced in 1940 by the slightly improved PPD 40, although both weapons saw service in Finland and in the Second World War. The PPD was time-consuming to make, and production was soon switched to simpler weapons.

2 PPSh 41

LENGTH: 33.1in (841mm)
WEIGHT: 128oz (3.63kg)
CALIBRE: 7.62mm (.3in)
CAPACITY: 35/71
MV: c.1600f/s (489m/s)

As they rebuilt their army after the disasters of July 1941, the Russians needed large numbers of weapons manufactured as quickly as possible. To meet this requirement, Georgi Shpagin took the PPD as the basis of a simpler design which was much easier to produce. The ensuing PPSh 41 is largely made from steel pressings although it retains a wooden stock. It has a slotted jacket around the barrel, ending in a simple compensator to reduce muzzle climb. A 35-shot box magazine can be used, although most were fitted with the 71-shot drum of the PPD. This specimen is an early model, with a selector lever in front of the trigger and a tangent rearsight. Later models fired bursts only, while their rearsight was a simple aperture. The PPSh was a great success, with over 5 million made.

3 TZ45

LENGTH: 33.5in (851mm)
WEIGHT: 115oz (3.26kg)
CALIBRE: 9mm (.354in)
CAPACITY: 20/40
MV: c.1250f/s (365m/s)

This Italian wartime design only went into production in 1945, and was mainly used by security troops in mopping up operations after the war. Crudely made, it incorporates a grip safety just behind the magazine housing, the lever of which has to be pressed for the bolt to be free to move.

4 Owen

LENGTH: 32in (813mm)
WEIGHT: 150oz (4.24kg)
CALIBRE: 9mm (.354in)
CAPACITY: 32
MV: c.1375f/s (420m/s)

When the Second World War broke out, Australia began making a version of the Sten known as the Austen. The Army were not impressed by the British design, and looked instead to an indigenous .22in (5.59in) weapon developed in the late 1930s by Evelyn Owen. Modified for 9mm (.354in) Parabellum, this became the Owen Machine Carbine, a heavy, robust blow-back submachine gun with a tubular receiver, metal stock and two pistol grips, The 32-shot magazine feeds from above, which makes for a more reliable feed than most other submachine guns. The bolt is also in a sealed chamber, sep-arated from the cocking han-dle by a bulkhead which pre-vents the ingress of dirt and moisture. The Owen served with the Australian Army well into the 1950s.

5 Type 50

LENGTH: 33.75in (858mm)
WEIGHT: 128oz (3.63kg)
CALIBRE: 7.62mm (.3in)
CAPACITY: 35
MV: c.1400f/s (472m/s)

In the late 1940s, the Chinese communists turned to Russia as the source of their infantry weapons. This is their Type 50, a copy of the PPSh 41, although it has a lighter stock and normally uses a 35-shot curved magazine. Many of these weapons were used by Chinese troops in Korea.

1 Type 54/PPS 43
LENGTH: 32.25in (819mm)
WEIGHT: 118oz (3.36kg)
CALIBRE: 7.62mm (.3in)
CAPACITY: 35
MV: c.1600f/s (489m/s)

During the 1941-42 siege of Leningrad, the Russian defenders had to improvise a supply of arms from whatever materials and machinery was available in the city. As a result, Sudarev designed this crude but effective blowback submachine gun, originally known as the PPS 42. It could be made by any reasonably competent workshop, being formed from simple metal pressings spot-welded and riveted together. It has a folding steel stock, and is only capable of burst fire, being fed by a 35-shot box magazine. A later improved version was the PPS 43, and over a million of these weapons served with the Soviet Army throughout the war. This specimen is actually a post-war Chinese-made Type 54. It is almost indistinguishable from the Russian, the only clue being the diamond marking on the grip.

2 BSA Model 1949
LENGTH: 27.9in (697mm)
WEIGHT: 103oz (2.9kg)
CALIBRE: 9mm (.354in)
CAPACITY: 32
MV: c.1200f/s (365m/s)

After the Second World War, the British looked to replace the Sten, and this was one of the weapons they considered. It is a neat blowback design, with a side-mounted 35-shot magazine. To cock the bolt, the grip is rotated then moved forward and back. It was not selected for service.

3 MCEM 2
LENGTH: 23.5in (598mm)
WEIGHT: 96oz (2.72kg)
CALIBRE: 9mm (.354in)
CAPACITY: 18
MV: c.1200f/s (365m/s)

The MCEM 2 was another unsuccessful attempt to replace the Sten. Designed by a Polish officer, it had a hollow bolt with the firing pin at the rear and which almost completely surrounded the barrel. While this 'telescoped bolt' made for a short weapon, the rate of fire was excessively high.

4 Sterling L2

LENGTH: 27.15in (690mm)
WEIGHT: 96oz (2.72kg)
CALIBRE: 9mm (.354in)
CAPACITY: 32
MV: c.1200f/s (365m/s)

Originally known as the Patchett, a few prototypes of this British weapon saw service during the Second World War before it was selected in 1953 as the replacement for the Sten. Designated the Sterling L2A3, it is robust and well made, and can almost be thought of as a Sten built to peacetime stan-dards. It is a simple blowback weapon with a folding steel stock and plastic pistol grip, above which is the selector lever. The bolt has ribs machined on to it which scrape out dirt and fouling, making the L2 extremely reliable in all conditions. The curved 32-shot magazine has the rounds in two columns, and is robust enough to prevent most of the problems associated with the Sten. The Sterling is in service with over 90 countries, and has been manufactured in India, Canada and elsewhere.

5 Madsen M50

LENGTH: 31.25in (794mm)
WEIGHT: 111oz (3.15kg)
CALIBRE: 9mm (.354in)
CAPACITY: 32
MV: c.1250f/s (381m/s)

The first indigenous Danish submachine gun was the Madsen Model 45, which was too expensive and complex to be successful. Madsen than produced the Model 46, a simple blowback weapon, made using modern mass-produc-tion techniques. Minor improvements resulted in the Model 50 (shown here) and the later Model 53. All these have a body made from two pieces which are hinged at the rear, and which can be opened for cleaning and maintenance. The side-folding stock is metal tube, while there is a grip safe-ty just behind the magazine housing. Madsens sold in rel-atively small numbers, although the M50 was trialled by the British as a possible Sten replacement. This specimen is one of those, and is fitted with a curved magazine rather than the normal straight one.

1 Carl Gustav M45

LENGTH: 31.8in (808mm)
WEIGHT: 122oz (3.45kg)
CALIBRE: 9mm (.354in)
CAPACITY: 36/50
MV: c.1210f/s (369m/s)

The Second World War spurred the neutral Swedes into developing a simple submachine gun suitable for mass production. The Carl Gustav factory eventually came up with the Model 45, a straightforward blowback design that mechanically owes a lot to the Sten. A simple tubular receiver holds the recoil spring and one-piece bolt, while the side-folding tubular metal stock is hinged above and below the wooden pistol grip. The Model 45 was only capable of burst fire, although a trained user could squeeze off single shots using the trigger. It was originally equipped with a 50-shot Suomi magazine, although this was soon replaced by a new design of 36-shot box. This was a successful and reliable weapon which was also built in Indonesia and Egypt.

2 MAT 49

LENGTH: 28.35in (720mm)
WEIGHT: 124oz (3.5kg)
CALIBRE: 9mm (.354in)
CAPACITY: 20/32
MV: c.1280f/s (390m/s)

The first successful French submachine gun was the pre-war MAS 38, which was replaced by this design in 1949. It is a straightforward blowback weapon, and the square outline indicates extensive use of welded and riveted steel pressings. There are a few unusual features in this design, however, including the safety lever at the rear of the pistol grip, which has to be depressed by the firer for the weapon to operate. The straight box magazine fits into a combined foregrip and housing, which can be hinged forward to lie under the barrel. This allows access for maintenance and is another effective safety measure. The MAT 49 was used by the French in all the post-war conflicts in which they were involved, and large numbers were captured by the Vietnamese communists.

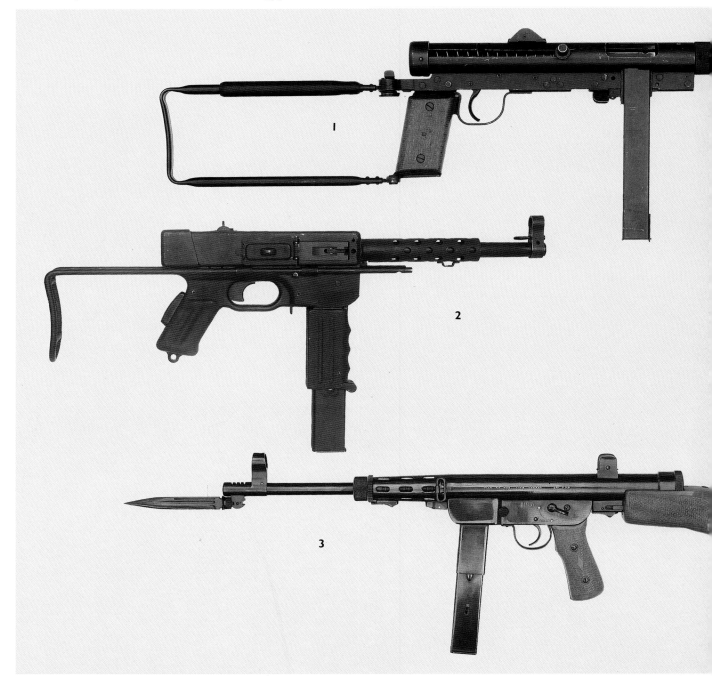

3 Rexim-Favor

LENGTH: 32in (813mm)
WEIGHT: 112oz (3.18kg)
CALIBRE: 9mm (.354in)
CAPACITY: 20
MV: c.1300f/s (396m/s)

A 1950s Swiss design manufactured in Spain, this weapon is rather complex for a submachine gun. It fires from a closed bolt, using a separate hammer and firing pin, although the operation is still blowback. Expensive and over-sophisticated, its only known use was by the Turkish Army.

4 Uzi

LENGTH: 25.2in (640mm)
WEIGHT: 123oz (3.5kg)
CALIBRE: 9mm (.354in)
CAPACITY: 25/32/40
MV: c.1280f/s (390m/s)

Designed by Major Uzi Gal, this neat blowback weapon was one of the early products of the fledgling Israeli Arms industry in the early 1950s. It was the first successful submachine gun to use a telescoping bolt which wraps around most of the barrel at the moment of firing. This allows for a reasonably long barrel in a short weapon, and has been used in many other designs since. The magazine feeds through the butt, and the weapon is so well balanced that controlled single-handed fire is easily achievable. Compact, reliable and effective, the Uzi has sold to many countries around the world, although most weapons are fitted with a metal folding stock rather than the fixed wooden one seen here. 'Cut down' versions are also available in Mini- and Micro-Uzi machine pistol forms.

5 Australian F1

LENGTH: 28.1in (715mm)
WEIGHT: 115oz (3.26kg)
CALIBRE: 9mm (.354in)
CAPACITY: 34
MV: c.1200f/s (365m/s)

The 1960s replacement for the Owen (see page 191), the F1 retained the upright magazine of the earlier design. It has a fixed butt level with the barrel, which improves accuracy but necessitates a high sight line. This is a reliable, effective and popular weapon made to a high standard.

1 VZ61 Skorpion

LENGTH: 20.47in (520mm)
WEIGHT: 46.4oz (1.31kg)
CALIBRE: 7.65mm (.301in)
CAPACITY: 10/20
MV: c.970f/s (294m/s)

Only 10.63in (270mm) long with the stock folded, this neat Czech blowback design was originally intended as a personal defence weapon for vehicle crews. Popular with police and security agencies (and terrorists), its only fault is the marginal stopping power of its bullet.

2 Ingram MAC 10

LENGTH: 21.57in (548mm)
WEIGHT: 102oz (2.84kg)
CALIBRE: .45in (11.4mm)
CAPACITY: 30
MV: c.900f/s (275m/s)

A simple weapon first seen in 1970, the Ingram uses a telescoped bolt and extending wire stock to keep the body length down to 10.59in (269mm). It failed to sell in large numbers, although a few special forces units showed some interest. This specimen is fitted with a suppressor.

3 H & K MP5

LENGTH: 26.77in (680mm)
WEIGHT: 102oz (2.88kg)
CALIBRE: 9mm (.354in)
CAPACITY: 15/30
MV: c.1312f/s (400m/s)

The modern Heckler & Koch MP5 is an unusual submachine gun in that it fires from a closed bolt, making use of the same roller-delayed blowback system as the G3 rifle (see page 169). It makes for an exceptionally accurate and reliable design, although one which is expensive and which demands a reasonable degree of care and maintenance. Nevertheless it has proven to be highly successful with police, security and special forces units around the world, and is available in a bewildering array of variants. There are extendable stocks, fixed plastic stocks and versions with three-round burst selectors, while there is also an extremely compact 'Kurz' (short) model for concealed carriage. The model shown is the MP5A5, with extendable stock and 3-round selector, and has the 15-shot magazine.

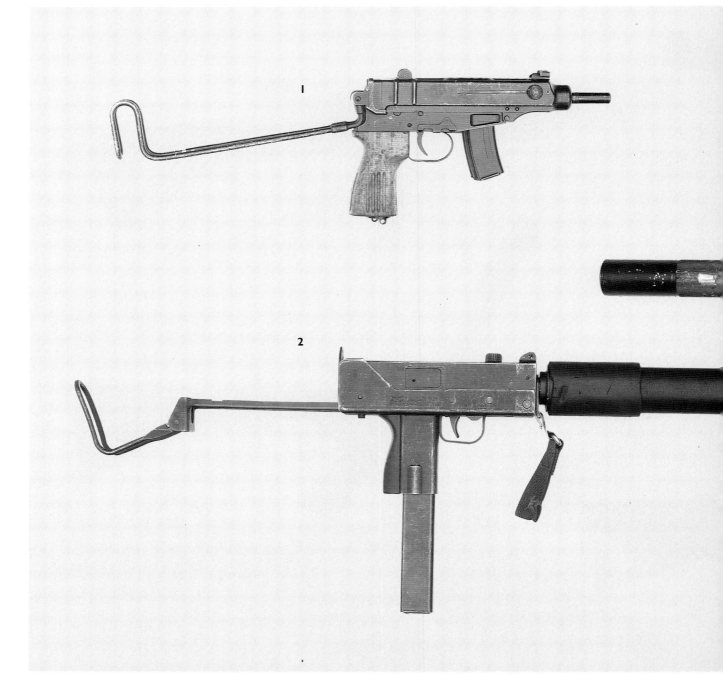

4 H & K MP5SD

LENGTH: 30.7in (780mm)
WEIGHT: 120oz (3.4kg)
CALIBRE: 9mm (.354in)
CAPACITY: 15/30
MV: c.935f/s (285m/s)

With the popularity of the MP5 in the special forces community, it was perhaps inevitable that a silenced version would be produced. The barrel has numerous small holes in it which vent gas into the surrounding silencer. They then leak into a front chamber before leaving the muzzle with greatly reduced energy. By the time the bullet exits the barrel it is subsonic, and the only sound is from the firing pin and the bolt as it recoils. As the MP5 shoots from a closed bolt, the accuracy of the first shot is superb up to about 220yds (200m), which makes the use of special telescopic, night vision or laser sights a worthwhile option. This is the MP5SD3 model with extendable butt. There are also variants with a fixed butt or no butt at all, or with a three-round burst selector.

5 Spectre

LENGTH: 22.83in (580mm)
WEIGHT: 102oz (2.9kg)
CALIBRE: 9mm (.354in)
CAPACITY: 30/50
MV: c.1312f/s (400m/s)

A 1984 Italian design, the Spectre is another blowback weapon firing from a closed bolt. It has a double action mechanism, in that once a round is chambered, the firing pin can be decocked to enable the gun to be carried in safety. There is no manual safety catch, the user just has to pull the trigger to fire, giving him the ability to react quickly to the unexpected. Some use a folding metal stock, although with the addition of a forward pistol grip the gun can be easily controlled without it. The Spectre also has an ingenious 50-shot magazine, which by using four columns in its lower section takes up as much room as a standard 30-shot item. This weapon combines firepower, safety and speed of reaction in a compact package, and has proven to be popular with security and police users.

MACHINE GUNS

The automatic machine gun appeared in 1884 as the Maxim gun, and this reigned supreme until about 1910, even after a number of other designs had appeared. The truth was that the armies of the turn of the century were not at all sure of the tactics to apply to machine guns; they were all very well for mowing down hordes of screaming savages in colonial wars, but their utility in European warfare was in some doubt. Moreover the water-cooled, belt-fed Maxim, with its tripod, was a cumbersome beast to carry about. Altogether it is surprising that armies adopted them at all, but a near-universal standard of two guns per infantry battalion seems to have become accepted by the early 1890s.

What gave the machine gun some impetus was the 1904 Russo-Japanese War, where machine guns were used by both sides to good effect. The Russians had the Maxim, while the Japanese had the light Madsen and the heavier Hotchkiss. There seemed to be little to choose between the Hotchkiss and the Maxim, but the Madsen was a much lighter weapon and far-sighted soldiers noted this fact.

Far-sighted inventors also noted the Madsen's success. Samuel MacLean of the USA began developing a light machine gun, capable of being carried by one man, fed with ammunition from a drum, and fired from a bipod rather like a rifle. He had other things to do, so he sold the design to a company which hired Colonel Isaac Lewis to perfect it; the result was the Lewis Gun. But America wasn't interested, and Lewis went to Belgium to have it manufactured.

The machine gun sprang to prominence in 1914-18 when, allied with impenetrable thickets of barbed wire, it decimated the troops of both sides whenever they attempted to attack. For defensive war, which 1915-17 essentially was for both sides, the medium machine gun was the ideal weapon. It could be emplaced in a suitable enfilading position. supplied with ample ammunition, and could fire for hours on end. But when warfare became more mobile in 1918 these weapons were less useful; what was wanted was a lighter gun which could move as fast as the infantryman. And by this time the demand had made itself sufficiently apparent for the various armies to have begun manufacture. The Lewis and Hotchkiss outfitted the British And French, while lightweight Parabellum, Dreyse and Bergmann

Below: *Lt. John Browning of the US Army with a Model 1917 designed by his father. This water-cooled, belt-fed machine gun saw service in both World Wars.*

Right: *The BAR was first used by the US Army in 1917, and served until the 1950s. Tough and reliable, it suffered from a limited magazine capacity of only 20 rounds.*

designs were adopted by the Germans.

These lighter guns varied in detail but all were intended to be man-portable and fired from a bipod. The Lewis and Hotchkiss used magazines; the Lewis a 47-round drum, the Hotchkiss a 24-round strip, several of which could be linked together. The Germans preferred to remain with the Maxim belt, which the soldiers understood, even though it was awkward to handle in the mud.

Subsequent analysis of the war's lessons suggested that the light machine gun was a desirable weapon, since it was generally assumed that the static warfare of 1915-17 had been an aberration and that mobility would return in future conflicts. The French, having had possibly the worst machine guns of any combatant, set about remedying this early in the 1920s, and by the end of the decade had the Chatellerault in service, a gas-operated, magazine fed, bipod-mounted weapon which also inaugurated a new and improved 7.5mm (.29in) cartridge.

The British were torn between the Lewis and the Vickers-Berthier, an Anglo-French design, but at a late stage in the deliberations the Czech ZB26 was brought to their notice. This, too, was gas-operated and bipod mounted, and featured a quick-change barrel to permit prolonged firing by allowing the removed barrel to cool down. Originally in 7.92mm (.31in) calibre, it was quickly modified to use the British .303in (7.69mm) cartridge, the rights were purchased, and as the Bren gun it became probably the best light machine gun of all time.

Germany adopted an entirely new viewpoint. Rather than adopt two different weapons, a medium gun and a light gun, it elected to adopt one gun but use it according to the tactical requirement of the moment. The MG34 was air-cooled, belt-fed, recoil-operated, and incorporated a quick-change barrel to allow prolonged firing. When mounted upon a tripod it acted as the medium support machine gun, but if a more mobile weapon was wanted, the MG43 was given a bipod to become the squad machine gun. The concept of the 'General Purpose Machine Gun' had been born.

The Second World War saw Germany armed with the MG34 and later MG42, Britain with the Bren and Vickers, while the United States adopted Browning's M1919 and light automatic rifle. Russia retained the 1910 Maxim, supplemented by Degtyarev light machine guns.

Postwar years saw the adoption of the 'General Purpose Machine Gun' idea in many armies, though by the 1980s the novelty had worn off and light machine guns were again coming into use. The current move is towards smaller calibres; rifles have virtually standardised on the 5.56mm (.223in) cartridge, and it makes some sense to use the same ammunition for the squad automatic weapon. It does, though, reduce the effective range of the machine gun to that of the rifle, and machine guns traditionally fire at rather more than rifle ranges. As a result, while the 5.56mm (.223in) standard is acceptable for the squad weapon, the 7.62mm (.3in) cartridge remains the general choice for the company support machine gun.

Heavy machine guns of 12.7mm/.5in calibre are generally used as air defence weapons or as the armament of light armoured vehicles; they are somewhat too heavy to be easily carried by the foot soldier. Two designs, the American Browning M2 and the Soviet DShK, more or less dominate this field. A design from Fabrique Nationale in 15.5mm (.61in) calibre was put forward in the mid-1980s; it was a formidable weapon, but it arrived just at the time when the Cold War ended and military funding began to dry up. In 1992 the project was shelved indefinitely.

Below: *The belt-fed AAT-52 is a French machine gun which uses delayed blowback.*

Right: *Singapore's Ultimax fires 5.56mm (.223in) ammunition from a 100-round drum.*

1 Colt-Browning M1895

LENGTH: 40.75in (1035mm)
WEIGHT: 35lb (15.87kg)
CALIBRE: .30in (7.62mm)
CAPACITY: Belt feed
MV: c.2800f/s (855m/s)

At about the same time that Maxim was harnessing the recoil of the cartridge to drive an automatic weapon, John Browning was experimenting with using the muzzle blast to carry out similar functions. In 1890 he produced a prototype air-cooled machine gun, which was then manufactured by Colt and adopted by the US Navy. Designated the Model 1895, this uses an unusual form of operation, where the gas is bled off through a port near the muzzle. Under this port is the end of a piston, which is hinged at the breech end of the weapon. The gas blows the front end of this piston down in a great swinging arc which provides the motive power for the mechanism (and gave it the nickname 'potato digger'). A lever connected to this piston unlocks the breech then moves it backwards to begin the reloading cycle. Ammunition is fed from a canvas belt, and the gun is normally mounted on a 61.25lb (27.8kg) tripod. The Colt was reliable enough, although the swinging piston prevented it from being properly emplaced, and being air-cooled it could not produce heavy sustained fire. It saw limited action in Cuba and China, but by the time of the First World War it was obsolescent, and US troops went into action equipped largely with automatic weapons designed and produced by their allies.

1

2 Maxim Model 1884

LENGTH: 46in (1169mm)
WEIGHT: 60lb (27.22kg)
CALIBRE: .45in (11.4mm)
CAPACITY: Belt feed
MV: c.1600f/s (488m/s)

Hiram Maxim was the American inventor of the first successful self-powered automatic 'machine gun' – a weapon which was to change the face of land warfare. After emigrating to England, where he felt the market was greater, he soon began manufacture of a small number of weapons.

The first Maxim to be used in action was reportedly an 1884 model purchased by a British officer, although the gun was not formally adopted by the Army until 1889. Chambered for the black-powder .45in (11.4mm) rifle bullet, the Maxim feeds from a canvas belt. When a round is fired, the recoil drives the barrel and the bolt a short distance to the rear, where a locking toggle hinges in the middle to release the bolt. This continues moving against a side-mounted recoil spring while extracting

the spent case and pulling a fresh round rearwards out of the belt. The spring then drives the bolt forward, pushing the new round into the chamber as the locking toggle snaps into position. This process continues as long as the trigger is pressed and there is ammunition in the belt. Most British Maxims were built by Vickers, and were either mounted on large wheeled carriages or on 15lb (6.8kg) tripods as seen here. Within a few years, many others had copied Maxim's concepts

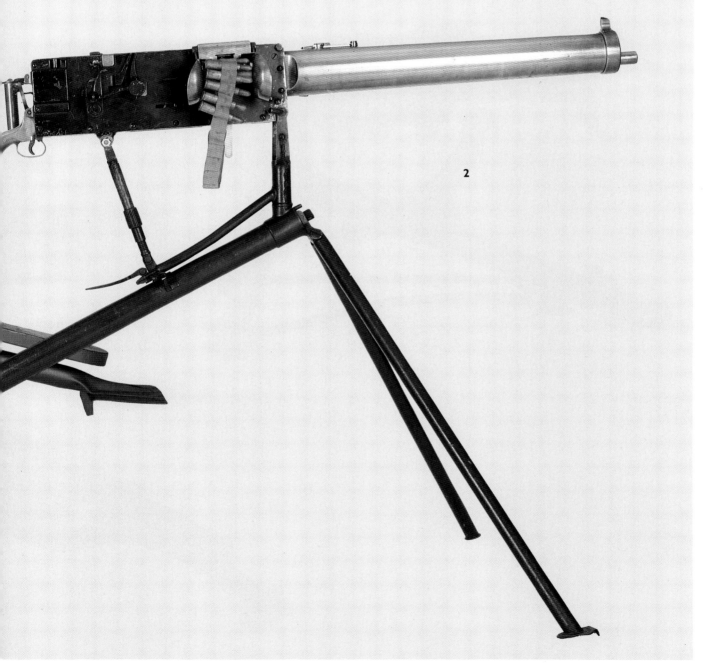

2

1 Schwarzlose MG05

LENGTH: 42in (1067mm)
WEIGHT: 44lb (20kg)
CALIBRE: 8mm (.315mm)
CAPACITY: Belt feed
MV: c.2000f/s (610m/s)

Designed in 1905 by Andreas Schwarzlose, this Austrian weapon was the only widely used medium machine gun to fire from an unlocked bolt. Instead of the recoil mechanism of the Maxim, the Schwarzlose uses blowback to drive the bolt back and begin the reloading and cocking cycle. This is a much simpler system requiring fewer moving parts, an important consideration for a service weapon. As it fires full-powered rifle cartridges, the MG05 needs an extremely heavy bolt to prevent the chamber opening while the gas pressure is still dangerously high. This is supplemented by a strong recoil spring and a mechanical lever to further delay the initial bolt travel. At 20.75in (527mm) the barrel is nearly 8in (203mm) shorter than that of the Maxim, which helps reduce the gas pressure at a cost of range and accuracy. To improve the extraction cycle a small oil pump is fitted to lubricate each cartridge before it is inserted into the breech, although this complexity was removed in a 1912 redesign. As with the Maxim, the Schwarzlose is normally seen with a water-filled cooling jacket around the barrel, and is normally mounted on a 44lb (20kg) tripod. An effective gun, it was used by a number of armies in different calibres during the First World War.

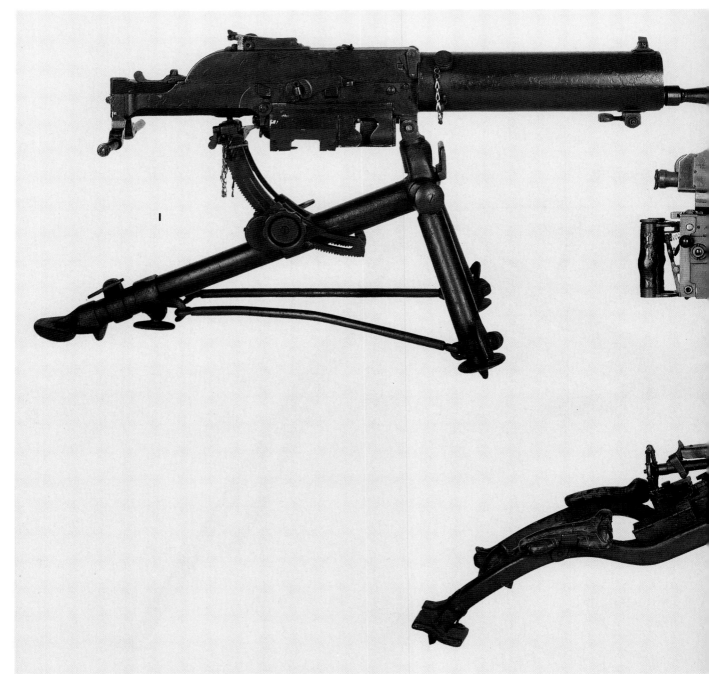

2 Maxim MG08

LENGTH: 46.25in (1175mm)
WEIGHT: 58.5lb (26.54kg)
CALIBRE: 7.92mm (.31in)
CAPACITY: Belt feed
MV: c.2925f/s (892m/s)

Maxim first demonstrated his machine gun (see page 201) in Germany in 1887, after which the Army carried out a sequence of field trials until formal adoption in 1901. After a few years of use, the weapon was modified slightly to become the MG08, which would become the backbone of the German machine gun force in the First World War. The Germans displayed as much hesitancy in deciding upon how to use the new weapon as did every other army, until reports of the 1904-5 Russo-Japanese War convinced them that machine guns had a vital part to play in modern warfare. A battery of six MG08s was attached to each infantry regiment, and by 1914 there were nearly 13,000 in service. The MG08 is a tough, reliable weapon which uses Maxim's recoil mecha- nism and locking toggle inside a large rectangular steel receiv- er. The barrel has a water-filled cooling jacket, which as long as it is topped up regularly, per- mits extended periods of con- tinuous fire. To prevent exces- sive barrel wear when hot, a spare is also normally carried, and can be fitted quickly dur- ing any lull in the fighting. All the Maxim designs were heavy weapons, but in the German case this is compounded by a 70.5lb (31.98kg) mount which could also be used by the crew as a makeshift sledge.

2

1 Hotchkiss Machine Gun

LENGTH: 51.6in (1311mm)
WEIGHT: 55.7lb (25.26kg)
CALIBRE: 8mm (.315in)
CAPACITY: Strip feed
MV:c.2325f/s (709m/s)

In 1893 an Austrian officer named Odkolek sold the French gunmaking concern of Hotchkiss the rights to a new automatic weapon. The weapon itself was impractical, but the chief engineer, an American named Laurence Benét, had spotted the worth of its method of gas operation, and within a few years had produced an effective machine gun. As the bullet moves up the barrel, gas is tapped off into a cylinder, which drives a piston backwards against the bolt. The bolt is unlocked by the piston opening a hinged flap, releasing it to move to the rear to begin the reloading cycle. Instead of a Maxim-style water jacket, the Hotchkiss uses air cooling, and has a row of thick steel or brass cooling fins around the breech end of the barrel. The feed system is also unusual, in that instead of a canvas belt there is a solid metal strip holding 24 or 30 rounds, which is ejected after passing through the receiver. The gun shown is the later M1914, which served with French and American forces during the First World War. This normally sat on a 60lb (27.24kg) tripod and was fed from three-round strips linked together. While the feed system was always a source of trouble, and overheating could be a problem, the Hotchkiss turned out to be a fine, reliable weapon which served its users well.

1

2 St. Etienne Modele 1907

LENGTH: 46.5in (1181mm)
WEIGHT: 56.75lb (25.74kg)
CALIBRE: 8mm (.31in)
CAPACITY: Belt feed
MV: c.2300f/s (700m/s)

The St Etienne was a misguided attempt by the French National Arsenal to improve upon the Hotchkiss and create a design which would be owned by the Government rather than by a private concern. The first try produced the Puteaux M1905, an unreliable and over-complex weapon which only stayed in service for two years. The St Etienne was intended to overcome the deficiencies of this weapon, but instead compounded them. It is another gas operated weapon, but in this case the designers chose to have the piston driven forwards by the gas pressure. This necessitates a system of gears and levers to translate the movement to the bolt (revealed here by the open receiver cover). In another departure from the norm, the main recoil spring lies around a guide rod underneath the barrel, originally covered by a steel tube. Heavy firing soon built up such a temperature that the spring lost much of its strength, so later models had it open to the elements – and the dirt and mud of the trenches. The only feature of the Hotchkiss that was retained was its weakest point – the rigid strip feed. The St Etienne was issued in large numbers to the French Army, but trench warfare soon pointed out its weaknesses all too clearly and it was quickly replaced by the reliable Hotchkiss.

2

1 Vickers .303in

LENGTH: 43in (1092mm)
WEIGHT: 33lb (14.97kg)
CALIBRE: .303in (7.7m)
CAPACITY: Belt feed
MV: c.2440f/s (744m/s)

The 1912 Vickers was an improved version of the Maxim (see page 201) but had the locking toggle reversed so that it bent up instead of down. This permitted a shallower receiver, and with the use of improved materials makes for a lighter gun. The barrel is surrounded by a water-filled cooling jacket, and the tin can shown here is used to collect and condense the steam for reuse. The tripod weighs 50lb (22.7kg), and when the spare barrels, dial sight, water and ammunition are added, the gun is barely man-portable. Nevertheless it is extremely tough and reliable, and capable of prodigious feats of continuous fire. It served with the British Army through until the mid 1960s, and was also used by many other forces. Variants included vehicle and aircraft mounted weapons.

3 Taisho 1914

LENGTH: 45.5in (1155mm)
WEIGHT: 62lb (28.1kg)
CALIBRE: 6.5mm (.256in)
CAPACITY: 30
MV: c.2400f/s (732m/s)

The Japanese had made good use of the Hotchkiss (see page 204) in their 1904-5 war with Russia, so in 1914 Nambu produced this copy in 6.5mm (.256in) calibre. It retains the 30-round strip and oil pump, but has more cooling fins around the barrel. The tripod weighs 60lb (27.25kg).

2 Browning M1917
LENGTH: 38.5in (978mm)
WEIGHT: 32.6lb (14.97kg)
CALIBRE: .30in (7.62mm)
CAPACITY: Belt feed
MV: c.2800f/s (855m/s)

After his experiments with gas operation and the Colt M1895 (see page 200), John Browning concluded that recoil operation was the best method for use in a medium machine gun. Gas was fine in a light weapon, but a piston system fouls very quickly, and would jam up during the long periods of sus-tained fire that a medium gun of the time was expected to produce. His first patent was in 1901, but it took another 16 years before the US Army could find the money for his new gun. The Model 1917 is a belt fed weapon which looks rather like one of the Maxim derivatives, with a water jack-et around the barrel and a 53lb (24kg) tripod. It operates using recoil, with the bolt fixed to the barrel by a camming lock plate. This is released in the first moments of travel to allow the bolt to proceed to the rear against the recoil spring. A buffer stop also protrudes from the rear, on which is mount-ed the pistol grip - a recogni-tion feature of Browning's medium guns. Simpler than the Maxims and extremely reliable, this was a fine weapon which was put into production too late to serve in large quan-tities during the First World War. The improved M1917A1 was introduced in 1936, and saw wide service in all theatres during the Second World War. There were also variants with no water jacket.

1 Browning M1919

LENGTH: 41in (1041mm)
WEIGHT: 31lb (14kg)
CALIBRE: .30in (7.62mm)
CAPACITY: Belt feed
MV: c.2800f/s (855m/s)

The Browning M1917 was a fine gun, but its bulky water jacket was a hindrance for mobile troops and aircraft. Modifications were made to the basic weapon to produce the M1919, which came too late for service in the First World War. The M1919 uses the same recoil system as the earlier weapon, although many of the components have been redesigned to reduce weight. The major change is a heavier air-cooled barrel surrounded by a light metal casing with cooling slots or holes cut into it. The first model was intended for use as a tank weapon, while the M1919A2 was to be carried by mounted cavalry. The classic Browning was the M1919A4, which became the main US medium machine gun of the Second World War. On fixed mountings it was used by fighter aircraft and tanks, while on flexible mounts it was fired from bomber aircraft, tanks, light vehicles and warships. The picture shows the infantry gun, which used the lightweight (14lb/6.35kg) M2 tripod in the ground role. There was also an attempt to make it into a light machine gun by adding a butt and bipod, but this was too heavy to be a success. The M1919 was tough, reliable, and easy to operate, while being popular with all its users, whether in the US forces or with their allies.

1

2 Breda Modello 1937

LENGTH: 50in (1270mm)
WEIGHT: 42.8lb (19.28kg)
CALIBRE: 8mm (.315in)
CAPACITY: Strip feed
MV: c.2600f/s (793m/s)

The Italian concern of Breda began making weapons as a subcontractor to Fiat in 1916, eventually turning to the development of their own designs. The Modello 37 was initially designed for use in armoured vehicles, but eventually became the standard Italian Army medium machine gun throughout the Second World War. It is a gas operated design, with a regulator which controls the bleed off from the barrel into the cylinder beneath. This drives a piston into the bolt, unlocking it from the barrel and pushing it to the rear. The space between the face of the bolt and the breech (the 'headspace') is not adjustable, and the initial pull on the empty case is very sudden, which could cause split cases and stoppages. To overcome this the Italians made use of an oil pump similar to that on the Schwarzlose (see page 202) which lubricates each round as it is loaded. The 20-shot strip feed system is also unusual, in that the empty cases are neatly laid back on the strip as it moves through the gun. Combining this idea with oiled cartridges would seem to be asking for problems, especially in the dusty environments where most Italian soldiers fought, but in practice the Modello 37 seems to have been a remarkably effective and reliable weapon which served well.

2

1 Browning M2HB

LENGTH: 65in (1651mm)
WEIGHT: 84lb (38.11kg)
CALIBRE: .5in (12.7mm)
CAPACITY: Belt feed
MV: c.2930f/s (894m/s)

Most armies fought the First World War with medium machine guns; tripod mounted belt-fed weapons firing rifle calibre bullets. Towards the end of that war there was felt to be a need for a heavier weapon firing larger bullets, for use against aircraft, observation balloons and armoured vehicles. By 1921, John Browning had modified his recoil system to produce a larger gun firing a .5in (12.7mm) cartridge derived from that used by the German Mauser anti-tank rifle. This water-cooled M1921 was then replaced in the 1930s by an air-cooled variant, which was itself soon replaced by one with a heavier barrel, better able to withstand the extreme temperatures caused by extended firing. Known as the M2HB (Heavy Barrel), this gun has been fitted to tanks, light vehicles, aircraft and light anti-aircraft mounts, as well as used in a ground role on a 44lb (19.86kg) tripod. It fought in the Second World War, Korea, Vietnam and the 1991 Gulf War, and still forms an important part of many national armouries. Now obsolete in the anti-aircraft role, it is still a powerful long-range ground weapon, able to penetrate light armour, masonry and other cover at remarkable ranges. Its only real competitor has been the Russian 12.7mm (.5in) DShK 'Dushka'.

2 SGM

LENGTH: 44.1in (1120mm)
WEIGHT: 29.76lb (13.5kg)
CALIBRE: 7.62mm (.3in)
CAPACITY: Belt feed
MV: c.2700f/s (823m/s)

From 1910 the Russians had made use of a Maxim variant as their standard medium machine gun, but the disasters of 1941 showed the need for a gun that could be made much more quickly using less industrial resources than before. Goryunov came up with this simple air cooled gas operated design which satisfied these requirements while being remarkably effective in use. Originally known as the SG43, it has the piston and cylinder under the barrel, with the piston impinging on the bolt, which is locked to the barrel by tipping sideways into a recess in the receiver. The piston unlocks this bolt before driving it back against the recoil spring. Its 7.62mm (.3in) cartridge is the Russian Model 1891, which being rimmed, has to be pulled backwards out of the belt. Extra complexity maybe, but the SG43 feed system works well enough. The weapon has a heavy barrel to absorb heat, which can also be changed in a few seconds for a cool one. Like the earlier Russian guns it is mounted on a 50.9lb (23.1kg) wheeled carriage, which can be tipped up to have the gun mounted on the trail in the anti-aircraft role. The picture shows the post-war SGM, which has a revised cocking lever and cooling flanges around the barrel. As such it served with many communist armies.

1 Madsen M1902
LENGTH: 46in (1169mm)
WEIGHT: 22lb (9.98kg)
CALIBRE: 8mm (.315in)
CAPACITY: 30
MV: c.2700f/s (824m/s)

This Danish weapon could be said to be the first true light machine gun, having been used by Russian cavalry during the Russo-Japanese War. It had an unusual mechanism similar to that on the Martini rifles (see page 141) in that the bolt was hinged at the rear so that it pivoted vertically.

When a round was fired the barrel and breech recoiled together, the latter being held in a steel frame which slid within the receiver. A cam system caused the bolt to tip up, and an ejector lifted out the empty case. As the frame moved forward again the next round was stripped from the vertical magazine and was pushed into the chamber. Unusually complex, this gun saw service in small numbers all over the world, although it was never formally adopted in quantity by any nation.

2 Chauchat M1915
LENGTH: 45in (1143mm)
WEIGHT: 19lb (8.62kg)
CALIBRE: 8mm (.315in)
CAPACITY: 20
MV: c.2300f/s (700m/s)

Thought to be the most unreliable machine gun ever produced, this French light recoil operated weapon was made to appallingly poor standards by a variety of inexperienced contractors. After disastrous service with the French Army, thousands were sold to the Americans in 1918.

3 Lewis Gun

LENGTH: 50.5in (1282mm)
WEIGHT: 27lb (12.25kg)
CALIBRE: .303in (7.7mm)
CAPACITY: 47
MV: c.2440f/s (744m/s)

In the early years of the 20th Century, an American named Samuel McClean developed a light machine gun, the design of which was completed in 1910 by Colonel Isaac Lewis. A few were sold to Belgium, but in general no army was interested. It was not until the deadlock of trench warfare that soldiers saw the need for a light source of automatic firepower that could be carried by one man when advancing over the shell-blasted terrain. It was adopted by the British Army in 1915 and soon proved to be popular and effective, although it was never a success with Lewis' own army. The Lewis gun was gas operated, with the piston lying in a cylinder under the barrel. At the rear of the piston there was a post which protruded through a cammed slot in the bolt. The bolt itself was locked to the breech by lugs which mated with recesses in the body. The first movement of the piston post rotated this bolt to unlock it, then pulled it back to extract the case. Ammunition was fed from a 47-shot drum above the receiver, while the gun could be rested on an adjustable bipod. A distinctive feature were the radial cooling fins along the barrel which were surrounded by a thin metal case. Complex and somewhat delicate, the Lewis was nevertheless an effective light machine gun.

1 M1918 BAR
LENGTH: 48in (1220mm)
WEIGHT: 19.5lb (8.85kg)
CALIBRE: .30in (7.62mm)
CAPACITY: 20
MV: c.2800f/s (855m/s)

In the early years of the First World War, John Browning had also seen the need for a light machine gun, and by the time the United States joined the fighting he had this design available. The Army called it the Browning Automatic Rifle, and intended to use it to provide 'walking fire', where a line of advancing soldiers would spray bullets at enemy positions to keep their heads down in the trenches. The BAR is a gas operated weapon with the piston and cylinder under the barrel. When the bolt lies against the breech, the rear tips upwards to lock, hence the 'hump' at the top of the receiver. Feed is from a detachable 20-shot box beneath the receiver, and the weapon can be supported in action by a short folding bipod. The original M1918 has a selector to enable single shots or bursts to be fired, although later models replaced this with the ability to select two rates of fire. There were a number of variants of BAR, including one with a finned barrel and others with butt rests and upper straps (the latter seen on this specimen). It is a fine, reliable weapon, although a little too light for a machine gun and too heavy for a rifle. Even so it remained in US service until the 1950s, fighting in the Second World War and Korea, and was also used by the armed forces of many other countries.

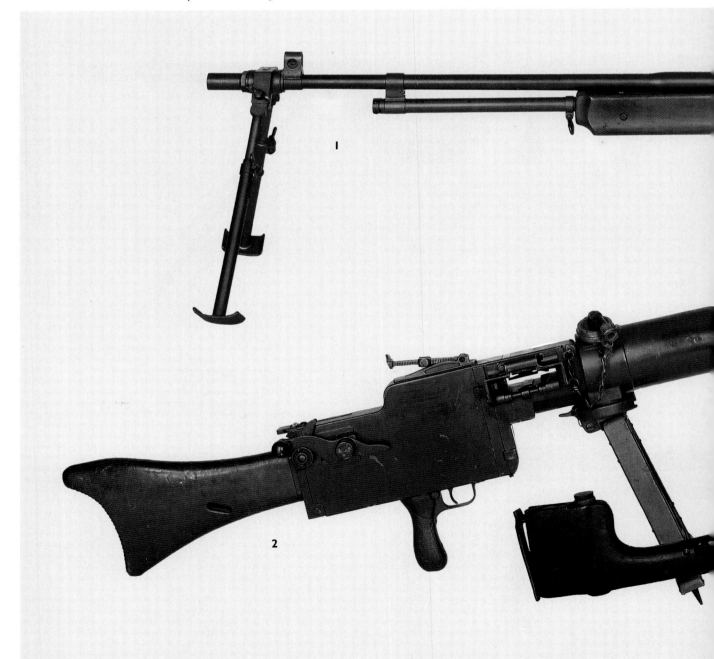

2 MG08/15

LENGTH: 55in (1398mm)
WEIGHT: 39lb (17.7kg)
CALIBRE: 7.92mm (.3in)
CAPACITY: Belt feed
MV: c.2900f/s (885m/s)

This was a German attempt to produce a light machine gun based on their Maxim MG08 medium, one which proved especially effective in their 1918 offensive. Components were redesigned and lightened, while a rifle style butt was fitted along with a pistol grip under the receiver. The water jacket was retained, although the sledge mount was replaced by a simple folding bipod. This is still a heavy weapon though, and demands a second gunner to control the belt feed when in action. An air-cooled version was used on aircraft and Zeppelins, and some were issued to ground troops towards the end of the war. While heavy and cumbersome for its intended role, the MG08/15 provided greater firepower than magazine fed weapons, and saw service until the mid 1930s.

3 Hotchkiss Mk. I

LENGTH: 46.75in (1187mm)
WEIGHT: 27lb (12.25kg)
CALIBRE: .303in (7.7mm)
CAPACITY: 30
MV: c.2440f/s (744m/s)

During the First World War, the British supplemented their Vickers and Lewis guns by building this version of the Hotchkiss. Initially intended for cavalry (hence the light tripod) it was later used on armoured vehicles. This gun was still in limited service in the Second World War.

1 Beardmore-Farquhar
LENGTH: 49.5in (1258mm)
WEIGHT: 19lb (8.62kg)
CALIBRE: .303in (7.7mm)
CAPACITY: 81
MV: c.2440f/s (744m/s)

A 1919 experimental design, this British gas operated weapon feeds from a distinctive drum magazine. Extremely light, it uses a spring between the piston and bolt to absorb the initial shock and give a very smooth action. Trials showed it to be unreliable and it was rejected.

2 Vickers-Berthier
LENGTH: 46.5in (1181mm)
WEIGHT: 20.8lb (9.43kg)
CALIBRE: .303in (7.7mm)
CAPACITY: 30
MV: c.2440f/s (744m/s)

Lieutenant André Berthier of the French Army had designed an effective light machine gun, but had difficulty in finding any takers until the British company Vickers bought the rights in 1925. It is a light and neat gas operated gun, fed from a vertical 30-shot curved box which protrudes above the receiver. The bolt is locked by tilting upwards into the receiver, and the action is remarkably smooth and positive. It uses few moving parts, and is easily maintained without the need for specialist tools. The VB was considered by the British Army, but in 1934 was rejected in favour of the Bren. It was, however, chosen by the Indian Army, and gave them excellent service throughout the Second World War. A heavier drum-fed variant was used by the RAF as an aircraft gun (the Vickers 'K' or VGO).

3 Chatellerault M1924

LENGTH: 42.5in (1080mm)
WEIGHT: 20.25lb (9.12kg)
CALIBRE: 7.5mm (.295in)
CAPACITY: 25
MV: c.2590f/s (790m/s)

The French Army ended the First World War with the notorious Chauchat (see page 212) as their standard light machine gun, a state of affairs which obviously needed amending. A new light gun was then developed by the Chatellerault national arsenal, although financial restrictions prevented formal issue until 1926. A 7.5mm (.295in) round was developed for it, based on the German Mauser 7.92mm (.31in). The gun built to fire this cartridge is a light gas-operated design, feeding from a distinctive straight box magazine above the receiver. The mechanism is based on that in the Browning BAR (see page 214), where the bolt locks to the breech by tilting upwards into a recess at the top of the receiver. There are two triggers, the forward one for single shots and the rear for auto-matic fire. After the usual teething problems suffered by any new design, the M1924 became a well-liked and reliable light machine gun, which served the French and their colonies throughout the Second World War. There was also the M1931 'fortress' variant which had a fixed mount and fed from a huge vertically-mounted 150-shot drum. During the German occupation, many M1924s were used by the Nazis, while after the war it fought extensively in Indo-China and Algeria.

3

1 ZB26

LENGTH: 45.25in (1150mm)
WEIGHT: 22.5lb (10.2kg)
CALIBRE: .303mm (7.7mm)
CAPACITY: 30
MV: c.2440f/s (744m/s)

The Czech firm of Zbrojovka Brno was formed after the First World War, and its most successful product was the ZB26 light machine gun. A gas operated weapon chambered for the 7.92mm (.31in) Mauser round, it taps gas from near the muzzle which gives a smooth, reliable action. It has a barrel which can be changed in a matter of seconds, and is fired from an open bolt to prevent overheating. The ZB feeds from a distinctive curved vertical magazine, and proved to be a reliable weapon popular with many armies. The ZB30 showed some minor improvements, while the ZB33 (shown here) was a prototype entered for the British Army trials of 1934. Chambered for the British .303in (7.7mm) round, it proved to be superior to all the other contenders, and was adopted as the Bren.

2 Besal Mk . 2

LENGTH: 46.63in (1185mm)
WEIGHT: 21.5lb (9.75kg)
CALIBRE: .303in (7.7mm)
CAPACITY: 30
MV: c.2440f/s (744m/s)

All Bren production was concentrated at Enfield, so during the Second World War, this weapon was developed as a back-up. Gas operated, it was made using techniques of pressing and welding later applied to the Sten. In the event it was never needed, and remained a prototype.

3 Bren

LENGTH: 45.5in (1156mm)
WEIGHT: 22.5lb (10.2kg)
CALIBRE: .303in (7.62mm)
CAPACITY: 30
MV: c.2440f/s (744m/s)

In 1934 the British Army decided upon a version of the Czech ZB26 as their new light machine gun, converting it to take the .303in (7.7mm) round. It was named Bren, from combining the first two letters of its place of origin (Brno) with those from its place of manufacture (Enfield).

The new weapon demanded sophisticated machining, and took some years to be widely issued, It was immediately popular though, proving to be simple, reliable and extremely accurate. The rate of fire is quite slow, and the gun can be controlled easily by a standing man, and even fired from the shoulder in an emergency. There were a few early problems with the ammunition feed, until it was discovered that these could be overcome by limiting the magazine to 28 rounds rather than the full 30.

Brens were also made in Canada, and equipped most units from the British Commonwealth. The weapon in the picture is mounted on a 26.5lb (12kg) tripod, although this was not a common method of use. Widely regarded as one of the best light machine guns ever made, a number were converted to 7.62mm (.3in) after the war. Obsolete in theory, these can still be found in British service, tucked away in remote corners by soldiers reluctant to finally give up this old warrior.

3

1 Degtyaryev DP

LENGTH: 50.3in (1290mm)
WEIGHT: 20.5lb (9.3kg)
CALIBRE: 7.62mm (.3in)
CAPACITY: 49
MV: c.2750f/s (849m/s)

Vasiliy Degtyaryev first began work on this light machine gun in 1921, and it was accepted by the Red Army in 1928. Designed to be manufactured by semi-skilled labour, it is of extremely simple construction and uses few parts. The DP is gas operated, with the piston underneath the barrel. The recoil spring is also wound around the piston, although the heat from the barrel can cause it to lose its strength during heavy firing. The bolt is locked by an unusual system, where two hinged flaps are forced outwards into recesses in the receiver as the firing pin moves forward. The main problem with the DP is that it has to make use of the Russian 1891 7.62mm (.3in) round with its large rim, a cartridge not suited to a box magazine. Degtyaryev got around this by using a flat 49-shot drum, although soldiers found that keeping the load to 47 rounds improved reliability. The DP can only fire in automatic mode, and the bolt is left open between bursts to improve cooling. An effective weapon, it had some problems with overheating and with an easily damaged bipod, difficulties which were overcome with the 1945 DPM, recognisable by its repositioned mainspring and wooden pistol grip. In this guise it served the Soviet Union and her allies and clients well into the 1960s.

2 Breda Modello 30

LENGTH: 48.5in (1232mm)
WEIGHT: 22.75lb (10.32kg)
CALIBRE: 6.5mm (.256in)
CAPACITY: 20
MV: c.2063f/s (618m/s)

This 1930 Italian light machine gun was a blowback weapon which used a cartridge lubricating system to ease extraction. The side-mounted magazine was fixed, having to be hinged open to have new rounds fed into it. Unreliable and awkward, this was not a popular weapon.

3 Type 96

LENGTH: 41.5in (1054mm)
WEIGHT: 20lb (9.07kg)
CALIBRE: 6.5mm (.256in)
CAPACITY: 30
MV: c.2400f/s (732m/s)

The first independently-designed Japanese light machine gun was the Nambu Type 11, a weapon with a number of unusual features. Based on the Hotchkiss gas system, it fed from a hopper, into which five-round clips of rifle ammunition could be inserted. It also had an oil lubricating

system to aid extraction. The 1936 Type 96 was an attempt to improve upon this, with the hopper replaced by a 30-shot top-mounted vertical box magazine. Oil lubrication is still required, but in this case it is applied by the magazine loading machine rather than at the gun. The weapon has a quick-change barrel with a carrying handle, and a one piece butt and pistol grip. The later Type 99 was an improved 7.7mm (.303in) version, but appeared too late to see much war service.

2

3

1 MG34

LENGTH: 48in (1220mm)
WEIGHT: 26.7lb (12.1kg)
CALIBRE: 7.92mm (.31in)
CAPACITY: Belt feed
MV: c.2480f/s (756m/s)

This 1934 German weapon introduced a new concept in infantry weapons, that of the 'general purpose machine gun'. This was to be capable of being mounted on a tripod and used in the medium support role, or being fitted with a bipod and a drum magazine as a squad-level light machine gun. It is air cooled and operated by a combination of gas and recoil. The barrel is driven a short distance back by the recoil, enough to rotate the bolt head to unlock it before sending it to the rear. This impulse is increased by the gas impinging on the cone shaped booster at the muzzle. There is no selector lever, instead the trigger is in two parts, the upper half being used to select single shots, the lower to fire bursts. In the medium role, feed is by a belt, made up from spring links which separate and are ejected from the gun as the round is loaded. In the light role, two 75-round drums can be fitted, joined by a 'saddle' which fixes into the feed tray at the top of the receiver. In practice the infantry preferred the extra firepower of continuous belt feed, and the drums tended to be reserved for the anti-aircraft role. An excellent and innovative weapon, its only fault was that it was too well made, the fine tolerances being vulnerable to dirt, sand and fouling. It served throughout the Second World War.

2 MG42

LENGTH: 48in (1220mm)
WEIGHT: 25.5lb (11.57kg)
CALIBRE: 7.92mm (.31in)
CAPACITY: Belt feed
MV: c.2480f/s (756m/s)

Wartime showed the need for a weapon similar to the MG34 but one which would be easier to make and more resistant to the rigours of combat. Made largely from stampings and pressings, the resulting MG42 uses a form of roller-delayed blowback, originally devised by a Polish engineer, Edward Stecke, and since used on most German post-war infantry weapons. While crude looking compared to its predecessor, the MG42 turned out to be a superb weapon, and features of it have been copied by many others since. It has a quick change barrel system, necessary because of the ferocious rate of fire (nearly 1200 rounds per minute). While such a rate reduces accuracy, it can produce a remarkable psychological effect on those exposed to its fire. Allied soldiers called this gun the Spandau.

3 RPD

LENGTH: 40.8in (1036mm)
WEIGHT: 15.6lb (7kg)
CALIBRE: 7.62mm (.3in)
CAPACITY: Belt feed
MV: c.2400f/s (732m/s)

This post-war Russian general purpose machine gun was the last Degtyaryev design. It uses a similar gas operating system to the DP (see page 220), but fires the 7.62mm (.3in) intermediate round used in the AK-47 (see page 164). Tough and reliable, it was made in very large numbers.

3

1 FN MAG

LENGTH: 49.75in (1264mm)
WEIGHT: 24lb (10.89kg)
CALIBRE: 7.62mm (.3in)
CAPACITY: Belt feed
MV: c.2800f/s (855m/s)

Like many others, the Belgian company Fabrique Nationale (FN) were highly impressed by the MG42, and after the war developed a similar type of general purpose machine gun. The MAG (Mitrailleur à Gaz) was first produced in 1957, and is a rugged gas operated gun which uses the feed system of the MG42 with a breech locking system derived from that of the BAR. It has a quick change barrel, and in the squad light machine gun role is fitted with a bipod and detachable butt. It has proven to be an unqualified success, serving with over 70 countries in infantry, vehicle- and helicopter-mounted roles. This specimen is the British-made L7A1 GPMG (known as the 'Gimpy') and is mounted on a 29lb (13.2kg) tripod. In the sustained fire role, it would also normally have a dial sight.

2 M60

LENGTH: 43.75in (1111mm)
WEIGHT: 23lb (10.43kg)
CALIBRE: 7.62mm (.3in)
CAPACITY: Belt feed
MV: c.2800f/s (853m/s)

Another 1950s design inspired by the MG42, this became the standard US machine gun from the early 1960s onwards. It is gas operated, and uses the feed system from the German gun, but in its early form was unreliable and awkward to use. It has an unusual gas system with no regulator, instead the

movement of the piston is supposed to control the pressure to the cylinder. In practice this system is extremely vulnerable to dirt and fouling. The barrel is lined with hard-wearing stellite, and when it is removed it takes the cylinder and bipod with it. This leaves the gunner having to cradle the gun or let it drop in the dirt, while his No.2 wrestles with a red hot barrel that has no carrying handle to protect his hands. The foresight is also fixed, so the gunner is supposed to reset the rearsight every time a barrel is changed, a task often ignored in combat. The later M60E1 overcame many of these problems, eventually giving the Army a gun they could rely on. It can be mounted on a tripod or vehicle, and a simple belt-box can be attached for mobile operations. The later M60E3 is a much lighter redesign, with a forward pistol grip and improved barrel. It has been adopted by the US Marine Corps and Navy, and many American soldiers feel it is the gun that the M60 should have been in the first place.

3 RPK

LENGTH: 40.5in (1029mm)
WEIGHT: 11lb (5kg)
CALIBRE: 7.62mm (.3in)
CAPACITY: 30/75
MV: c.2410f/s (735m/s)

Unlike most countries, the Russians never abandoned the light machine gun. In the 1960s they produced the RPK, basically an AK-47 with a heavier barrel, a bipod, and the ability to use a 75-shot drum. It shares all the Kalashnikov virtues of reliability, ruggedness and simplicity.

2

3

1 FN Minimi

LENGTH: 40.56in (1040mm)
WEIGHT: 6.83lb (15.05kg)
CALIBRE: 5.56mm (.223in)
CAPACITY: 30/200
MV: c.3000f/s (915m/s)

With the advent of 5.56mm (.223in) assault rifles, armies are having to decide whether or not to switch to the smaller calibre for their squad fire support weapon. If they do, they also have to decide whether to simply use a heavier version of their rifle or procure a completely new weapon. For those following the latter route, the Belgian Minimi is one of the most popular choices. It is a simple gas-operated weapon designed from the outset as a machine gun rather than converted from a rifle. It combines the firepower of belt feed with low weight and compact dimensions to make a neat but powerful package. There is a plastic rifle-style butt, a pistol grip and a folding bipod, while it is easily mounted on a tripod or vehicle pintle. An unusual feature is the ability to insert an M16-style magazine in a lower feed aperture, which could be useful in an emergency. It also comes as standard with a clip-on belt box holding 200 rounds, which improves portability and allows one man operation. There is also a 'para' version with a shorter barrel and extendable butt. The Minimi has turned out to be exceptionally reliable, and is in use with many armies. It is designated the M249 in US Army service, and is replacing the M60 as the squad-level general purpose machine gun.

1 FN Minimi

2 L86A1

LENGTH: 35.43in (900mm)
WEIGHT: 11.9lb (5.4kg)
CALIBRE: 5.56mm (.223in)
CAPACITY: 30
MV: c.3182f/s (970m/s)

For their latest section-level machine gun, the British Army adopted a heavier version of the 'bullpup' L85A1 assault rifle (see page 175). Most components are identical, although the L86A1 Light Support Weapon can be fired from an open bolt to aid cooling. The barrel is longer and heavier than that on the rifle, and has a support with a folding bipod underneath. The butt has a wire top strap, while there is also an extra rear grip. The L86 feeds from the same 30-shot box as the rifle, and has the standard optical sight. As with the L85, there have been reports of unreliability in service, although these may just be normal teething problems. A more justified question may be whether or not any magazine-fed weapon with a fixed barrel can effectively fulfil the fire support role.

3 AUG/HBAR

LENGTH: 35.43in (900mm)
WEIGHT: 4.9lb (10.75kg)
CALIBRE: 5.56mm (.223in)
CAPACITY: 30/42
MV: c.3280f/s (1000m/s)

The 'bullpup' Steyr AUG has already been described (see page 175), and this is the light machine gun variant with a longer heavier barrel, bipod and 42-shot magazine. It can also be modified to fire from an open bolt, while a variant is available with a mount for telescopic or infra-red sights.

INTO THE FUTURE

Looking back over the advances in firearms which have taken place since, say, 1870, one is tempted to wonder what the 21st Century is likely to show us. Surely, the argument may run, if the limited mechanical aptitudes of the 1890s produced such things as the automatic machine gun, the automatic pistol and the repeating magazine rifle, the modern technology of the 1990s ought to be able to produce some comparable advances?

Not necessarily. In the past, technical advance was often driven by what armies wanted or needed (and the two are not the same), but today the technical advance is more usually due to manufacturers who can see a possible improvement more easily than can non-technical soldiers. But making that technical advance into a workable weapon can, today, be a fearsomely expensive business. And in a world where military budgets are shrinking by the hour, it would be a bold manufacturer who would sink millions of pounds or dollars into a revolutionary weapon without the certain prospect of military adoption. The past decade has thrown up three cases which illustrate this problem.

In the first case the German company Heckler & Koch set out to develop a caseless cartridge rifle,

which subsequently became the Gewehr 11. They began in the 1970s, had a workable rifle by 1980, and, with the promise of general adoption by the German Army in 1990, spent the next few years perfecting the design for production. They had spent tens of millions of their own money in the development. But then came the collapse of the Berlin Wall, the integration of former East Germany, and the government demand for money with which to begin the economic recovery of their new eastern provinces. An easy target - as always - was the defence budget, and the Gewehr 11 contract was severely curtailed. Instead of outfitting almost all the German Army, purchase was restricted to about 1000 rifles for the Special Forces. As a result, Heckler & Koch got into financial difficulties which were only solved by their being bought up by British Aerospace. And the G11 rifle has vanished into limbo.

In the second case the French munitions consortium GIAT (as it then was) began a systematic study of caseless cartridge rifles. They spent three or four years on it, examining every conceivable method of operation, abandoning those which were totally impractical, finally arriving at a suitable

technical solution. At which point they announced that whilst they had a feasible design, one which toolroom models and laboratory tests had shown to work, they could not contemplate development any further unless they had financial assistance from another country And since none appeared, the French pursuit of a caseless rifle ended right there.

The third case is that of the American search for an Advanced Combat Rifle (ACR) which began in the early 1980s with the decision to seek a new design for adoption in about 1995. Multi-million-dollar contracts were awarded to a number of companies to develop caseless rifles, and, later, further contracts to other companies to examine non-caseless solutions. The designers were given a free hand within broad limits of weight and size, the primary stipulation being that the rifle had to give a 100 percent improvement in first round hit probability over the current M16A1.

Eventually, in 1989, four candidate weapons were tested, from Heckler & Koch of Germany, Colt and the AAI Corporation of the USA, and Steyr-Mannlicher of Austria. The Heckler and Koch design was virtually the German G11 with some minor improvements and modifications. The Colt design was derived from the existing M16A2, with some ergonomic improvements and with a special 5.56mm (.223in) round which carried two bullets. The AAI entry was a gas-operated rifle based

broadly upon some earlier research work and which fired a sub-calibre flechette - a small finned dart. The Steyr-Mannlicher design also fired a flechette but used a unique plastic cartridge case and a new design of rising-chamber breech mechanism. Tests and firing trials then continued until mid-1990; it was not until 1992 that a formal announcement of the results of these trials was made public. The overall conclusion was that whilst all four rifles were excellent designs and worked well, none gave sufficient advance over the performance of the existing M16A2 rifle to warrant further development to production standards. The Advanced Combat Rifle project went into suspended animation, after costing the US government something in the order of 375 million dollars. How much of their own money the four contestants had put into the project is not recorded.

With examples like these before them it is scarcely surprising that manufacturers are reluctant to make any major advance in firearms technology. Moreover, it is hard to see where such an advance would appear; the present service rifles in use around the world (and the pistols, submachine guns and machine guns) are all perfectly adequate for their purpose. One can well see the reason for the American demand for a one hundred percent improvement - anything less would be almost imperceptible and certainly not worth the expense

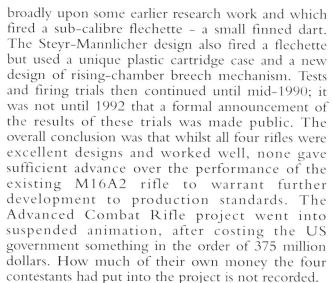

Left: *Heckler & Koch's G11 has the barrel and breech enclosed in a plastic case. The caseless telescoped rounds are held in the horizontal magazine.*

Right: *AAI's entry looked more conventional, but also fired a new design of flechette round, from the standard 5.56mm (.223in) cartridge case.*

Below: *Steyr's candidate for the US ACR programme was another plastic-cased rifle. It fires a specially designed flechette round which has a very flat trajectory.*

Below right: *Colt used the M16A2 as the basis for a new rifle, building on a well-proven system. Their ACR candidate fired a 'duplex' round with two bullets in one case.*

and trouble of replacing existing weapons.

But in spite of this gloomy forecast, there are occasional rays of light. Whilst it may not be sensible to try and develop a complete new weapon system, there are still a few areas which can be profitably explored; what, in commercial circles, are called 'market niches' which no existing weapon or equipment quite fills.

As an example of this philosophy, the FN P-90 Personal Defence Weapon (PDW) can be quoted. Fabrique National of Belgium (now known simply as FN Herstal SA) took time to consider what few people had, apparently, thought about before – how many soldiers actually need a high-powered assault rifle? And the answer appears to be "Apart from the assault infantryman, very few." All the rest of the army – and this could be up to seven-eighths of the total force – only need a weapon if ambushed or suddenly pitchforked into a situation where they need to defend themselves. A pistol is not good enough for this, and neither is the usual type of submachine gun firing a pistol cartridge; the pistol lacks range and demands a fair degree of skill, training and constant practice, while the submachine gun has a better range but, like the pistol, poor accuracy except in the hands of an expert.

FN therefore concluded that the weapon had to be light (otherwise the owner would be inclined to leave it in his truck instead of carrying it with him),

simple to use and maintain, accurate, with a low recoil force and yet with ample power out to a reasonable range. No existing cartridge fitted this concept, and FN designed a completely new one in 5.7mm (.224in) calibre resembling a tiny rifle round. The bullet is a compound type with a synthetic core and metal jacket, and has sufficient power to pierce a steel helmet at 150yds (138m) or a bullet-proof vest at 100yds (92m). Yet because the bullet is very light the recoil force is no more than that of a fairground .22in rifle; there is little jump and even the most gun-shy will scarcely flinch, so there is a good chance of an accurate shot.

The gun is shaped in a far from traditional manner. The transparent magazine lies on top of the body, and uses a turntable to align the rounds to the feedway. Although it looks peculiar, once in the hands it fits well and points instinctively; the weapon also being fitted with an optical collimating sight which allows the firer to keep both eyes open and simply place a luminous ring on the target in order to aim. High velocity means a flat trajectory and thus there is no need to fit any range adjustment to the sight.

Unfortunately, completion of development coincided with the economic malaise of the late 1980s and the end of the Cold War, so that major armies expressed interest but kept their cheque-books firmly closed. It took some time for the P-90

Left: *The Calico M960A is an advanced 9mm (.354in) submachine gun which uses a unique 50- or 100-shot cylindrical magazine.*

Right: *FN took a fresh look at the requirements for a PDW, and came up with a new 5.7mm (.224in) cartridge, tand the radical P90 to fire it.*

Below left: *This picture shows the inside of the Calico 50-shot magazine. The rounds are fed forward on a helical track, driven by an internal spring.*

Below: *Steyr's entry into the PDW field is the TMP, a machine pistol made largely from advanced plastics. Short and light, it uses delayed blowback.*

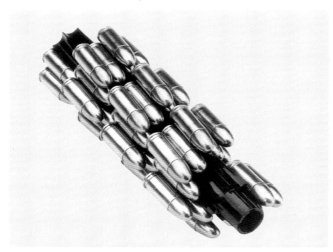

idea to gain acceptance, and this began in smaller armies, but eventually the concept was understood and P-90 production began in earnest in the early 1990s. Since then a number of major NATO armies have begun looking more closely at this 'market niche' that FN uncovered, and a number have expressed formal requirements for such a weapon. And since the P-90 is still the only serious contender in this field, their research might be said to have paid off. Which is perhaps just as well, since another market niche explored by FN at the same time has remained closed.

In the late 1970s FN looked seriously at the heavy machine gun. At that time there were only two heavy machine guns worth considering; if you were within the Soviet sphere of influence it was the 12.7mm (.5in) DShK, if you were a westerner it was the .50in (12.7mm) Browning M2. But the Browning was developed in 1919 and its cartridge had not seen much improvement since then, so that there was a distinct need for a modern heavy machine gun. At about this time some manufacturers developed improved ammunition, but there is only so much that can be done within the confines of the case and bullet, and there was very little juice left to be sucked from that particular orange. Moreover the battlefield predicated in the late 1970s saw an increase in light armoured vehicles and armoured ground attack helicopters, against

which the M2 was at best marginal.

FN therefore reasoned that an increase in calibre might be in order; this would improve the armour-piercing range to deal with light armour and provide a sufficiently destructive bullet to defeat helicopters at ranges from which the helicopters themselves could not threaten the gunner. A 15mm (.59in) weapon was developed, using dual feed so that two belts of different types of ammunition were constantly on the gun. The gunner could switch instantly from one to the other; and thus could carry a belt of armour-piercing rounds for dealing with hard targets and a belt of plain ball for personnel targets.

Unfortunately the design, which appeared in about 1985, ran into a severe barrel erosion problem. This was eventually traced to the ammunition, which was a scaled-up small arms bullet. A new design was developed using a plastic driving band to spin the bullet instead of forcing it to engrave in the rifling; at the same time the calibre was increased to 15.5mm (.61in). But, again, by the time this had been done the 'Peace Dividend' was on everyone's tongue, and the armies of the world could not begin to contemplate the cost of replacing all their .50 Browning machine guns when no apparent threat appeared to justify such a change. In 1992 FN finally gave up the struggle, placed the 15.5mm machine gun on the shelf and concentrated

their efforts on the P-90.

Another approach to the market niche: most submachine guns are, except for experts, uncontrollable in automatic fire. This is due to the rise of the muzzle as the weapon recoils, intensified by the mass of the bolt moving backward and forward at high speed. The nett result is an upward movement of the muzzle so that only the first few shots are on target, the remainder flying over it without performing any useful task. Attempts have been made to cure this by slowing down the natural rate of fire in light weapons by using various mechanisms which delay the return of the bolt for a fraction of a second. This helped, but did not cure the problem.

An American designer, working in Britain, concluded that the submachine gun, like most mechanisms, should have a natural frequency rate at which they would be controllable. He designed an adjustable electronic controller which would arrest the bolt of a submachine gun, just as had the mechanical devices, but which would be infinitely adjustable so that trials could be performed at varying rates of fire in order to determine whether such a natural frequency existed. It did; and the result is the 'Bushman' PDW, a one-hand automatic weapon which fires the standard submachine gun 9mm (.354in) Parabellum cartridge at 1400 rounds per minute with no regulator and is practically uncontrollable. But with the regulator installed it fires at 450 rounds per minute and rocks gently in the hand, delivering all its shots into the same area of the target with no rise or deviation at all. The regulator has been applied to other, more conventional, designs of submachine gun and works just as well, though, of course, at a different rate of fire – whatever the particular natural frequency is for that individual weapon.

Ammunition Changes

The past fifty years has seen a gradual reduction in the calibre of the standard rifle bullet, from an average of 8mm (.31in) to 5.56mm (.223in), with a concomitant rise in velocity in order to preserve momentum and thus deliver the same striking velocity. But not everybody has been convinced that the change has been for the better. Although figures prove that the lighter bullet strikes as hard as its larger predecessors, the fact remains that the results in combat belie the figures; a man hit with a 5.56mm (.223in) does not necessarily stop attacking, whereas a man hit with a 7.92mm (.31in) bullet did. From time to time boards and committees have studied the 'ideal calibre' question, and it is strange that almost all of them arrive at the same solution – 7mm (.276in) – and that this calibre has never been adopted. Britain formally approved it in 1949 for the EM2 rifle, but this was rescinded very quickly in the interests of NATO standardisation, and the 7.62mm (.3in)round was the result. American tests in the 1960s suggested a 6mm (.236in) round, and this was found to be efficient, but, again, political

Below left: *The Bushman has its rate of fire electronically regulated to the natural resonance of the weapon.*

Right: *Combat shotguns seem set to find a niche in the modern armoury. This is Franchi's SPAS 15, a gas-operated design.*

Below: *The advanced Glock 17 has a light plastic frame. The slide, barrel and parts of the mechanism are steel.*

Below right: *The Pancor Jackhammer is of more radical appearance. It has a cylindrical 12-shot cassette behind the grip.*

and economic decisions over-ruled the ballistic choice and the 5.56mm (.223in) bullet became the US standard, and was later adopted almost universally.

In about 2010 or so the armies of the world which adopted new rifles in the late 1980s will be seeking a new rifle, and the question of the ideal calibre will once again be raised. It is therefore interesting to see that in late 1993, the Russians, who adopted a 5.45mm (.215in) calibre cartridge in the late 1970s, have developed a new rifle and machine gun both firing an entirely new 6mm (.236in) cartridge. Neither is out of the prototype stage at this time, but the move to a slightly larger round, which is claimed to give longer range and better penetrative effect, is significant.

It should be borne in mind that the change to 5.56mm (.223in) calibre was less from ballistic necessity than from a demand to improve the chance of obtaining a hit from soldiers who were receiving less and less training in marksmanship. The American projects of the 1950s and 1960s were attempts to find a mechanical solution which would compensate for the poor state of training of the troops of the period, and much of this attitude remains. The soldier of today is so encumbered with high-tech equipment that the basics such as rifle shooting tend to be neglected.

If, therefore, the Russians are contemplating a move to a larger calibre it suggests that perhaps they have realised that firepower is no substitute for marksmanship, and we may be in for a revival of the old soldier-like virtues in the 21st century. In any case, it will be instructive to see what the next round of committees consider to be the ideal calibre.

New Directions

Traditionally the soldier's golf bag contains the pistol, submachine gun, rifle, light machine gun and heavy machine gun, a collection which ought to cover practically every eventuality. However, situations do arise in which none of these is quite right, and there are two other weapons which are currently being evaluated in various armies which are intended to fill certain gaps; these are the combat shotgun and the long-range sniping rifle.

The shotgun has a spotted history in military use; it appeared in the trenches in 1915-18 in limited numbers, and again in the Malayan campaign of the 1950s against the Communist insurgents, and then

in Vietnam in the 1960s. But the principal complaint in all these affairs was simply that the commercial shotgun was not designed for the hurly-burly of military life; it was too long, too delicate, and restricted in its ammunition capacity. The ammunition, too, was not of a military nature, nor made to military standards – the common paper shotgun cartridge had a short life in the humidity of the Malayan jungle.

From time to time military establishments would suggest that a militarised shotgun might be useful, but the manufacturers rarely did more than strengthen an existing commercial design. It was the usual story of reluctance to sink money into development without the assurance of a military contract at the end of it.

In the 1970s the US services began a project for a militarised shotgun under the title CAWS – Close Assault Weapon System. The demand was for an automatic shotgun firing much-improved ammunition with an effective range of some 300yds (277m). Two designs eventually appeared, but the whole project then appears to have died from lack of interest and nothing has been heard of it for several years. But private designers have also tackled the problem, some with excellent results. One such is the 'Jackhammer' combat shotgun, a 12-bore (70mm/2.75in) weapon with automatic feed which loads from a drum-like 'ammo cassette'. This cassette is pre-loaded and can be dropped from the gun and abandoned when changing to a new one.

The weapon has an automatic rate of 240 rounds per minute and is chambered for the standard 12-bore cartridge, though special ammunition has been developed. An additional bonus is a pressure plate which can be clipped to a loaded ammo cassette, turning it into a formidable anti-personnel mine.

It is possible, therefore, that the military use of shotguns may yet come to something and purpose-built shotguns be produced. Since the present military scenarios largely appear to be predicated upon limited warfare, intervention, ant-terrorist operations and similar short-range, small-scale situations, there is certainly ample scope for a short-range quick response weapon of this nature.

The long-range sniping rifle is an entirely different case. It is unfortunate that the first people to develop this class of weapon, in the USA in the early 1980s, elected to use the word 'sniping', since this immediately suggests anti-personnel firing. In fact, these weapons are designed to be used against delicate and vulnerable equipment rather than against people; the Steyr-Mannlicher company got it right when they named their version the 'Anti-Materiel Rifle'.

The original, and majority, of these weapons come in .50in (12.7mm) Browning calibre, using the standard machine gun rounds. They are heavy bipod-mounted rifles, usually with muzzle brakes and other recoil-absorbing devices, and their role is to launch the heavy bullet to ranges of 1200-1500yds (1100-1380m) with reliable accuracy. The

Left: *The basic M60 design was improved to become the E3 model.*

Below left: *The Negev is an Israeli 5.56mm (.223in) light machine gun similar to the FN Minimi.*

Below: *The Barrett M82 long range sniper or anti-materiel rifle chambered for .50in (12.7mm) cartridge.*

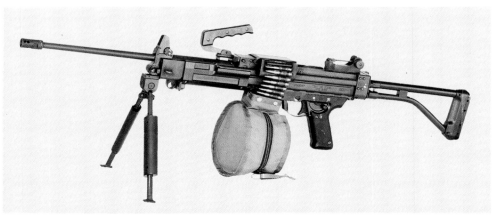

role envisaged for them might be best explained by the following scenario: a three-man squad of Special Forces, carrying one of these rifles and a handful of ammunition penetrates enemy lines and moves deeper into enemy territory until it can overlook a forward airstrip holding a flight of ground attack aircraft. From a range of about a mile, half-a-dozen shots from the rifle will effectively put half-a-dozen aircraft out of action – the .50in (12.7mm) bullet is sufficiently destructive to do immeasurable damage to a jet engine or to the complex and expensive electronics of a modern aircraft – after which the squad simply abandon the rifle and make their way back to base. Six high-tech jet fighters for a $5000 rifle is a fair rate of exchange.

Once the idea found a home – and the US Army employed these rifles in Grenada, Panama and the Gulf – other gunmakers began to iron out some of the defects in the original concept. The primary defect lies in the ammunition; .50in (12.7mm) machine gun ammunition, as it comes from the factory, is not sufficiently accurate for this sort of task. Hand-loading to a higher degree of consistency helps, but, as with the FN machine gun described above, the best way would be to abandon the .50in (12.7mm) idea entirely and start with a new calibre properly designed for the task in hand. This was the approach chosen by Steyr-Mannlicher with their Anti-Materiel Rifle, which uses a special 14.5mm sub-calibre flechette rounds in heavy metal which is capable of piecing 1.6in (40mm) of steel armour at 1000yds (920m) range. The weapon is, of course, considerably heavier than a .50in (12.7mm) rifle, but within the capabilities of two men and is superlatively accurate. It remains to be seen whether the idea will gain acceptance, or whether, like so many others, it will be paralysed by the current military/financial conditions.

Altogether, the prospects for dynamic advances in the firearms field within, say, the next twenty years are not good. Most of the world's armies are sufficiently well equipped to meet any threat that they can envisage, now that the Great Threat of East-West confrontation appears to have evaporated. The existing threats are all low-intensity and can be easily contained within the existing technology. With no pressing demand, and with governments reluctant to spend money on armies, there is no incentive for manufacturers to develop any new weapons; they are quite satisfied to improve existing designs where such improvement can be shown to reduce production costs, but since the chances of making major improvements in performance are small, it is economics alone which will count.

Below: *Instead of the radical (and expensive) G11, the German Army have chosen the Heckler & Koch G41, an improved version of the HK33.*

Below: *Another form of PDW is represented by the shortened MP5K variant.*

Bottom: *The South African BXP is yet another blowback submachine gun.*

INDEX

(Numbers in **bold** refer to main entry, numbers in *italics* refer to illustration captions.

The publisher is grateful to all the individuals and organisations that supplied weapons and photographs for inclusion in this book, especially the following:

Accuracy International; Armscor; The Armouries, HM Tower of London; Barrett Industries; Beretta SpA; Calico Firearms Company; CETME; Colt Industries; Civil War Library and Museum, Philadelphia, Pa; FN Herstal; GIAT Industries; Glock; Heckler & Koch; Ian V. Hogg; Israeli Military Industries; The Museum of the Confederacy, Richmond, Va.; New Zealand MoD; Pattern Room, RO Nottingham; Russ Pritchard; The Royal Military College of Science, Shrivenham; Royal Ordnance; Saco Industries; Singapore Industries; Steyr-Mannlicher; UK MoD; US DoD; Virginia Historical Society, Richmond; Va.; The Weapons Museum, School of Infantry, Warminster.